time's up!

an uncivilized solution
to a global crisis

time's up!

an uncivilized solution
to a global crisis

keith farnish

green books

First published in the UK in 2009
by Green Books Ltd,
Foxhole, Dartington,
Totnes, Devon TQ9 6EB

ISBN 978 1 900322 48 5

Text printed on 100% recycled paper
by TJ International, Padstow, Cornwall, UK

DISCLAIMER
The author and publishers accept no liability
for actions inspired by this book.

Contents

Acknowledgements

Thanks to the following people for inspiration and help in writing this book:

Professor Bob Altemeyer, The Ant, Bob Barrows, Bridget Box, Paul Brannon, Raymond Brettman, Phil Buck, Emma Chappell, Charlotte Chappell, Jacqui Cosgree, Mike Courtney, John Elford and all the staff at Green Books, Dennis Emery, Joyce Emery, Christine Farnish, Ron Farnish, Dr Simon Gowen, Kevin Grandia, Andy Griffiths, Mick Harding, David Johnston-Smith, Shane Jordan, Bob Lane, Lucy Luck, Peta Mason, Barbara McCarthy, Karen Pinder, Ana Salote, Bonnie Turner, David Wasdell, Dr Martin Wiselka, everyone on the A Matter Of Scale Facebook group, all my friends on the Talkawhile Folk Music Forum, and anyone I might have forgotten . . .

Special thanks to the following people who mentored me throughout the writing of this book, and so much more – you have no idea how important you are:

Angela Farnish, Helen Mulley, Shaun Qureshi, Tony Seels, and my two biological imperatives, Sophie and Becky.

Introduction

Let's start at the end.

The first ending has happened before. Vast groups of humans, all taking part in a single, complex system, thrive for a short while; they take what they want until there is nothing left to take, and the system collapses. This has happened time and time again in the fruitless rise and fall of human ambition. The greatest of these civilizations is the one we are living in now. The end is when it falls, and the fall is coming soon. With this ending, we stand little chance of survival.

The second ending is something we're becoming sadly familiar with: the one in which the ice caps melt, the forests disappear, the oceans rise and countless species wake for the last time before leaving the Earth forever. This is an environmental catastrophe. We can bat it away, think it has little to do with us and carry on as before. But the environment is not another place: it is what we depend on for our survival, and we are part of it, whatever anyone might say. An 'environmental' catastrophe is a human catastrophe. With this ending, we also stand little chance of survival.

The third ending is one you get to choose. There is a chance that we might survive.

*   *   *

Life on Earth exists in a vast continuum, with individual organisms ranging from the sub-microscopic to those that are colossal. Each organism functions as part of a complex web of interconnected ecosystems, some of which are truly global in extent. What is most astonishing of all is that almost everything we are now doing to our environment is affecting something else at some scale or another, and it is coming back to bite us in more ways than we can imagine. We are causing our own demise. Part One of this book will tell the story of that multi-scaled, multi-dimensional impact: it is not a pleasant story, but it is one that we all need to learn.

Humans, like all other life forms on this planet, act in order to benefit the continuation of their genes. Humans, unlike all other life forms on this planet, have managed to go beyond what seems possible for such a recently emerged species. Part Two will go right to the heart of what it means to be human and then, bit by bit, attempt to work out whether humans are vital, relevant, or just an irrelevant scourge upon the Earth. Given what we know about human history and the nature of humanity, the answer might come as a surprise.

Despite our knowledge of the imminent collapse of the global ecology and its impact on human life, and despite the clear and natural human imperative to ensure our continued survival, we have become totally incapable of connecting these two inseparable factors. Part Three aims to correct this. First it will describe how these two things are connected at so many different levels, and then will explain how we can allow ourselves to create the most important connection of all – the one that binds us to the very things we depend upon for our survival. It will then take you on a journey into the darkest parts of the most powerful civilization in history – a civilization that has created a synthetic, disconnected view of humanity to serve the needs of a few. Here also lies the answer to one of the most profound questions of modern times: who is in charge?

It seems obvious that the only acceptable future for humanity is one in which we survive. We are in a position where we have to choose between the short-term greed of Industrial Civilization or the long-term survival that humans are capable of, and in order to make this choice freely, we must first be able to resist the influence of those who seek to deny us that choice. Part Four will describe, at a range of levels never assembled before in one place, how we can simultaneously breathe new life into both our own lives and the Earth, and also how we can break down those things that are preventing us from connecting with the real world and having a genuine say in our future. Part Four contains the keys to human survival.

I didn't choose the title of this book lightly: time is up for humanity if we don't change the way in which we are now living – change it in such radical terms that, once complete, the so-called 'civilized' world we have grown up in will be but a distant and bitter memory. As you will find out later, there is nothing wrong with being uncivilized . . . if it means having a future.

Now read on, and enjoy the journey.

Keith Farnish, November 2008.

Part One

The Scale of the Problem

Chapter 1

One Ten-Millionth of a Metre

Breathe in, and your body starts a battle. Countless micro-organisms hitch a lift on every stream of air being pulled into your lungs, seeking out a place where they can embed themselves and multiply. Once inside, every potential form of nutrition is fair game: blood cells, fat cells, skin, bone marrow, lymphatic fluid – all hosts for the army of invaders that just want to find a way of increasing their numbers. You are alive because your body has evolved ways of fighting them off. No medicine can match the efficiency of your own army of defenders across such a vast range of attackers, without killing off its host as well.

HIV, the virus responsible for AIDS, is a beautiful thing to look at; rather like a three-dimensional cog with rounded buds spread across its spherical surface. In cross-section the central capsid, which contains the genetic material responsible for allowing HIV to fight off all but the most sophisticated drugs, is coffin-shaped. So beautiful, so appropriate, but so terrible that it is able to cut through an entire country in just a few years, leaving a scarred, distressed and dying landscape of human beings in its wake.

In South Africa, 19% of the population of 44 million are infected with HIV.[1] In Lesotho, 23% of the two million inhabitants have HIV. In Botswana, 24% of the population of just under two million – that's nearly a quarter of every person in this tiny country; adults, children, even new-born babies – have a virus that will eventually kill most of them.[2] Over a million of these tiny viral entities could fit, side by side, on this full stop. We may have evolved defences against the oldest and most common viruses, but human evolution is a slow process; we have no natural defences against HIV.

Here is another statistic. The World Health Organization estimate that Dengue Fever, caused by four types of closely related virus, is a risk for around two-fifths of the world's population.[3] Without treatment, Dengue Fever is deadly in 20% of cases, and there are around 50 million cases of the disease every year. Dengue Fever is spread by mosquitoes, as is Yellow Fever, which kills 30,000 people a year. Japanese Encephalitis is also spread by mosquitoes, but develops in pigs and birds before being passed to humans by the same species of mosquito that infected these other animals. This kills around 15,000 people a year and leaves another 25,000 permanently paralyzed.

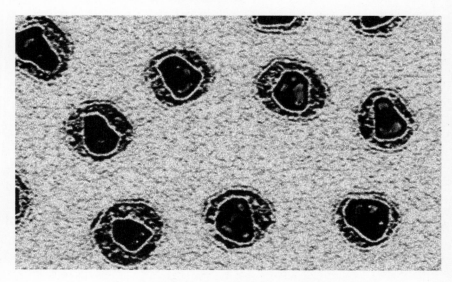

Figure 1: Electron microscope image of HIV virus,
showing the central coffin-shaped capsids

Influenza is not spread by mosquitoes; it is spread by birds, humans and many other mammals, including domestic dogs and cats – in fact any warm-blooded animal can potentially harbour and pass on influenza in its many forms. The worry about the potential for a catastrophic influenza pandemic (global infection), quite rightly expressed by epidemiologists and other health professionals, is not based on some abstract idea that bears no resemblance to reality; it is a genuine fear that echoes fiction in so many ways. Compare this quotation:

> By midnight the barriers were set up, and by dawn the next morning, the morning of the twenty-fifth, several people had been shot at the barriers, most just wounded, but three or four killed. Almost all of them were people coming north, streaming out of Boston, stricken with fear, panic-stupid. They were dealt with.
>
> But by that evening, most of the men manning the barricades were sick themselves, glowing bright with fever, constantly propping their shotguns between their feet so they could blow their noses. Some…simply fell down unconscious and were later driven back to the jackleg infirmary that had been set up over the town hall, and there they died.[4]

with this one:

> The Boston Globe reported that in the twenty-four hours preceding 7:00 am of September 23, 66 men, all of them probably in the peak years of physical prowess, had died.

> The statistics boggled Welch's mind: the sight of the lines of sick men shuffling through the cold, penetrating rain to the hospital gave him no encouragement about the immediate future. He needed no stethoscope to conclude that the problem for many of them was lung failure. He could see that at a dozen paces: some of them, stumbling along, the blankets over their shoulders soaking up the fine drizzle, were turning blue and even purple.[5]

It would take a brave person to tell which of the two reports is fictional: it is actually the first one, from Stephen King's doomsday epic *The Stand*. The second quotation is from an American study of the 1918 'Spanish Flu' pandemic, which took 25 million lives globally, or 1.5% of the world's population. The general public seem to have only recently grasped the deadly potential of the seemingly innocuous flu virus. A healthy person can catch one of the more benign and common strains of flu and spend a few days in bed, albeit with considerable discomfort, before making a full recovery.

Up to a billion people worldwide may be infected every year[6] with influenza, of which half a million will die. Such is the population of the Earth (6.6 billion and counting) that half a million people is a global 'hiccup' – a mere 0.008% of humanity; yet the Indian Ocean tsunami, which took 300,000 lives in December 2004, is still remembered as a world-changing event. Less than 1% of the annual global toll from influenza died in the World Trade Center attacks of September 11, 2001. Nineteen hijackers in four aircraft making a co-ordinated attack on the military and financial centres of the USA are tangible targets upon whom we can conveniently pile our collective wrath. Unknowably vast numbers of sub-microscopic viruses do not a tangible target make.

What is a Virus?

With an irony that speaks volumes about the direction we are heading as a species, the simplest description for a virus comes from the world of computers. Such is the extent to which we have substituted our ancient love of nature for the modern love of technology, that we often have problems seeing the real world without a technological analogy to help us along the way. So, for the uninitiated in technology, a computer virus is a small, simple piece of computer code (a program) that attaches itself to a larger piece of code in order to duplicate itself and spread. At the time of writing, there were about 74,000 computer viruses in the 'wild' [7](now there's a bizarre use of the term 'wild', if ever there was one). For the uninitiated in biology, a natural virus is an organism that has no means of reproducing other than by using another organism as a host; generally that organism is a cell within a larger organism, such as a person, plant or fungus. Viruses reproduce by convincing a cell, by use of its protein coating, that it is a desirable object to welcome into the cell's interior. Once inside, the virus loses its protective coating, revealing the genetic code, which is then copied by the cell's nucleus, just as though the cell is copying its own genetic material. The cell then ejects the newly replicated viral material through its walls and *voilà*!, replication is complete. This is clever stuff, especially considering that a virus may not, in fact, be a living thing.

Obviously something that is less than a micron (a millionth of a metre) across couldn't be considered an animal even by the most imaginative biologist; but whether something that is not even capable of reproducing on its own or with another virus, let alone being able to move, excrete or grow, should be considered 'living' is another matter. Scientists cannot agree with each other on this, largely because the definition of 'life' is unclear: is it the ability to be self-aware – in which case things could get very complicated due to the limited ways in which this can be tested (try holding a mirror in front of a sightless creature to understand the problem); is it the ability to grow, move, excrete, respire, reproduce and all those good things; or is it simply "the ability to move a genetic blueprint into future generations, thereby regenerating your likeness"? [8] We do know that there are probably more different viruses than all (other) types of life, and that there are certainly more individual viruses than all (other) individual life forms put together; so, if viruses are living then they are most certainly the most successful life forms that there have ever been.

The thought that my entire body is teeming with viruses that my own defence systems are having to constantly fight off, and that if I find my immune system to be compromised in any way – whether from lack of nutrients, or the Human Immunodeficiency Virus – I could fall foul of them, is not the kind of thing that makes for a restful state of mind. Most people only knowingly come into contact with a virus when they have a cold or other minor infection, so have little reason to be aware of their existence. Our ignorance of viruses, though (and we are tremendously ignorant, despite the great strides that have been taken in bringing immunization to the masses) is something that could be our undoing.

Take the polio virus, the cause of Poliomyelitis. I have some home movies of my sister and me happily playing on the beach at Margate, a middle-sized seaside resort in England, during the hot summer of 1976. Dutifully we would stack up lumps of chalk into makeshift dams in the shade of the Victorian sundeck and then fill the resulting inundations with handfuls of the white foam that gathered in lines at the water's edge. The source of the foam was a short sewage outfall not half a mile away, which also deposited partially-treated human excrement a few metres out to sea, only to be washed back inshore with the foam by the rising tide.

Across the Thames Estuary, about 30 miles away, lies Southend-on-Sea. It was on the coast of this town in the late 1940s that the legendary songwriter and performer Ian Dury contracted polio, a life-threatening disease that is carried in faecal matter, and can be caught merely by swallowing a small amount of infected water. It was almost certainly from a poorly chlorinated swimming pool near the Spanish town of Altea that my own father contracted transverse myelitis, a related viral disease of the nervous system, which led to him being partially paralyzed from the waist down. All the time I happily played in the sewage-ridden waters of Margate no one thought to warn me that I should perhaps be careful.

Fortunately I am fit, healthy and (so far) free of disease, and that is thanks to my immune system working in the way it should. Whether it will keep up with changes that happen in the future is another matter.

A World of Change

The world is heating, and change is happening faster than expected. The signs are there for everyone to see: a polar icecap that opens up enough to allow ice-free navigation for the first time since humans colonized North America; the accelerated calving of icebergs in the Southern Ocean; the early emergence of bulbs and other spring plants in temperate zones; even the wine trade is feeling the change, as southern Europe dries up and northern Europe warms. It doesn't take a big change in global temperature to make a difference – as of the end of 2007, the average global temperature had risen 0.7°C above the mean for the previous 200 years – because this is a planet of carefully balanced systems. Thresholds that are a hair's breadth from being breached are ready to tip like houses of cards in a breeze.

The British Antarctic Survey, about as sanguine and level-headed a body as you could find, reported this in 2006: "Adélie penguins, a species well adapted to sea ice conditions, have declined in numbers and been replaced by open-water species such as chinstrap penguins. Melting of perennial snow and ice covers has resulted in increased colonization by plants. A long-term decline in the abundance of Antarctic krill in the SW Atlantic sector of the southern ocean may be associated with reduced sea ice cover."[9] Three separate findings, and a whole web of changes that spawn from them: webs that you will find everywhere, and many of which I will discuss in this book.

*   *   *

Come and visit Suffolk, England, on a warm day in September 2007:

> The Department for Environment, Food and Rural Affairs (Defra) said last night that tests had confirmed bluetongue in a second cow at the Baylham House Rare Breeds Farm, near Ipswich, Suffolk. It was immediately slaughtered to limit the chances of the disease spreading. Bluetongue has already spread across the Continent to Britain. On Sunday, Debbie, a ruddy-haired Highland cow who was a favourite with visitors, was put down after being found to be suffering from the midge-borne disease.
>
> While tests continue to see if more animals have been infected, Defra announced that from 3.30 pm today a huge bluetongue surveillance area restricting the movement of animals will be established over a 150km radius around the Suffolk farm where the disease was first found. This is the maximum distance that midges can fly, but if they have spread from Suffolk, biting animals as they go, the infection could be much more widespread. It has spread like wildfire across farms in Germany, France, Belgium and the Netherlands, having originated in Africa. Thousands of animals have died or been destroyed, causing massive losses for Continental farmers.[10]

Bluetongue is an arbovirus, short for 'arthropod-borne virus'. Arthropods include spiders, centipedes, shrimps and crabs; but most importantly they include insects, the most diverse group of animals on Earth. Anything that assists the spread of a disease is known as a 'vector', which essentially means the movement of something in a specific direction. Mosquitoes are notorious vectors for diseases, and not just those caused by viruses. Midges, which are closely related to mosquitoes, range from the harmless (to humans), non-biting *Cecidomyidae*, to the painfully persistent Highland midge, which has been suggested as the reason for much of Scotland being undeveloped.

The midges that are responsible for the spread of the bluetongue virus are temperature-sensitive: based on the global 'temperature gradient', a tenth of a degree increase pushes breeding grounds north by at least ten kilometres. If there are anomalies in temperature caused by local warming, insects can be pushed far further. Temperature gradients also operate with height above sea level, with every ten metres in height causing a drop in temperature of 0.1°C. That means that with 0.7°C of additional heating midges, or any other temperature-sensitive organism, can range over land that is up to 70 metres higher than previously. That makes a lot of difference in hilly areas.

Fortunately for humans, midges can be easily killed off by frost, but as frosts have been starting later and later in the year in the Northern Hemisphere, the midges have been able to extend their breeding cycles into stormier times of the year. This effectively means that they can be blown across seas and into previously unaffected areas. If that wasn't bad enough, warmer temperatures also cause faster breeding.

A study carried out in 1999 found that mosquito larvae were extremely sensitive to temperature in determining how quickly they developed into adult mosquitoes.[11] At 15°C the average development times for two types of mosquito were 44 and 61 days respectively. When the temperature was increased to 22°C this development time was reduced to 32 days for the first type and 24 days for the second type. At 30°C, the second type of mosquito was able to go from larva to adult in a mere 14 days. The significance of this is mind-boggling when you consider how quickly mosquitoes can breed. If a 7°C increase in temperature is able to reduce the breeding cycle of a mosquito by 37 days, then that means a mere 1°C increase in temperature could allow for one additional breeding cycle during the breeding season. Given that a female mosquito can lay hundreds of eggs in its short lifetime, one extra breeding cycle is a frightening prospect: one more generation of mosquitoes can mean a thousand-fold increase in numbers. A thousand-fold increase in West Nile Virus, Yellow Fever, Dengue Fever, and Japanese Encephalitis. Am I scaremongering?

> Valere Rommelaere, 82, survived the D-Day invasion in Normandy, but not a mosquito bite. Six decades after the war, the hardy Saskatchewan farmer was bitten by a bug carrying a disease that has spread from the equator to Canada as temperatures have risen. Within weeks, he died from West Nile virus.

> Paul Epstein, a physician who worked in Africa and is now on the faculty of Harvard Medical School, said that, if anything, scientists weren't worried enough about the problem.

> "Things we projected to occur in 2080 are happening in 2006. What we didn't get is how fast and how big it is, and the degree to which the biological systems would respond," Epstein said in an interview in Boston. "Our mistake was in underestimation."[12]

Am I scaremongering, then?
I really don't think so.

Packing Them In

Figure 2: Liverpool Street Station, London

For fourteen years I travelled into London by train, for the most part alighting at Liverpool Street Station in the heart of the Square Mile, the financial centre of the UK. It took me a while to get accustomed to the constant threading, dodging and occasional colliding of thousands of people heading to and from work within the concourse and on the noisy, hectic streets outside. The density of travellers is modest, though, compared with the tumult of people thronging the platforms, concourses and pavements of southern and south-east Asia. In India, suburban trains still dominate, transporting over 3 billion people a year across the cities of the nation,[13] while the cross-country and cross-state lines are rightly known as the arteries of the nation. But there is a price to pay in terms of comfort: 'intimate' would be a good word to describe a rush-hour journey. This pen picture written by a Mumbaian describes the experience wonderfully:

> When train arrives on platform, one starts by praying to one's favourite God. The arrival of the train is marked by a sudden change in the atmosphere at the station. Everyone, including the seemingly docile auntie pulls up her (ahem) socks, clenches her fists and gets ready for THE GREAT CHARGE. This sight can easily make initial non-supporters of evolution great believers of Darwin's Theory, for what follows is nothing but living proof of Darwin's idea of 'Survival of the Fittest'.

Another reason I believe that the rails offer too much for the measly sum we pay for the tickets is that they provide free exercise, body massage and stretching aerobics early in the morning (as well as all day through) which is definitely an advantage for today's health-obsessed generation.[14]

The battery conditions of human transportation throughout the world – whether on foot in London, bicycle in Beijing, underground railway in Tokyo, car in Los Angeles or train in Mumbai – are symptoms of an overcrowded planet full of time-dependent, job-dependent, money-dependent people. Intimacy is rarely of our choosing: the lives we are increasingly shoehorned into by economic necessity (in other words, 'work or die') are often led in squalid conditions. It is a blessing that the notorious walled city of Kowloon, with a population density approaching two million people per square kilometre, is no longer with us, but similar, much larger urban areas exist, and they are growing. One part of Mumbai in India squeezes 200,000 people into just 1.7 square kilometres;[15] an area half the size of New York's Central Park. Kowloon still accommodates over two million people at a density of 118,000 people per square kilometre – six times as cramped as central London.

Battery conditions are not restricted to humans. As we treat people, we also treat animals. Karl Taro Greenfeld described the method of storing wild animals for food in Guangzhou, China as 'industrialized':

> In one cage in Xin Yuan, I counted fifty-two cats pushed in so tightly that their intestines were spilling out from between the wire bars. There were fifty-five such cages in this one stall. There were fifty-two stalls down this one row of vendors. And there were six rows in this one market. There were seven markets on this street.[16]

Over six million animals in a single street is an astonishing estimate, but not when you consider the scale of battery farming in China. According to the US Department of Agriculture,[17] in 2004 there were 85 poultry farms in China each with over a million birds being bred for meat, and a total of four billion birds slaughtered in that one year. The battle against 'bird flu' or the H5N1 virus is being waged in the backyard farms of eastern Europe and south-east Asia, with mandatory housing, and sometimes slaughter taking place at the first sign of a diseased bird; yet these free-range conditions are merely the stopping-off points for wild birds that have already contracted the virus. The source of the virus and the cause of the most lethal strains of influenza are bound up in the way that viruses operate on large, densely packed populations of animals.

The process by which organisms evolve starts with the mutation of a piece of its genetic material. Mutations cannot be predicted, but can be encouraged to happen more or less frequently: for instance, certain types of radiation are able to change the chemical make-up of an organism's DNA, so can be said to accelerate the mutation process. By their nature, mutations only involve a single gene at a time; multiple genetic changes require multiple mutations. In most cases genetic mutations have little or no effect on the organism; in other cases the mutation may be damaging to the organism, for instance it may lead to excess cell division, which can lead to cancer, or it may impede the organism's ability to reproduce. In some cases, though, the mutation is a positive step for the organism, and it is this type of mutation that is generally considered to be 'evolutionary'. In order for a virus to pass to a species other than the one it is currently hosted by it may have to undergo a number of mutations, none of which can be damaging to the virus itself. Eventually the virus may have changed sufficiently to make the hop to another species.

Evolution through mutation is a slow and haphazard process and, in normal population densities, more often than not the virus will end up as a benign scrap of DNA, unable to do its genetic duty. In vast populations of birds that are pecking, flapping and depositing faecal matter upon each other, a veritable viral beanfeast can take place. Viruses are rapidly passing from bird to bird, and back again, mutating and evolving as they go. A single incidence of highly pathogenic (deadly) bird flu can wipe out an entire shed of birds within 48 hours, according to the World Health Organization (WHO). The WHO goes on to say: "Apart from being highly contagious among poultry, avian influenza viruses are readily transmitted from farm to farm by the movement of live birds, people (especially when shoes and other clothing are contaminated), and contaminated vehicles, equipment, feed, and cages. Highly pathogenic viruses can survive for long periods in the environment, especially when temperatures are low. For example, the highly pathogenic H5N1 virus can survive in bird faeces for at least 35 days at low temperature (4°C)."[18] The long survival time at low temperatures helps explain why influenza outbreaks occur more frequently during temperate winters in the Northern Hemisphere (the other reason, particularly for rapid spread, is that people stay indoors and crowd together more when it is cold). For once, global warming is not to blame. The same cannot be said for human behaviour.

The book *China Syndrome* by Karl Taro Greenfeld contains a superb analysis of the social and biological conditions that led to the global outbreak of SARS in 2003, and then the inevitable spread of H5N1 from 2006 onwards. He writes: "For a microbe, a city is a target-rich environment, with slabs of human meat stacked literally one over another in apartments and houses, waiting to be consumed. Of the four major modes of disease transmission – waterborne, vector-borne, airborne or direct contact – each is facilitated by urban life."[19] We create perfect environments for viruses to spread and thrive, right down to the artificially moist and putrid environments without which such agents would die in minutes.

When you bring the kind of rich pathogenic soup that can be found in cities in close proximity to the kinds of bird farming described above then the likelihood of cross-species transmission is greatly increased. If a human influenza virus evolves sufficiently to infect a bird, and that bird is infected with H5N1 bird flu then the two viruses can mix and 'swap' genes.[20] The resulting virus will then have enough common characteristics to both infect humans *and* create the kind of turmoil that H5N1 has caused in flocks of birds. It only takes one person in the vast genetic pool of our major cities to contract a transgenic virus for it then to become a human epidemic.

It only takes one flight across the world for an epidemic to turn into a pandemic. Humans like to fly; it has become one of the key aspirations of the consumer society to take long trips to different parts of the world and experience the way that other nations move to the rhythm of the tourism machine. We travel to distant lands to lie on distant beaches, then come home and tell our distant friends all about it. Tourism is not just big business, it is the primary business of many countries; and God help anyone who tries to stop flights from continuing to feed their economic boom! Air travel, which is excluded from all international targets – and the vast majority of national ones – to reduce greenhouse gas emissions, is expected to account for 15% of all greenhouse gas emissions by 2050, up from just 3% in 2006.[21] It is illegal for an individual country to tax aircraft fuel and aircraft parts.[22]

A study published in the scientific journal *Nature* in 2006 found a remarkable drop in the numbers of early-onset influenza cases amongst humans in the period following the World Trade Center attacks in September 2001. "The 27% drop in passenger numbers on international flights delayed the normal peak of flu deaths by nearly two weeks, from February to March. And the fall in domestic air travel meant that the disease took 16 days longer to spread throughout the country."[23] Incredibly, and almost certainly due to economic pressure from business and business-friendly governments, restricting air travel does not form part of international plans for preventing the spread of any potential strains of highly pathogenic influenza.

While scientists watch the skies for migrating birds that may harbour avian flu, the same skies are filled with people who may be carrying something equally lethal.

Death by a Thousand Cuts

The H5 strains of avian influenza are often called the 'Ebola of the birdworld'. The Ebola of the human world, and also that of a number of other primates, is something that almost defies description, such is its brutality:

> A nurse brought a bag of whole blood. Dr Musoke hooked a bag on a stand and inserted the needle into the patient's arm. There was something wrong with the patient's veins; his blood poured out around the needle. At every place in the patient's arm where he stuck the needle, the vein broke apart like cooked macaroni and spilled blood, and the blood ran from the punctures down the patient's arm and wouldn't coagulate. The patient continued to bleed from the bowels, and these haemorrhages were now as black as pitch.[24]

Ebola is a type of haemorrhagic fever, the type that leads to the liquefaction of the internal organs while the sufferer 'bleeds out', infecting almost everyone who comes into contact with the copious quantities of blood that the sufferer emits. There are other forms of haemorrhagic fever, with the most common types, Dengue and Lassa, being far less deadly than the much rarer Marburg, Rift Valley and Ebola. The reason that Ebola has not caused more deaths overall (about 1,200 deaths since it was first discovered)[25] is because of the speed with which it kills the victim – as little as four days from first exposure. HIV, on the other hand, can lie dormant for years, being passed from person to person without any symptoms showing.

But while HIV can only be passed from human to human in its current configuration, Ebola can seemingly pop out of nowhere, cause a spate of deaths in many different species, and then disappear with epidemiologists none the wiser as to precisely where the original infection came from. Rift Valley Fever is harboured in cattle, goats, sheep and other hoofed animals; Lassa resides in a species of West African rodent; Ebola's primary source is officially 'unknown'.

Martin Wiselka, a consultant in infectious diseases at the Nuffield Hospital in Leicester has little doubt over the reasons for Ebola's emergence. He says: "Exploiting wild habitats such as the tropical rain forests allows interaction between human hosts, animals and vectors of infection, such as rats and insects. This can increase the likelihood of certain infections such as yellow fever, hantavirus and Ebola, which are normally carried by animal hosts." [26]

* * *

The Congo River sweeps round in a continuous arc from the northern heights of Zambia in the heart of Africa, through the ignominiously-named Democratic

Republic of Congo (formerly Zaire) until finally, after 4,700 km, emptying into the Atlantic Ocean at the small town of Muanda in the Republic of the Congo. Covering the bulk of its catchment area, swelling its volume with incessant rainfall, is the second largest continuous area of forest in the world: the Central African Rainforest. This great block of green canopy contains some of the richest plant and animal habitat in existence. This area of forest also contains, potentially, around 37 billion tonnes of carbon, more than the whole of Southeast Asia and the USA combined;[27] that is over five times as much carbon as all human activity on Earth produces each year.

The extent of this vital carbon 'sink' is shrinking each year.[28] In 1990 the Central African Rainforest occupied 2.5 million square kilometres; in 2005 it occupied less than 2.4 million km^2, a reduction of about 5% in total area.[29] This may not seem like a lot, but when you look at the speed the forest is degrading at the same time, you realize something fundamental is happening. According to a report published in 2007,[30] over a quarter of this unique habitat had been earmarked for logging, while only 12% was officially protected – in practice not protected at all. From a disease point of view, the expansion of logging tracks and other roads is equally disturbing: "[the study] found that road density had increased dramatically since the 1970s and that around 29% of the remaining Congo rainforest was 'likely to have increased wildlife hunting pressure because of easier access and local market opportunities' offered by new logging towns and roads."[31] Access to forest means access to disease vectors, and in this part of the world that means a potential outbreak of Ebola is never far away.

The way that humans are exploiting the rainforests of Central Africa, for tropical timber, for minerals like coltan (a key component in micro-electronics) and gold, and increasingly for 'bush meat', beggars belief. Yet, it seems as though any price is worth paying for economic wealth: climate change, degraded habitats, silt-laden rivers, even a disease that could strike at any time, kill off an entire town in days, and then disappear again. And there lies a vital message: if we don't exercise discretion in the way we treat the planet, its animals and its plants, then we may fall foul of the smallest, yet one of the most effective killers that there has ever been: the not-so-humble virus.

Chapter 2

One Millionth of a Metre

I didn't know this until I watched a BBC television documentary a few years ago called 'The Private Life of Plants', but lichen – the patches of variously shaded matter that grow on gravestones, roof tiles and paving slabs – are not individual organisms, but a combination of algae and fungi. They function in a tightly woven, lifelong embrace from which neither can ever escape; nor would they want to, because neither could survive independently any more. This is called endosymbiosis. The alga provides the food energy, created through photosynthesis, and the fungus the protection to see the joint organism through the harshest of conditions. There are lichens that exist (I hesitate to use the word 'thrive') in Antarctica[1] where, incredibly, they manage to carry out photosynthesis at temperatures as low as -24°C. An organism that exists in near stasis for most of the year, and below freezing conditions all year round, still manages to have a net benefit on the planet by consuming carbon dioxide and producing oxygen.

Imagine if, rather than independent beings that could pick and choose what we ate and what we surrounded ourselves with, humans had an endosymbiotic relationship with another organism. How would it feel to be part of another organism, or have organisms living inside you, doing work without which you would die?

Say hello to your mitochondria. Don't be shy, they won't answer back – they are far too busy converting amino acids and sugars into energy for your cells to use. Tucked away within the cells of probably all animals, mitochondria are effectively the 'boiler rooms' of your cells; yet they didn't evolve like the majority of the components of your body, gradually changing or adapting their functions to suit their host organism, instead the mitochondria 'hijacked' specific types of bacteria and used them in order to extract oxygen from surrounding molecules.[2] It may be that such bacterial entities are being used in other parts of cells as well, which seems to make a mockery of how we view evolution overall – could it be that large organisms evolved by using other life forms to give them a head start? We simply don't know enough about these processes to say for sure; however, we do know enough to make some people feel rather queasy.

Consider your gut: approximately six metres of grey and green muscle and mucous membrane, which ensures that the nutrients from the food you eat are absorbed correctly into your body, and the waste that your body doesn't need is expelled in a similarly efficient manner. It seems that a day doesn't pass without a newspaper, television or magazine advertisement telling people that they should keep their internal 'flora' intact. What a horrible thought – it conjures up images of delicate fronds of algae and other plant matter gently waving as the intestinal juices flow past. On a bad day, the images are more akin to the giant orange fungus that exploded out of the body cavities of scientists working in the crater of a volcano during an episode of the X Files.

Distressingly, it is the latter image that the yoghurt advertisements are closer to. The many forms of fungi and 'bad' bacteria that threaten to make our digestive experience an unpleasant one are not alone. A recent study on the nature of micro-organisms in the human body found that most of the individual cells in our body do not, in fact, belong to our bodies at all;[3] they consist of myriad fungi, bacteria and viruses (viruses are not really cells, but you get the idea) so numerous that, "because our bodies are made of only some several trillion human cells, we are somewhat outnumbered by the aliens."[4]

What Are Bacteria?

If you divided all definite forms of life into 'bacteria' and 'everything else' you would still have far more life in the former group than the latter. Everything teems with bacteria – sterilization is just a temporary respite, for they will come back relentlessly so long as there is something from which they can obtain nutrients. Obviously, bacteria are extremely small; typically they are about one micrometre in length – meaning you could fit hundreds of them end-to-end in the width of a human hair – although they can be as 'large' as half a millimetre.

The main difference between bacteria (including the very ancient and robust types, known as *Archaea*) and other forms of life is that bacteria don't have a nucleus in their one cell. Other single-celled organisms, such as amoebas, do have a nucleus, which puts them in the same group of life as all other non-bacterial organisms. The lack of a nucleus means that the bacterium's genetic material is in close contact with the rest of the organism's components,[5] such as those which convert food into energy. This makes a bacterium more vulnerable to attack and change, but on the positive side the simpler structure means that less energy and time are required for it to reproduce.

The reproduction process for bacteria is without emotion and turmoil: they simply divide when they reach a certain size. If you consider that there is a marine bacterium called *Pseudomonas natriegens* that can produce another generation in just under ten minutes[6] and that within one day a single bacterium (not a pair, we are talking asexual reproduction here) could become . . . well, I started working this out, and by 6 o'clock in the morning the number had already reached 68,700,000,000 individual organisms, and I realized that there was not enough room on Earth to accommodate one day of this single rapidly reproducing specimen! Compare this to the mosquitoes in Chapter 1, which reproduced fully in fourteen days under ideal conditions, and you get an idea of the kinds of things we are dealing with. Obviously the world would just be a mass of grey goo if bacteria could multiply according to their habit but, fortunately for us, most bacteria are *heterotrophs*, meaning they cannot make their own food. When their food runs out, the bacteria cannot multiply.

Like all tiny things, we have absolutely no idea how many different bacteria there are in the world. The likelihood is that because of their fragile genetic protection there are different kinds of bacteria being created faster than we could ever hope to count them. Certainly most hospitals struggle to keep up with the mutations that take place within their walls such that a single outbreak of a new antibiotic-resistant strain is cause for a national emergency. The human body copes admirably with its own harvest of integrated and not-so-integrated bacteria for the most part. When we lose control, though, we really lose it.

The phrase 'flesh-eating bug' may have been a newspaper seller for a short period in the early 1990s, but the bacteria that cause Necrotizing Fasciitis have always been with us, and will remain with us forever. If you have ever had a severe sore throat, then that will probably have been the result of a form of *Streptococcus* bacteria; hence the term 'strep throat'. In the vast majority of cases, time, rest and if necessary, a course of antibiotics will deal with strep throat. If the *Streptococcus* bacteria responsible for strep throat enter a wound on the skin, that can lead to something far worse. Eric Cornell, physics Nobel laureate, takes up the story:

> On Oct. 24, 2004, I came down with what I thought were flu symptoms – fever and a sense of malaise. The next day, I developed an aching pain in my shoulder. The pain steadily got worse and on Oct. 27, I was referred to the emergency room at Boulder Community Hospital. There I was diagnosed with necrotizing fasciitis and I underwent operations to cut away infected flesh, including amputation of my left arm and shoulder. However, even so, the infection continued to spread and I was very near death. In the afternoon of Oct. 28, I was airlifted to the Burn Intensive Care Unit at the University of Colorado Hospital in Denver. Two more operations removed more skin, muscle, and subcutaneous fat from large areas of my left torso.[7]

Professor Cornell survived his ordeal, after a three-week coma and intensive therapy. Others do not. Fatality rates, according to the US Centers for Disease Control are around 25%, extremely high for an infectious disease. The number of deaths each year from Necrotizing Fasciitis is probably around 150,000 to 200,000 [8] – far less than the annual total for influenza, but a lot more deadly. Nevertheless, it pales into insignificance when you consider the overall number of deaths that result from bacterial infections, both directly and indirectly.

Direct Killers

As a fourteen-year-old school student, I remember the little needles, the tiny sharp bunch of concentric spikes that pierced my skin with a click. Phew! That's over. But it wasn't, because like most of my friends, I didn't have the right antibodies, meaning that I had never had the disease before, had never been vaccinated before, or didn't have natural immunity to the infection. The second needle was longer. A prefect held me, with my left arm down at my side, while the nurse inserted the metal spike into my upper arm and filled a void under the skin with milky-white fluid. A synthetic blister, the legacy of which is still with almost every person who went to school in the UK up to the mid-1990s, as a small scar.

Vaccinations don't always work. The BCG vaccination, named after its French inventors (hence Bacillus Calmette-Guérin), protects against some types of tuberculosis (TB) but not others. The most common and most infectious type – pulmonary tuberculosis – is poorly controlled by BCG, but for the moment BCG is the best vaccine widely available. Unfortunately, TB is a widespread and devastating killer, with an average of 1.7 million reported deaths a year between 1995 and 2005:[9] and one-third of the world's population thought to be latently infected with the bacteria.[10] The reason for the endemic presence of TB is likely to be related to its long history as a human pathogen. Of the 85 mummies exhumed from a number of tombs in Egypt, 25 were found to have probably been infected with tuberculosis, with another twelve that definitely were infected.[11] The specimens from the oldest of the tombs showed that even 4,000 years ago, the infection had been caught from other humans rather than (as previously thought) cattle.

Given the length of time that humans have had to adapt to the TB bacterium in its various forms, it is not surprising that most carriers do not actually contract the disease; but given its reputation as the most deadly infectious disease on Earth, it has to be taken seriously. Africa is the heartland for TB: Zambia had 118 TB deaths per 100,000 people in 2005 (down from 208 in 1999, but still over 5%

of all deaths); 140 people out of every 100,000 died in Kenya in the same year from TB (13% of all deaths); and in Swaziland in 2005, TB accounted for 304 deaths per 100,000 people, or 10% of its already terrible death rate. Overall rates are dropping because of better health education along with more widespread vaccination and antibiotic availability, but the killer still lies dormant, only needing a little nudge to wake it up and wreak further havoc.

That nudge may come in the form of global warming.

Bacteria love heat. Bacteria need heat, and some thrive in conditions that would be deadly to any other life form. *Pyrodictyum* grows best at 105°C, while others cannot reproduce if their temperature drops to less than 80°C. Truly creatures of Hades,[12] these 'extremophiles' may occupy niches in which no other organism has a chance of survival, but the majority of bacteria have very specific temperature requirements well within the realms of humans. Speaking to Martin Wiselka of the Nuffield Hospital, Leicester, it becomes clear that our warming world will increasingly become a haven for many types of harmful bacteria. He says: "Most bacteria which are pathogenic to humans survive and reproduce optimally at around 37°C (in other words, they are adapted to humans). Bacteria maintained at this temperature are likely to grow faster and become more infectious than those at a lower temperature which is why we refrigerate our food to make it last longer. Certain bacteria will only survive in warm climates."[13]

The relationship between the growth rate of bacteria and temperature is remarkably consistent, such that it is possible for scientists to develop general rules to predict how quickly a specific type of bacteria will multiply at a certain temperature. For example, if a certain type of bacteria doubles in number every fifteen minutes under a certain set of conditions, e.g. in a test tube full of milk at 10°C, then under the same conditions but at 15°C the growth rate of that strain of bacteria can be very accurately predicted. David Ratkowsky and his colleagues at the University of Tasmania found the relationship held true in their own samples, and also in the 29 other examples they extracted from various pieces of scientific literature.[14] In short, under ideal conditions, for every 5°C increase in temperature, bacteria divide between 50% and 100% faster. A mere 1°C increase can therefore increase the division rate of bacteria by around 20%. For a common pathogen like Salmonella (1.4 million cases per year in the USA),[15] this kind of change is vital when working out the time that food can be kept out of cold storage, and also how many people are likely to be infected under a range of conditions. Salmonella is not just responsible for the illness caused by undercooked meat and eggs, though: serious as these strains can be, others have an even darker side.

Typhoid fever is caused by the bacteria *Salmonella typhi*, and is the cause of

over half a million deaths worldwide every year.[16] Unlike tuberculosis, typhoid
will happily live outside of the body, specializing particularly in standing water
containing human sewage. A pond, well or ditch only has to contain a fragment
of faecal matter from the unwashed hands of a child for the entire water source
to become infected; and the warmer the water is, the faster it will become
infected until every person drinking that water is fated to ingest the bacteria.
Vaccinations are an effective preventative measure against typhoid, and antibiotics can bring most cases under control, but studies carried out in Vietnam and
throughout Africa have found numerous strains of antibiotic-resistant typhoid
throughout the population, and even bacteria that appear to be changing the way
that they evolve in order to survive.[17] As I discussed in Chapter 1, the increased
density and mobility of humans is also creating the conditions for bacteria to
mutate more rapidly:

> In 1989, multidrug-resistant *S. Typhi* appeared, with the emergence of strains
> resistant to chloramphenicol, ampicillin, trimethoprim, streptomycin, sulfon-
> amides, and tetracycline. The prevalence of multidrug-resistant *S. Typhi* has also
> increased among travellers. The rate of multidrug-resistant *S. Typhi* infection in
> American travellers acquired in India increased from 30% in 1990–1994 to 35%
> in 1996–1997, and 4 of 5 travellers with typhoid fever acquired in Vietnam were
> infected with multidrug-resistant strains.[18]

Not only are most antibiotics useless against the newest strains of typhoid,
but it also won't be long before, as with influenza, vaccines themselves have to be
updated regularly in order for them to be effective against the disease. With the
Earth due to heat up by another 1.3°C by the middle of the twenty-first century
– twice as much heating as experienced in the last 200 years – we can confidently
overlay the heating effect upon the dual microbiological horrors of overcrowd-
ing and excessive travel. Now imagine what that will do to the activity of our bacterial colleagues.

How do you feel? Let's go on.

Indirect Killers

Like any good horror story, sometimes you need a bit of comedy to give your
mind a rest from the constant torment it is suffering. When I was in my twen-
ties, I read the war diaries of the unique and sadly-missed comedy genius Spike
Milligan over and over again. Such was his skill as a writer that you could be
lifted straight out of a terrible battle scene into a nugget of sparkling wit, barely
having time to draw breath. Never forget that you always have time to laugh – it

really helps when contemplating annihilation.

One moment that has stayed with me concerned the outbreak of pubic lice, or 'crabs', amongst the cable-laying team which Spike's best friend, Harry Edgington, was part of. Their work was relentless, repetitive and filthy. As Harry said: "We hadn't had our clothes off for some considerable time, much less our underwear, and a bath was only something we vaguely remembered from long ago." [19] He then goes on to tell in vivid but hilarious detail of how the British army dealt with such an outbreak – modesty and a low pain threshold are two attributes that wouldn't have held the soldiers in good stead. Pubic lice certainly qualify as a considerable irritation and, like most personal problems, are a ripe target for comedians. Lyme Disease, another animal-borne infection, is perhaps less likely to be the target of comedy, although I do recall it featured in an episode of The Simpsons.[20] Humour aside, Lyme Disease *is* a very serious illness if left untreated, causing heart problems and a variety of nervous conditions, but is very rarely fatal. As a major risk factor, Lyme Disease is not something that should worry most people. But it is an important indicator.

Figure 3: Deer Tick

Lyme Disease in the USA is carried by black-footed or deer ticks, which in turn are carried (or 'hosted') by deer, mice, squirrels and other rodents. In Europe and northern Asia, other ticks, including the castor bean and sheep tick, harbour the bacteria that are then passed on to humans and other animals through their bites. These ticks are hosted by a variety of animals. Ticks, lice, fleas and other arthropods are sensitive to temperature and other environmental conditions, including moisture, habitat type and the availability of hosts, but they cannot migrate on their own, relying instead on their hosts to move for them.

As I have said, Lyme Disease is not a serious threat to life, but it has been on the increase in the USA, steadily growing from less than 10,000 cases in 1991 to 23,000 in 2005.[21] This is partly due to better reporting methods, but also the intrusion of humans into the native habitats (mainly woodlands) of the ticks and their hosts. This bears a striking resemblance to the way that Ebola has spread in central Africa. There is also good evidence to show that as humans degrade the habitats they intrude upon they reduce the number of different species in that habitat – its biodiversity – and thus the competition for food also reduces. The outcome of this is that one species tends to dominate, and in the case of the woodlands of north-east USA, that is the white-footed mouse.[22] The white-footed mouse hosts the deer tick, and the deer tick can infect people more easily due to the invasive habits of the mouse.

Some animals carry Lyme Disease; others carry Bubonic Plague. You would be forgiven, if you live in the Western industrial world, for thinking that plague is just a bad memory from the past that, thankfully, no longer threatens lives. Sadly, plague is most certainly alive and well, and is living in Africa: "Globally, the number of cases of human plague has remained stable from year to year and, in comparison with other infectious pathologies, can be considered weak. Nevertheless, human plague remains a public health problem worldwide. The re-emergence of human plague in Algeria in 2003, fifty years after its last occurrence, further demonstrates that the geographical distribution of natural foci is not immutable."[23] In other words, plague is out there, and it could emerge anywhere.

But bacteria don't even need to infect humans to affect them.

The majority of people on Earth drink milk or eat dairy products. A sizeable minority eat meat products from cattle, and this proportion is growing as people in newly industrialized countries start to see the 'Western' meat-rich diet as a symbol of luxury and success. Such a diet is actively promoted by the meat processing and producing industry throughout the world, partly because many people in the most industrialized nations are reducing their intake of both meat and dairy. Approximately 15% of global calories derive directly from the consumption of meat,[24] of which a quarter is from cattle. In addition, a significant chunk of the world's total calories comes from dairy products. A major cattle disease would be tragic for those who have become accustomed to a cattle-dependent diet.

Cattle farmers in tropical and subtropical regions fear the deadly and debilitating disease called cattle anaplasmosis, but have to accept it as a known hazard for their herds. Such is the threat of this disease to commerce, that as far back as 1906 the US government carried out a complete eradication of the disease and placed strict quarantine measures on its borders to ensure that no infected cattle could cross into the USA from Mexico. The potential of the disease for economic damage is truly momentous. Back in 1981 the United Nations Food and Agricultural Organization (FAO) stated: "The figure must be staggering. Mortality rates range from 5% in some herds where the disease has been prevalent for many years to as high as 70% during severe outbreaks in herds where the disease has not occurred previously. Though death losses are sometimes overwhelming, they can also be minor as compared with weight, milk, and calf losses among surviving cattle."[25] Current reports suggest that the disease is still endemic in tropical areas and will readily infect, and kill, any cattle that are introduced alongside immune animals.

The most deadly form of cattle anaplasmosis is caused by the bacterium *Anaplasma marginale*, and most commonly carried from animal to animal by the tropical cattle tick *Boophilus microplus*. Like all other ticks, this one is sensitive to environmental conditions,[26] and will not lay eggs in temperatures of less than 15-20°C. As with mosquitoes and midges, a small rise in regional temperature will allow the ticks to breed further north, at a higher altitude and potentially on animals that have not been able to host them in cooler temperatures. If a disease with the virulence of cattle anaplasmosis appeared in humans, then we would be considering a pandemic on the scale of the 1918 influenza outbreak, or the aforementioned bubonic plague. Interestingly, the bacteria that are readily spread by the tropical cattle tick to cause cattle anaplasmosis are of the same genus[27] as the bacteria that are spread by the deer tick to cause the potentially lethal human form of anaplasmosis. The more you look into it, the more complex the web becomes.

Typhus is nothing to do with typhoid. The two are often confused, and both are caused by bacteria; but whereas typhoid fever is spread via infected watercourses, typhus is most usually carried by the human body louse, spreading the bacteria when its faeces are scratched into a louse bite. Typhus is at its worst when it causes epidemics of disease; typically where sanitary conditions are poor, clothes are rarely changed, and floor coverings and furnishings filthy. Such conditions prevail during wartime, in prison camps, ghettos, trenches and concentration camps – the physical and mental brutality carried out by the guards in the Nazi concentration camps of World War II is only part of the tale:

Maj. William A. Davis, MC, while serving as liaison officer from the U.S.A. Typhus Commission to the 21st Army Group, recorded the typhus fever epidemic that occurred at the Belsen Concentration Camp, Belsen, Germany. This camp was taken by the British Second Army on 15 April 1945. Among the 61,000 inhabitants, there was widespread suffering from starvation, typhus, dysentery, tuberculosis, and other diseases. Typhus had been prevalent in the camp for four months, and there were approximately 3,500 cases at the time of liberation. Practically all of the internees were heavily infested with lice.[28]

At the start of World War I, Serbia was literally decimated by typhus, killing 200,000 of its people. Worse was to come: after cutting through much of the eastern war front in Europe, it ravaged post-war Russia, killing around ten million people with a 50% fatality rate.[29] War stories are awash not only with experiences of awful living conditions, but also of delousing: the use of toxic powders and other chemicals, including DDT; hair being forcibly shaved off; clothing and blankets being burnt. These methods were often brutal and always uncomfortable, but were usually the only rapid way to prevent disease epidemics in such conditions.

The kinds of conditions that much of the world's population has to put up with are creating new breeding-grounds for diseases like typhus. The cramped, unserviced slums skirting Mumbai, Sao Paolo and Jakarta are barely acknowledged by the same authorities that pride themselves on their city's economic opportunities. These shanty-towns, favelas and ghettos are the result of a multitude of individual aspirations that never came to fruition because the dream-sellers failed to deliver on their promises. Instead, the aspirant slum-dwellers get disease and a way of life that is often far worse than the one they wanted to escape from.

Most poignant of all, the bacteria that cause these explosive diseases are almost certainly the same kind of bacteria that first found their homes in our cells millions of years ago.[30] In a striking example of the wheel of life turning full circle, the mitochondrial bacteria that we rely on to provide our cells with energy have evolved to also be devastating killers.

Bacteria will continue to evolve and occupy every niche that exists on Earth long after we are gone. We depend on them, and we fear them. If we dare to alter the environments in which they exist, you can be certain they will win the first assault before we have the chance to fight back.

Chapter 3

One Thousandth of a Metre

We're coming back to familiar things now. The great blobs on the lens that were just misty patches are finally slipping into some sort of focus, and a whole raft of life forms is dropping by the wayside as we pull out and change our scale to something far larger: the tiny fragments of plankton that fill the oceans; the dusty fungal clouds in the evening air; the singular amoebas that live wherever there is moisture – all wonderful subjects, but for another time. I just can't seem to get the focus right though: the nematodes are everywhere. Where should I start?

What about soybeans?

I have just found out that The Society of Nematologists is advertising the 4th National Soybean Cyst Nematode Conference: a whole conference about the egg-filled bodies of a specific nematode worm that affects a specific crop. This being the fourth such conference, you might be forgiven for accusing the organizers of being a little over-enthusiastic – maybe they are scientists ensuring they have their research grants for another year; maybe they are companies trying to sell a product; maybe soybean cyst nematodes are actually very important indeed. Actually it's all three. Scientists need to justify their work so they can keep on working: unfortunately, whereas justification used to be on mostly scientific grounds, justification in many modern universities requires evidence of commercial potential. Pest control companies need to raise the profile of the 'pests' they sell control products for, so they can sell their products to worried consumers.[1] Finally, according to the US Department of Agriculture, the cultivation of soybeans is not economically possible unless soybean nematode cysts are sufficiently controlled.[2]

A glance at the literature on nematodes reveals two things: they are apparently almost all damaging pests, and there are an awful lot of them. In regard to the latter point, many writers turn to the words of Nathan A. Cobb, the legendary nematologist and stalwart of the US Department of Agriculture in the first half of the 20th century:

In short, if all the matter in the universe except the nematodes were swept away, our world would still be dimly recognizable, and if, as disembodied spirits, we could then investigate it, we should find its mountains, hills, vales, rivers, lakes, and oceans represented by a film of nematodes. The location of towns would be decipherable, since for every massing of human beings there would be a corresponding massing of certain nematodes. Trees would still stand in ghostly rows representing our streets and highways. The location of the various plants and animals would still be decipherable, and, had we sufficient knowledge, in many cases even their species could be determined by an examination of their erstwhile nematode parasites.[3]

Stirring stuff, indeed. Nathan Cobb could certainly move the soul when writing about his foremost passion; and he needed to, because if ever a biological subject needed a higher profile, it was the much-maligned but utterly fascinating world of nematodes. Cobb himself recognized this problem, writing: "[nematodes] offer an exceptional field of study, and probably constitute almost the last great organic group worthy of a separate branch of biological science comparable with entomology."[4] But was Cobb right? Do nematodes really create this film of organic matter around every object in contact with the Earth?

There is a certain difficulty in gaining realistic statistics about the variety and quantity of nematodes; after all, nematodes were not formally discovered until 1808, principally because they are too small to observe properly with the naked eye. Victor Dropkin made a more sober assessment than Cobb of the nematode population in 1980, stating: "Take a handful of soil from almost anywhere in the world . . . and you will find elongate, threadlike, active animals. These are nematodes. Or catch a fish, a bird or a mammal almost anywhere in the world...and in most cases you will find some nematodes inside."[5] Although nematodes are aquatic animals, in that they need water to survive, the best place to find them is in soil. Simon Gowen of the University of Reading tells his students that in temperate grasslands there are around nine million nematodes for *every square metre of soil* – then the same students are expected to count them for themselves (not all nine million of them, I hasten to add), just to get an idea of what this means. That is an astounding figure for something that is not a virus or a bacterium, but an animal. This means that the lush grasslands of New Zealand that produce rich butter, high quality lamb and 150 thousand tonnes of wool each year,[6] but only constitute 5.5% of New Zealand's land area, also hold something like 132,660,000,000,000,000 nematodes. That's 132 quadrillion, for those of you who ever wanted to know how large a quadrillion is. Compare this with the apocryphal (but believable, and slightly disturbing!) figure of one million spiders per acre of grassland, and you find that nematodes outnumber spiders by 36,000 to 1.

Globally – and I'm going to have to take a stab in the dark here – you are probably looking at between 100 quintillion (that's 20 zeros) and 1,000 quintillion (21 zeros) nematodes on and in the land. To put this into perspective somewhat: for each human on Earth, there are something like a trillion nematodes. Nematodes in the oceans are far less abundant, but there are still lots and lots of them – they may, in fact, account for 90% of all life at the bottom of the sea.[7] Apologies for boggling you with figures, but that's what often happens in nematode-land.

The pest-control industry ensures that the dangers that would be unleashed in a world where nematodes are not controlled are writ large in the minds of farmers, so it is the 'pest' nematodes that are given the biggest exposure, at the expense of other types. Despite the commercial world's propensity to invent problems in order to sell products, they may in this case be right – but for all the wrong reasons. The pressure we place on already exhausted soils and the effort we go to in order to extract every last gram of nutrition from industrially farmed crops to feed a growing human population (both in number and, in rich countries, appetite), means that the slightest drop in the production of a staple crop is treated as a potential catastrophe.

In the majority of European countries, the impact of the potato cyst nematode (PCN) is such that the movement of untested seed potatoes and the planting of potatoes on untested land is banned, and the quarantine of land on which PCN is found is mandatory.[8] PCN is a global problem for potato growers, being found across Europe (since 1913, and possibly the 1880s), in Australia (since 1986), in the USA (since 1941) – in fact just about everywhere that potatoes are grown on a large scale. There are quite a few varieties of potato that are naturally resistant to the effects of PCN, which essentially means not being in danger of having entire crops wiped out within two seasons of growing on the same spot; and there are lots of sensible, non-chemical methods of avoiding the problem, such as the aforementioned quarantine, crop rotation and the use of natural predators. But the chemical companies persist in pushing their wares, both in the form of pesticides and genetically modified organisms (GMOs):

> The chemical group BASF has expressed optimism that within a few weeks the European Commission may approve the genetically modified 'Amflora' potato to be grown in Europe. In early December, Hans Kast, Managing Director of BASF Plant Science, spoke with journalists in Brussels and stated the expectation the decision be made in any case early enough for the growing season of 2008.[9]

It won't be too long before natural resistance to PCN is engineered into non-resistant potato varieties. Now, I am no scaremonger when it comes to genetic modification, but when economic gain comes before concerns for environmental welfare – the GMO-producing companies still obstinately refuse to accept liability for any negative effects of their products – and the number of discovered nematode species is less than 10% of the number that potentially exists in the wild, then I start to get a little worried.

Then there is the question of pest versus friend:

Figure 4: Nematode Adverts

Yes, those are adverts from Google. It's remarkable what is advertised on the internet: not so much the availability of salacious activities and products to enhance your performance in all sorts of ways, but the wide range of friendly nematodes that you can use in your garden, and can buy on-line: nematodes in a box. I think it's about time we stopped for a little, and went back to first principles.

What Are Nematodes?

Remember me saying that I had problems getting the focus right? There are teeny-tiny nematodes and there are, relatively, very large ones indeed. I admit the title of this chapter takes a few liberties, but there are many species of nematode that are around a millimetre in length. There are many that are less than a millimetre, and some parasitic types that are a few centimetres long. One type (which no one alive seems to have seen) was measured at eight metres long, in the placenta of a sperm whale. This species is, unironically, known as *Placentonema gigantissima*.

Nematode is the name given to any one of at least 20,000 species of unsegmented worm, which have a single end-to-end digestive tract, no limbs or other appendages, and a surprisingly well-developed nervous system, considering their antiquity. They are commonly known as 'roundworms', which describes their cross section, not their overall shape, and which distinguishes them from many other types of worm, including flatworms and bristle worms.

Such is their age and diversity (although this does not always follow) that they occupy their own Phylum, separate from the arthropods (insects, spiders etc.) and molluscs. There are as many as twenty different Orders of nematode, ranging from those that attack plants and fungi, to those that feed on other animals, to those that drift around feeding on whatever bacteria or single-celled animal might be available. Despite nematodes being aquatic in origin, the vast majority of Orders describe land-based varieties. This strange inconsistency is most likely simply because the world's oceans have been so poorly researched compared with the landmasses we are so familiar with. Our natural, possibly ancestral attraction to the sea, a place that has always (until recently) provided us with a rich source of food, only goes so far. Without technology to help us breathe humans immersed in water – like gasping fish on the water's edge – will only survive for a minute or so. Maybe it is for the good that much of the vast oceanic world has been left unexplored – the level of exploitation by the oil, gas and industrial fishing industries is a dire warning of what can happen – but it does leave us with a large empty space in our knowledge, and the consequent skewing of information that suggests that the oceans are a vast, barren place. Sadly, that lack of knowledge also hides the inexorable, and possibly irreversible changes that we may be causing to the oceans.

Because nematodes can look very similar, regardless of their size, they are most commonly distinguished by their mouth-parts, which define what they are able to eat. Nematologists do have what some might consider to be an unhealthy obsession with mouth parts, but when you have a great mass of seething, wormy matter to identify, then it's usually best to take the easy route. Such efforts are not without their rewards though: success in the field of nematology can be quite lucrative if you don't have any qualms about taking the corporate shilling.

The multi-segmented tapeworm that can live for years inside humans and most other mammals is not a nematode; human parasitic threadworms and hookworms, on the other hand, are nematodes. I'm sorry to enter the bowel, as it were, at this stage of the chapter, but if you have had anything to do with children's health or education, then you will probably have come across threadworms. Unfortunately for human health, children have a propensity to pick, scratch and probe anything and everything with their fingers: noses, scabs on knees, eyes, bottoms. Under the nails of a good proportion of kindergarten children just about anywhere in the world lie a little cluster of threadworm eggs waiting to be passed into the digestive system (you can guess how) of that child, or any other person they may meet: "How do you do?" and with a shake of the hand the eggs are passed on. Fortunately for us, threadworms are relatively harmless.

There are a number of other parasitic nematodes that infect humans and other mammals: in dogs, hookworms can cause severe anaemia, and in both dogs and cats the roundworm *Toxocara* is endemic. The latter is of particular concern to humans because of the potentially severe symptoms that the resulting Toxocariasis can lead to, including blindness and pneumonia. Studies carried out between 1985 and 2000 found that children's sandpits in public parks contained Toxocara eggs a minimum of 25% of the time, with one study in Greece finding 97.5% of play parks infected.[10] A child who touches dog or cat faeces will almost certainly have nematodes on his or her fingers. This level of infection may be shocking, but it is the hygiene failures of humans that have turned something pretty benign into something approaching epidemic proportions in certain parts of the world. This lack of hygiene makes the little press nematodes get predominantly negative – which is a shame because, like humans, not all of them are bad.

The Good Guys

Good organic gardeners know how to deal with pests – the kinds that damage the crops they are trying to grow. A piece of fruit or a vegetable is at its most appealing to birds, insects, slugs and snails at just the time when it is at its most appealing to us; the sugar-rich strawberry, the fat-to-bursting pea pod, the succulent red tomato, the crisp crimson and white radish – all perfect for eating, regardless who the final consumer may be. Good organic gardeners don't need to spray chemicals across their gardens, to be caught by the wind and misted across the neighbouring crops, flowers and ponds, and into the lungs of playing children: they just need to understand the natural interactions between plants, soil, weather and the organisms that may protect or attack what they are trying to grow.

The history of pesticides (that kill animals), herbicides (that kill plants) and fungicides is littered with toxins that no sensible people would let anywhere near their mouths. We see arsenic being widely used for pest control on plants, and even as sheep dip; mercury, formaldehyde and hydrogen cyanide used to fumigate buildings and glasshouses; and the surprisingly lethal copper sulphate applied as a common weedkiller.[11] Paris Green derived its name from its colour and its use as a rat control agent in the sewers of Paris in the 19th century. Alternatively known as Parrot Green and Emerald Green, amongst other names, it is a compound of copper and arsenic, and is still widely used as a barnacle prevention measure on the hulls of ships, and as a wood preservative, as well as an insecticide. Seven drops of this (surprisingly unregulated) substance is enough to kill a normal-sized human,[12] and its death toll almost certainly includes many artists who keenly made use of its vivid tones; not to mention the poor souls who made the stuff. It seems that if a substance is useful enough, then being lethal in tiny doses is not enough reason to regulate it.

The use of cyanide, mercury and formaldehyde may have been dramatically reduced during the 20th century, but given the boom in the use of organophosphates and organochlorines ('organo' simply means something that is carbonbased), such substances were not required much anyway. The world now had cheap, highly effective and controllable – so it seemed – agents that could be applied at will. Of course, as we know now (and, no doubt, the manufacturers already knew early on), the legacy of these chemicals was passed into the water and from mother to child in countless animal species, including humans. There is no way of knowing how many cancer deaths have been caused by chemical pesticides, nor any way of predicting how many more deaths will come as their legacy lives on both in the bodies of fish and marine mammals, and also those parts of the world where such pesticides are still commonly used with relish.

Organic gardening and farming have been practised for far longer than chemical-based growing, and nematodes can play an important part in this. Remember those I mentioned that feed on other animals? Well, there is a whole range of different species that not only leave the plants you are growing well alone, but also actively destroy the very creatures that would otherwise cause damage. Technically, these are known as entomopathogenic nematodes,[13] and there are two main species that are used: *Steinernema* and *Heterorhabditis*. They are similar in form and effect, both killing a wide range of insects and related organisms, such as caterpillars, by entering their bodies as juveniles then releasing bacteria that are toxic to the host. These bacteria kill the insect, after which the nematode is free to mate or, in the case of *Heterorhabditis*, reproduce alone.

The downside? Well, there really isn't one, unless you count having to make sure they are not fried by ultraviolet light, or overheated. I include this quotation from Cornell University, just to show I am not overstating the advantages of these wonders:

> Entomopathogenic nematodes are extraordinarily lethal to many important soil insect pests, yet are safe for plants and animals. This high degree of safety means that unlike chemicals, nematode applications do not require masks or other safety equipment; residues, groundwater contamination and pollinators are not issues. Most [other] biologicals require days or weeks to kill, yet nematodes, working with their symbiotic bacteria, kill insects in 24-48 hrs.

> Dozens of different insect pests are susceptible to infection, yet no adverse effects have been shown against non-targets in field studies. Nematode production is easily accomplished for some species using standard fermentation in tanks up to 150,000 litres. Nematodes do not require specialized application equipment as they are compatible with standard agrochemical equipment.[14]

"But wait!", you may say, "if these creatures are such efficient killers, then surely they can multiply, spread and kill off everything they touch, even human-beneficial insects." A fair point, but one that isn't backed up in practice. The aim of applying commercially available biological control nematodes is in order to overload the natural system and kill many more insects than would be killed by nematodes naturally.[15] After they are applied, they do indeed destroy their targets very quickly, but once the target is destroyed then there is little for the juvenile worm to mature within and nematode numbers rapidly decline.

So why aren't nematodes used all over the world, making most types of pesticide redundant? There are three reasons. First, not a lot of widely read research has been carried out on the usefulness of such nematodes; in fact many nematologists still believe that every nematode is a pest.[16] Second, although nematode insect parasites were identified as effective controls in the 1930s, the availability of cheap, effective chemical pesticides in the 1940s caused this research to be largely ignored, and it was not until some chemicals were banned that research started up again.[17] Finally, and linking these two together, it is clear from the continued lobbying of powerful companies like BASF, Monsanto and Syngenta, that the chemical industry will not give up without a fight. It is no coincidence that DDT was not widely banned until 20 years after clear evidence of its terrible impacts on wildlife was made public, and that the 2007 European Union REACH legislation – which enforces the control of hundreds of previously uncontrolled chemicals – took ten difficult years to come into force. Industry still calls the shots, even in an age when it is so obvious that natural ecosystems cannot cope with the torrent of chemicals being washed into them day after day.

Moving with the Climate

How fast can a nematode move? One study suggests that 3cm in five hours is a fair guess;[18] although there are so many variables that all we can truly say is they move pretty well considering their size. Despite their elegant, sinuous propulsion method, the problems nematodes have in movement are manifold, largely related to their diminutive length. Even in water, something about a millimetre long will experience considerable pressures from all sides, and have to swim through the thick soup of tightly interconnected molecules to make any headway – if you have ever tried to run in the sea then you will understand how it feels. In the soil the problems are multiplied: air gaps have to be traversed, boulder-like grains circumvented and anything like a solid object simply accepted as impassable. Viruses and bacteria can be carried in water flows, or in droplets through the air, but animal vectors are the smart way to travel, whether this be within parasitized insects or the gut of a human. A flying insect, bird or aircraft will lap up distance with ease, meaning that anything able to take advantage of a mobile host is definitely one more rung up the evolutionary ladder. Nematodes are also easily transmitted from one place to another on plants, as they are moved from nursery to farm and on agricultural equipment. The latter is particularly significant. It only requires a farmer to plough a field infected with, for instance, root-knot nematode, and then plough an uninfected field with the same plough, for the nematode to become ensconced in the next field.[19]

The rate of global heating, although significant in its impact on the forces that drive weather and other processes that rely on heat, is only slowly creeping across the Earth; slowly but inexorably altering environments as the swathe of change moves across the land and the sea. Gradual movement is what nematodes can best take advantage of, and that gradual movement is what is starting to concern farmers. There is a concept used by phenologists (people who study the timescales and cycles of natural events) called Degree Days. A degree day is simply a measure of the amount of time available for an event to occur depending on temperature: one day at one degree above the lowest temperature an organism will breed at is one degree day. Using this system it is possible to predict the lengths of the life cycles of many organisms, including nematodes, according to the measured air temperature. For example, if a certain nematode requires the temperature to be above 5°C and below 30°C to carry out its life cycle, four days at a constant 10°C makes 20 degree days.

Using degree days, not only is it possible to work out how long the life cycle of a nematode will be at different temperatures, but you can also determine whether an area of soil is warm enough for the life cycle to take place at all. The root-knot nematode is widely regarded as one of the world's most destructive pathogens.[20] If a particular species of root-knot nematode needs 1,000 degree days to produce an entirely new generation of worms in a new crop of potatoes or carrots in a new field,[21] then a 1°C average temperature increase could certainly make the difference between a new field being a favourable breeding-ground or not, and the difference between a crop being successful or not. One ploughing is enough to distribute a few plants' worth of nematodes across an entire field; just because nematodes move slowly, doesn't mean that they can't spread extraordinarily quickly. If temperatures in a field never drop below the lower threshold for root-knot nematode, then the nematode will happily keep multiplying there all the time food is available: impervious, because of sheer numbers, to all but the most toxic applications of pesticide. I'll leave you to imagine what the impact of increasing temperature on our food supply could be.

A Singularity of Bananas

Here are some facts about bananas:

1. They grow on ground-loving plants, not trees.
2. The fruit of the banana plant can be yellow, green, purple or even red.

3. In their natural form, bananas have large seeds.

4. A single variety, 'Cavendish', accounts for the vast majority of the world's banana trade. It is virtually seedless.

5. Bananas are an analogy for the whole of the industrial economy.

OK, that last one you won't find in any textbooks or scientific journals, but I'm not just making this up on the spot; you may consider society to have gone 'bananas' in more ways than one, but even that isn't what I'm getting at. The simple fact is that the bananas that most of us eat are in deadly peril, and it is likely that the global supply will be largely wiped out within a few years. It was only in the 1950s that the previous reigning variety 'Gros Michel' was almost totally destroyed by a fungus called Panama Disease. Gros Michel had many of the characteristics of Cavendish, except it wasn't resistant to the particular type of fungus that Cavendish is; but that is set to change dramatically. The problem is that every Cavendish plant is genetically identical to the original variety that was brought to the Caribbean from south-east Asia in the early 19th century,[22] regardless of the small differences in texture, size and colour that derive from different growing methods and climates. In order for genetic variety to occur in plants that reproduce sexually, two sets of chromosomes, one male, one female, have to be combined. Making cuttings doesn't create genetic variety, and this is basically the reason why family interbreeding amongst humans has been outlawed in most human cultures for centuries, possibly even thousands of years. It is not possible for different sexes to be genetically identical, but if brothers and sisters, or other close relatives breed over a number of generations, then any damaging genetic mutations will remain within the family line, eventually leading to a much higher rate of abnormalities, including poor resistance to disease.

Evolution occurs in order to ensure that a particular species remains hardy enough to continue its line. The Cavendish, and the Gros Michel before it, are perfect examples of what happens when evolution is not allowed to occur. In the 40 years since Gros Michel was almost wiped off the map, the fungus that caused Panama Disease in that plant has evolved so that it can now do the same to Cavendish. In the words of one writer: "the banana is too perfect, lacking the genetic diversity that is key to species health. What can ail one banana can ail all. A fungus or bacterial disease that infects one plantation could march around the globe and destroy millions of bunches, leaving supermarket shelves empty."[23] Lack of bananas may not cause huge numbers of deaths, but lack of genetic diversity most certainly can:

> From 1845 to 1846 Ireland's potato crop consisted of one or two closely related varieties. Both were wiped out by blight. In the ensuing famine, nearly a million

people died and more than a million others were forced to emigrate. By 1851 Ireland's population had diminished by 23%. If Irish farmers had been growing many varieties of potatoes with different genetic backgrounds the disaster would never have happened.[24]

You may ask why this is an analogy of the industrial economy. The reason is that throughout the 20th century and into the 21st century, money and the possession of material goods have come to dominate the way societies are run, especially in the industrial West. The market economy, which governs the way most commerce and a great deal of politics in the world operates, does not favour diversity – positively discourages it, in fact. The spoils almost always end up going to the individual, company or country that can provide the most of some thing or another – whether that be a raw material, a consumer product, a service, or a variety of banana or potato – at the cheapest price, in the shortest time and, often as a result, at the lowest quality. This is the way this type of economic system works: if you want genuine variety (and quality) then you have to operate outside the market economy.

Of course there are notable exceptions, for instance products that fail strict safety guidelines in one country will not be sold there, but that does not mean they cannot be successful in countries where those guidelines don't exist. The much-touted sub-$2,000 car will, no doubt, be a roaring success in India, its country of manufacture, but can never be sold in Europe, Canada or the USA due to its poor construction. But in the main, big, fast and cheap wins out; so while the Cavendish banana is the type chosen by the largest producers, who effectively have the banana market cornered, then that will be the banana that sits on supermarket shelves, market stalls and in fruit bowls around the world.

You may also ask what all this talk about bananas is doing in a chapter about nematodes. Like almost all types of food crop, bananas are vulnerable to attack by nematodes; and in many countries they can cause losses of 30% to 60%[25] – that is the difference between making a living from banana sales, and not being able to afford to grow the crop. Two particular species of nematode, *Pratylenchus coffeae* and *Radopholus similis*, exist right across the world, from the Caribbean, to Ecuador, to Central Africa, to the Philippines – in fact everywhere bananas are grown on a commercial basis. There can be little doubt that this vast distribution is the result of a single, genetically identical variety of banana having a virtual monopoly. Even if the new strain of Panama Disease doesn't finish off the world's banana crop, then a tiny writhing worm may well do so; a tiny little worm whose relations we hardly notice, but which exist in uncountable numbers in almost every animal, every piece of soil, every plant and all the way down at the bottom of the ocean.

Chapter 4

One Hundredth of a Metre

Imagine a spring day.

See it in your mind: the haze of warmth at the edge of the field disturbing the patterns of air and giving the impression of water, a narrow strip of silvery light in a verdant land that has drunk in the rains of April. Smell it: the heady scent of open flowers releasing their aroma as the bleached sun reaches its apex. Breathe it in: the sharp tang of a distant coast mixed with the moisture of a dew-laden lawn. Feel it: the rough woody trunk of the tree at your back, the dampness on your hands that lie in the grass, the hope of a season of life and continuity.

Hear it. Hear the pulsing drone of a distant light aircraft crossing the sky; hear the evidence of habitation, the mowers and the moan of traffic, just out of sight; hear the tolling church bells drift across the land, striking the noon, sending out a message of time and divinity; hear the honey-bees. Silence. The aircraft drone lessens, the mowers halt, the traffic stops, the bells lose their voice, but the bees' wings are not beating. The empty silence that was once full of humming life is total. This year the pollen will not be shared.

A vision of countryside hell, perhaps, but something that is becoming more likely with each passing season. The multiple enemies of agricultural intensity, climate change, insect parasites, genetic modification and many other possible adversaries, make life as a bee far less kind than their sonorous hum would suggest. The signals of a potential apian catastrophe have only just started emerging, and they are amplified with every bee colony that undergoes CCD, or Colony Collapse Disorder.

VISALIA, Calif., Feb. 23 — David Bradshaw has endured countless stings during his life as a beekeeper, but he got the shock of his career when he opened his boxes last month and found half of his 100 million bees missing.

"I have never seen anything like it," Mr Bradshaw, 50, said from an almond orchard here beginning to bloom. "Box after box after box are just empty. There's nobody home." [1]

Like colic in children, Colony Collapse Disorder describes a number of symptoms but no specific cause. Colony Collapse Disorder is a condition by which a honey-bee colony – usually defined as a fully functioning social order including a queen – dramatically reduces in numbers over a very short period, sometimes overnight. The really odd thing is that the hives are abandoned: there are few if any bodies and the abandonment is almost total, to the extent that larvae are left in sealed cells, all of which will eventually die of starvation. Often the queen remains along with just a few loyal workers.

The impact of CCD worldwide is becoming more dramatic as it spreads – bear in mind that this isn't a disease as such, but it is nevertheless spreading – since 2006 it has moved rapidly across the USA and into Canada, and also affected Australia and many European countries. Because there is no central beekeeping 'agency', details and statistics tend to be sketchy, but there is little doubt that the types of events being reported bear the hallmarks of CCD. What actually causes it is another matter. Many theories have been expounded, from the highly feasible (pesticides, parasites, viruses and fungi), to the bizarre (mobile phone signals) to those that are very difficult to show much evidence for at all (genetically modified crops and climate change).

We can easily rule out the mobile phone issue: bees do indeed use some form of electromagnetic navigation system, and mobile phones (cellphones) and their masts do indeed use a form of electromagnetism – microwaves – but given that the majority of hives affected are in rural areas, which have few masts, then we can safely ignore some of the wild speculation that purports to be science.[2] Pesticides seem an easy target, and their impact on the habitats and food sources of many traditional farmland birds since wide-spectrum pesticides came of age is incontestable; but again, evidence of their impact on bees is sparse and contradictory. On the other hand, the presence of numerous types of disease-causing organisms, including common types of fungi that had been absent from hives for more than 70 years[3] and also a particularly virulent pathogen called Israeli acute paralysis virus[4] in most affected colonies, give the impression that there are common factors involved. As I write no single cause has been identified, but that does not mean that the cause has to be particularly complex and alien: as you will see in this chapter, bees are a lot more similar to you and me than you may realize.

What Are Bees?

Everyone knows something about bees: in Western cultures, the term 'the birds and the bees' is used to mean sex, when speaking to children; 'Royal Jelly' is sold in many health food shops as a supposed miracle food, although it can cause a severe and potentially fatal allergic reaction in some humans;[5] being stung by a bee can be very painful, and fatal for the perpetrator, although beekeepers are more than happy to shrug off such stings as just part of the job; bees create hexagonal cells in which they raise larvae to become members of their colony, and to store nectar which turns into honey. Winnie the Pooh loves honey, and it never, ever goes off if kept dry; which makes Pooh, with his honey-filled clay pots, a very sensible bear indeed. Generally speaking we love bees, even though apiphobia (fear of bees) is extremely common. What a strange and wonderful relationship we have with them!

Getting down to the science: bees are closely related to ants and wasps, although many types of wasp and ant are carnivorous, or at least omnivorous, whereas bees feed solely on nectar and pollen. All bees occupy a single family called *Apoidea*, which, although it includes certain types of wasp that look as though they are wearing corsets, mainly contains bees, of which there are around 20,000 varieties. Nectar is secreted by flowers to attract insects; bees feed on the nectar directly and also carry it back to the nest or hive (an artificial type of nest) which then ferments to make honey. The reason plants produce tempting nectar is to encourage the visits of pollinating insects, like bees, which then distribute their pollen to other flowers and thus fertilize the plant. As hummingbirds are also pretty good pollinators, the use of birds and bees as a euphemism for sex seems rather apt. Pollen, which is produced by every flower, is rich in protein, and is used by bees to feed newly-emerged larvae, fattening them up before they pupate.

Bees work very hard collecting food, building their combs and bringing up youngsters, but surprisingly they may spend a large amount of time back at the nest resting, collecting information and awaiting instructions for finding a good source of food.[6] When the food source is identified by a worker, the bees dance, and the dance varies depending on the distance and direction of the food source. Some types of bee are solitary or live in small groups, but the vast majority, in terms of absolute numbers, are social – living in large communities, or colonies. It is the social bees that produce honey, and provide the bulk of the pollination that humans depend upon for many types of plant food. If you eat honey then you are eating the product of a complex and highly evolved animal community.

The Need for Bees

Has this ever happened to you: someone you idolize or deeply respect, for whatever reason, is making a public appearance close to where you live, or maybe you just see them walking along. You take the opportunity to speak to him or her and rather than the wonderfully formed nuggets of wisdom you are expecting, what comes out of their mouth is something that totally throws you off balance – it's nothing like you were expecting, and you no longer feel the same about that person.

> "If the bee disappeared off the surface of the globe, then man would only have four years of life left. No more bees, no more pollination, no more plants, no more animals, no more man." [7]

This statement is commonly attributed to Albert Einstein and, after reading it, I thought: "What is he going on about? Call yourself a scientist." A little research later finds that Einstein probably never said any such thing, and whoever did say this was certainly not a biologist of any repute (which, incidentally, Einstein was not). But stop there! If you happen to be a viewer of the PBS television network in the USA, which is watched by 73 million people a week and provides "high-quality documentary and dramatic entertainment",[8] then you may have come across a documentary called 'Silence of the Bees,' which showed the potential impact of Colony Collapse Disorder. I hesitate to quote from the trailer, but here goes:

> "Life as we know it, I don't think will exist."
>
> "You won't get any fruits, and you won't get any vegetables."
>
> "We're scared to death!"[9]

I hope those people were quoted out of context because they really looked like they were gearing up for global collapse. Actually, that may not be such a stupid idea, but it probably won't have anything to do with bees. The sober truth is that if the world's bees disappeared, we would be faced with a disaster of sorts, but that disaster would be far more economic than ecological.

Despite our claim to be omnivores, humans eat a surprisingly small number of different food items. This was certainly not the case before industrial agriculture became the norm, leading to a focus on the easiest to grow, the most disease- and pest-tolerant, and the most profitable crops – in fact ease of growing along with disease- and pest-tolerance are just different ways of ensuring a steady, reliable stream of income in the modern age. Diets prior to the industrial agricultural system tended towards local availability, which is obviously the only type of availability in hunter-gatherer societies; and even up to very recent times in the industrial West, widespread kitchen gardens and home-growing maintained a wide range of different food types, as well as a huge range of different varieties of similar crops. Not only that, but it seems that the earliest human diets, with their dependence on local availability may also have been far healthier than modern diets which literally have the whole world on a plate: Palaeolithic diets (we are talking tens of thousands of years ago) had more fibre, less sodium, more vitamins and minerals, and a virtual absence of refined sugars.[10]

Consumption of animals (meat and fish) and vegetables varies around the world depending partly on the particular culture, but especially on the level of industrialization.[11] In the least industrialized parts of the world, meat consumption is around 13% of total calories, whereas in industrialized countries, as a whole, the percentage of meat calories is 28%. In the USA virtually all consumed meat (excluding fish) derives from cows, chickens and pigs.[12] You won't be surprised then to hear that just 57 single vegetable crops (including all cereals, pulses, tubers, leafy vegetables and fruits) account for 94.5% of global vegetable-based food production.[13] Not quite a monoculture world, but a far cry from the thousands of potential food sources that exist: if it ain't farmed, it ain't eaten.

Despite the blinkered attitude to crop variety in industrial cultures, as far as pollination goes this attitude seems not to have caused too many problems up to now. Around 60% of the world's production of crops is completely independent of animal pollination (where the term 'animal' includes many types of insect and, to a lesser extent, birds and bats),[14] relying instead on wind or self-pollination. This in itself is an issue – especially where genetically modified crops that rely on wind pollination are grown, and inevitably cause contamination wherever the pollen enters a non-GM area. But – and this is a medium-sized 'but', that could become a big 'but' – something like 20% of all crop production does require animal pollination in order to improve yield, and about 15% requires pollination to improve seed production.[15]

In Chapter 3 I said that we were pushing the soil and natural plant varieties ever harder in order to maximize food production. As well as this, humans are wantonly using vast amounts of synthetic fertilizer to the same ends. The result of fertilizer overuse leads to the twin threats of nitrous oxide being sent up into the atmosphere – which accounts for around 8% of anthropogenic global heating (that which is caused by humans) – and the eutrophication, or oxygen starvation, of the waters into which nitrogen-rich rain and irrigation water flow. Genetically modified crops are a typical response by the agricultural industry to increased food stress: rather than suggesting that we reduce the amount of animals we eat that are fed the very crops humans are striving to grow in ever greater quantities (that would mean reducing output, which is no way to do business), agribusinesses and governments together try to persuade us that fiddling around with genes is the way forward.

That the margin between potential crop production and actual crop consumption is getting ever narrower is not in doubt – witness the startled reaction to fuel companies buying up land and food crops from which they can make biofuels – so it is easy to understand why the extra advantage, however small, that honey-bees and other animal pollinators provide for farmers is actually very important indeed. The United Nations Food and Agricultural Organization put this starkly:

> Most high-quality agricultural land is already in production. The marginal benefit of converting new land diminishes. Available land and water resources are declining in many developing countries. Future food production growth will primarily depend on further intensification of agriculture in high potential areas and to a lesser degree in low potential areas.[16]

Fertile land being such a scarce resource for humans – even for humans that have no qualms about removing tropical rainforests and draining marshland to obtain fertile soil – means that something like Colony Collapse Disorder could just as appropriately be renamed Production Collapse Disorder; but in this case the disorder would most definitely be one of our making.

Why Collapse Happens

Collapse, as the name implies, is not something that is gradual, but to a certain extent, it may be possible to predict it. If you have a sea-cliff made of porous chalk, underneath which is a bed of clay through which rainwater cannot penetrate, and the fissures or joints in that chalk are angled downwards towards the cliff face, then collapse is pretty much inevitable. There is a maximum weight and a minimum amount of friction that the blocks of chalk can cope with before they start to slide apart, and if you have ever run your finger along a piece of wet chalk then you can understand how slippery the edges of the rock at the fissures will be after a period of heavy rain. After a while the water, which has not been able to sink further than the layer of clay, starts to rise again as a water table, and that perfect combination of factors – the saturated chalk base, the slipperiness of the joints and the weight of the chalk – means that it is not a case of whether, but when the cliff will collapse.

The same pressures and limitations apply to all sorts of simple and complex systems. A cliff face is a system: it has inputs (rain, wind and waves, road traffic above, burrowing animals below), processes (erosion, changes in friction, movement of materials) and outputs (water, rock, soil), but it is a relatively simple system. The global atmosphere, on the other hand, although still a system, is a devilishly complex one, which explains why all the computing power in the world can only hope to accurately predict small parts of it even over small timescales. Thankfully, we do have the experience of many people, along with numerous tools and models that can allow us to make pretty good guesses as to what will happen in the future.

A bee colony is a system, and also a pretty complex one, involving as it does a large number of living organisms each of which has its own behavioural variations, as well as a range of different 'colony behaviours' such as collecting pollen and nectar, raising young bees, keeping the colony cool or warm, protecting the colony and so on. That said, you can simplify the processes of the colony and easily demonstrate what happens when different factors affect it. The type of model in Figure 5 may look familiar to some people, but to others it may be unfamiliar – I'll explain it.

The picture shows a graph with three different dimensions, or axes. Each axis indicates the relative strength of a particular factor. The horizontal axis, running from right to left, shows the stress caused by the various diseases that normally affect the colony: stresses that would affect the ability of a colony to sustain numbers. These diseases include a range of different parasites such as the notorious Varroa mite plus the viruses and fungi mentioned earlier. The vertical axis shows the number of bees that the colony is capable of maintaining at any one time. The number is limited by the size of the hive or nest, beyond which some of the bees are forced to swarm in order to find a new location. Finally, the axis on the left – the depth axis – shows all the other stresses, on top of the normal diseases, that may make the difference between the size of the colony *gradually* decreasing, and the colony undergoing a *collapse*.

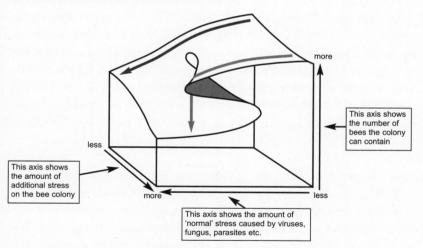

Figure 5: Bee Colony Cusp Diagram

Because honey-bees have evolved certain defences, both physiological and social, against the various 'normal' disease stresses, then the appearance of one or even two different disease-causing organisms won't necessarily be devastating – in most cases there will be a reduction in the overall numbers in the colony, but collapse is unlikely unless a new enemy emerges to which the bees have no defence. This type of scenario is shown by the upper path (thick arrowed line), which gradually curves downwards as the normal stresses increase. On the other hand, if the colony is already weakened in some way, such as from a very poor summer which provides only small amounts of nectar and pollen, then the same diseases can have a much more destructive effect on the colony. The appearance of a major infestation of the Varroa parasite could, under these circumstances, cause a dramatic reduction in bee numbers, as could a virulent fungal infection exacerbated by cool, moist weather. The lower path shows how precipitous a drop this can be, suddenly changing from a gradual decline to a collapse in numbers.

As I said earlier, the jury is out on genetically modified organisms and pesticides as a causal agent for CCD, but if you use the cusp diagram then it would seem that climate change is another matter. Cool, moist weather is not something you would expect from the current trends in climate change, but shifting climate patterns are increasing the likelihood of flash flooding in almost all parts of the world, which can have a considerable impact on the availability of flora. According to the Intergovernmental Panel on Climate Change: "Widespread increases in heavy precipitation events have been observed, even in places where total amounts have decreased. These changes are associated with increased water vapour in the atmosphere arising from the warming of the world's oceans, especially at lower latitudes. There are also increases in some regions in the occurrences of both droughts and floods." [17] The longer, drawn-out summer droughts that are already apparent in large parts of China, Australia and Canada, for instance, are also bad for flower production, which can be significant in moving bee colonies from the relative safety of the 'upper path' to the dangers of the 'lower path'. Professor Eric Mussen, Secretary of the American Association of Professional Apiculturalists, agrees:

> "I am pretty concerned about it this year because, at Davis, in January we only had 0.17 of an inch of rain and we should have had 4 inches. The early mustard – we never got it."

> "In many situations the bees were weakened by not being able to get a nice mix of nutrients that they needed from the pollens, and I think that weakened them. Under those circumstances you can take all the other (causes), and there are plenty of them, and combine them together and down go the bees." [18]

Temperature change alone, as I have shown in earlier chapters, can provide an excellent opportunity for parasites to breed more quickly and frequently: the resulting exponential climb in parasite numbers, particularly in the case of Varroa (something beekeepers universally dread) would likely turn the problem from something that is currently manageable into one that could silence entire hives in a matter of days.

The power of the cusp diagram is such that it can be applied to subjects as diverse as a chalk cliff, a bee colony or even human civilization. Change the hor-. izontal axis to indicate the normal impacts of endemic disease, food availability, quality of healthcare and sanitation, and even government or cultural attitudes, on population, and you can follow the upper path quite happily up and down to show how these affect the human population of a country or a region. Change the depth axis to include unpredictable factors like the incidence of catastrophic flooding and storms, the outbreak of war or civil unrest, the sudden unavailabil- ity of energy supplies that feed every system in Industrial Civilization,[19] or any other factor that can increase the sensitivity of a population, and you can be hurtling straight into the drop zone quicker than you can say, "I want to get off". And this is certainly not idle mathematical speculation: human civilizations have undergone collapse after collapse, in almost all cases with the post-collapse soci- ety left as a shadow of its previous might. The Ottoman Empire, the Mayan civ- ilization and the Roman Empire all collapsed for different reasons, but all of the collapses were sudden and uncontrollable.

The British Empire collapsed from having dominated a vast area in excess of 35 million square kilometres in the late 1930s to little more than a few scattered territories within the space of ten years. The sheer size of such an empire, which constituted a civilization controlled according to the rules of the Parliament of Great Britain, could only be maintained while the populations of the different countries were relatively placid – often through a combination of military force and political corruption. With the British navy and army fully occupied in the war effort between 1939 and 1945, such control was no longer feasible. This combined with the growth of a number of civil protest movements to make col- lapse almost inevitable. "It is hard to say that any one of [the many pressures] was decisive but, without an awakening of national consciousness in a great many colonies, several external pressures would have lost much of their importance."[20] In essence, it was not the normal stresses that caused the collapse of the British Empire; it was those extraordinary additional stresses that moved it from the manageable upper path to the uncontrollable, catastrophic lower path.

The true cause of Colony Collapse Disorder may never quite be resolved – the ideas presented above are, after all, just educated guesses – but the silver lining for the bee is that many are likely to have escaped the hive in time to be able to form a new colony somewhere else. As I see it, the collapse of a human civilization may not provide such a clear-cut opportunity to escape: some people might make it, but a lot more may not have the chance to get out in time. Before you go on to the next chapter, it's worth taking some time to consider which path you think you're on.

Chapter 5

One Metre

My second favourite moment from the charming and beautifully animated film *Finding Nemo* is when Marlin, having found the perfect spot for a hatchery, shows with pride to his expectant partner their view. From the coastal shelf, the seabed tumbles steeply down to the great yawning abyssal plain that stretches into the distant watery haze: the depths of the ocean foretelling the story to come without a word needing to be spoken. The efforts of a small team of computer animators manage to illustrate the all-embracing vastness of the ocean far more effectively than any TV documentary or piece of writing I have yet encountered. Call me a philistine if you wish, but I'm still a sucker for a good movie.

My favourite moment in *Finding Nemo* is when the little boy in the dentist's waiting-room lets his mouth fall open at the terrifying events taking place in the surgery the other side of the tropical fish tank. I love that bit.

Finding Nemo was about many things: love, courage, the beauty of the natural world, the uncaring attitude of certain humans, and the ability of many different species to communicate (so it would seem – they certainly passed on messages more efficiently than many electronic systems). What *Finding Nemo* was *not* about was encouraging children to go out and buy clownfish, but that's what happened: "Sales of clownfish across America increased almost overnight, with eager parents harassing pet shops for a 'Nemo' of their own. But in contrast to the common goldfish, clownfish need a saltwater environment – plus a lot of complicated equipment – to survive. In the hands of inexperienced owners, countless fish perished."[1] We have no way of telling whether any of the dominant messages in the film were taken up by movie-goers, but I would be willing to bet that once immersed again into a world of advertising, those messages would sadly have been pushed to the back of even the most caring child's mind.

Whether it is from the use of explosives, the application of hydrogen cyanide or the casting and dragging of miles of fine-meshed net; the pillaging of tropical waters to feed an insatiable desire for attractive, exotic fish in the front rooms of the richer nations' consumers is big business. The death toll is so large from ocean to fish tank – the UN estimate that 30% of fish are killed in transit – that, were profit margins not so great, no one would be interested in doing this kind of thing on a large scale. According to the United Nations Environment Programme, 20 million tropical fish are removed from the sea each year, destined for fish tanks, along with 10 million other animals and 12 million specimens of coral – themselves collections of tiny animals called polyps.[2]

Over 70% of all tropical fish are caught in Indonesian waters, a figure that the third largest producer of carbon dioxide – if you include the amount of carbon released by forest destruction – would have to be proud of, if astonishingly bad environmental records were anything to be proud of. On the flip side, and with astounding irony, the recipient of 73% of the world's tropical fish is the USA; a nation that, at the time of writing, still produced more greenhouse gases than any other nation on Earth, and had done more than any other nation to prevent global agreements being struck to reduce the emissions of these greenhouse gases. When you combine the ills of coral cyanide poisoning to stun tropical fish with the increase in global temperatures caused by greenhouse gases bleaching (effectively killing) large areas of sensitive reef, then you find that the USA is number one in the world at destroying coral reefs. The gas-guzzling, coal-burning, tropical fish-keeping customer is not always right – especially when it comes to the care of the most important oceanic habitats on Earth.

If the 10cm-long clownfish is a symbol of the way consumers disregard nature to feed their pastimes, then the one-metre-long cod is surely a symbol of the way consumers disregard nature to feed their appetites.

I mentioned the way that the consumption of meat seems to mirror economic development a while ago, but didn't really touch on the problems that this brings. In a nutshell, meat requires a far greater amount of food energy to produce compared with plants grown directly for consumption – this can vary from about five times more, in the case of battery-farmed chickens, to 25 times or more for the finest quality beef.[3] The reason for this is simply that in order to rear an animal for food, you have to feed it; and animals, though efficient users of food energy, need time in order to produce the muscle, which comprises the meat. The food that these animals eat has to be planted, usually using machinery that consumes oil and produces carbon dioxide; grown, mostly with the aid of fertilizers, pesticides, herbicides and so on, which take energy to produce and contribute to global heating; harvested, pre-processed and transported, just like all food destined directly for our kitchens, all of which produces more carbon dioxide; and then finally fed to the animal. If it takes ten pounds of grain or beets to produce one pound of food then, even allowing for the extra protein in animal muscle, the consumption of meat (and most dairy products, for that matter) is considerably worse for the environment than the consumption of vegetable matter. Not surprisingly – if you ignore the beneficial subsidies given to the meat and dairy industry by most of the governments in the industrial world – calorie for calorie, meat also costs far more to produce than fruit, vegetables or grains.

This is a major reason why fishing is a vital part of the economies of so many countries, rich or poor, subsistence or industrial. Catching fish is an effective and relatively cheap way of feeding a population – or rather, it was.

What Are Cod?

Cod are just a type of fish, like humans are a type of mammal. That seems obvious, but it's vitally important to realize that the reason cod are seen as such a significant type of fish, possibly above all others in importance, is simply because humans have probably eaten more of this type of fish than any other throughout history. We need to differentiate the economic or cultural significance of an animal, like the lion or blue whale; a plant, like an oak tree or stem of wheat; or any other organism, from what it actually is. Cod don't know that they are economically or culturally significant, so for now, let's just treat them as a type of fish.

There are only three true species of cod, namely the Atlantic, Greenland and Pacific. Each have distinctive breeding and schooling areas, such as the Barents Sea, and the waters around the Faroe Islands and Newfoundland; and each grow to a different maximum size – the Atlantic Cod being the biggest, at up to two metres in length, and the Pacific Cod the smallest at around 50cm. There are also a number of related species, which aren't strictly cod but do have many similar characteristics, including the Arctic Cod and Polar Cod. For commercial reasons, they are usually bunched into the same category, but then commerce never was very good at understanding nature!

Cod are known as demersal fish, meaning they spend most of their lives near to the bottom of the sea, feeding off other marine animals rather than the rich flora nearer to the ocean surface. Other types of demersal fish include haddock, whiting and monkfish. Far larger, by total mass, are the pelagic fish, which spend most of their time closer to the surface making the most of the food energy that derives from sunlight, which is largely absent from the deeper areas of the ocean. Pelagic fish include anchovies, sardines, mackerel and tuna, all of which are heavily fished wherever they occur in the world. As you can see, the vertical location of the fish doesn't really have any bearing on size: tuna are some of the world's largest fish, growing up to 2.5 metres in length and weighing in excess of 200kg, whereas adult anchovies are often no larger than the size of a child's finger. The 1-2 metre Atlantic Cod is no match for the largest tuna, but at 20kg or more, is no tiddler; but when was the last time you saw a 20kg cod on a plate?

Cod can take five years or more before they reach full size, and may live for 20 or 30 years – no one is quite sure. If you catch a cod before it reaches full size then you are effectively catching a child or a growing teenager that has years of development ahead of it. But far worse than any ethical issue you may have about eating a youngster (most meat eaten is immature, be it from a cow, a pig or a tuna), because cod take at least three years before they are able to breed, by catching and eating cod before they reach sexual maturity, you are putting a brick wall in the way of the breeding cycle. This is now the acceptable face of fishing; according to the Scottish Fisheries Research Services: "By the time they reach two years old, young cod are fully exploited by the commercial fishery and many are caught long before they have the opportunity to spawn." [4]

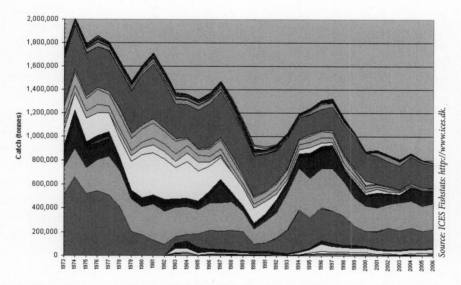

Figure 6: Atlantic Cod Catch by Fishing Area 1973-2006. Different shadings denote the various fishing areas in the North Atlantic.

Looking back to the beginnings of the mass fishing industry, one is filled with a sense that something was bound to go wrong. Tales of being able to drop buckets into the sea off Newfoundland, the edge of the now defunct Grand Banks fishery, and bring them back up full to the brim with fish may not have been far off of the mark during the spawning season – although the explorer John Cabot, who pondered whether he could have walked from one side of the Atlantic to the other on the backs of the cod, would almost certainly have come to grief. The point is, though, that the fishermen (and they were all men up to only a few years ago) really thought that there was an endless marine bounty. Fishing has always had an air of sentimentality, courage and permanence to it: men were made and broken, in dreadful conditions of isolation, wild storms, tiredness and constant pressure, only partly eased by songs, whisky and the thoughts of the family back home. Yet it most certainly was, and is a way of life: "Some guys couldn't wait 'til the last day of school so they could join the boat," says Michael Coe, a former trawler skipper at Peterhead in the north-east of Scotland, with genuine excitement.[5] A way of life, but nevertheless an industry, partaken of by thousands of boats across the great fishing grounds of the North Atlantic, Southern Ocean, Arabian Sea, Mediterranean and wherever a mass of marine life is there for the taking.

But business and especially the search for profit now take precedence in almost all formerly traditional and self-sustaining occupations. Whereas the shops and restaurants would in the past have paid the going rate for fish and kept the industry alive for another season, it is now the supermarkets and fish-processors who call the shots – culling prices and progressively smaller fish until the skippers have no choice but to search deeper, further and with more technology; in the sad knowledge that their search for a high-volume, low-price resource is destroying the very thing that kept them going for countless generations.

In the last 35 years, as shown vividly in Figure 6, the volume of Atlantic Cod retrieved from the water has plummeted from a high (for that period) of two million tonnes, to less than half that. The type of fish now being caught disguises the real volume – the smaller, immature fish may keep the industry ticking over for a few years, but the future looks barren. Fish colonies are in jeopardy around the world, with over half of all 'stocks' (a term used by governments to imply humans own these natural habitats!) fished to full capacity, and a quarter in decline or endangered.[6] There is such a fine line between 'near' capacity and 'over' capacity that it is fair to say that three-quarters of the world's major fish colonies are in an unsustainable state: they are not self-regulating – their numbers are being regulated by humans.

This is known as 'The Tragedy of the Commons': the inevitable outcome of the oceans being used as an infinite resource, compounded by the wilful ignorance of a market economy that refuses to see the inevitable outcome of its greed. To paraphrase Garrett Hardin, the originator of the concept: the business benefits from its ability to deny the truth even though society as a whole, of which it is a part, suffers.[7] Amongst those people affected by the decimation of stocks, this denial is not so much malicious as pathological, according to Mark Kurlansky, author of Cod. They do not want to see this happening, so they just shut it off. Michael Coe says he only noticed a drop in the cod numbers around the year 2000; before then he claims he was able to fish pretty much the same areas year after year for over thirty years. This certainly doesn't match the statistics. In 1996, the Canadian fisheries minister claimed that he knew "for sure" that the decline in the Newfoundland cod fisheries had ceased. It had done nothing of the sort – there were something like 15,000 cod counted, compared with 1.2 million ten years before.[8]

The rapid expansion in farmed fish, or aquaculture, tells the true story of the panic growing within the fishing industry. Buy farmed fish and, just like farmed meat, it will have been fed far more protein than it actually brings to your plate – sucking smaller and smaller fish out of the sea. This 'hidden' catch allows us to pretend there isn't a problem at all. China is the global giant of aquaculture, accounting for two-thirds of the world's volume of farmed fish.[9] Most of these fish are freshwater carp which, unlike in the fish-collecting West, are used as a major source of protein, especially in landlocked countries and inland areas. The global volume of farmed fish produced in 2004 was 48 million tonnes, out of a total of 140 million tonnes of fish consumed. Much of the fish production is carried out using plankton as a food source, but there is an increasing trend towards the production of carnivorous species that are fed on wild caught fish: two million tonnes of salmon, trout and related species were farmed in 2004, and well over two million tonnes of shrimp and prawn in the same year. These carnivorous species eat between two and five times more fish protein than they contain at the point that they are killed for food.[10] The farming of salmon and trout alone requires over eight million tonnes of wild caught fish, or about 9% of the global catch.

There is a myth that industrial farming, whether of fish, meat or vegetables is an efficient way to produce food. No doubt it is a way to produce lots of food at a greater density and lower cost (mainly in terms of labour), but it is clear from the behaviour of the parties involved that industrial farming exists to maximize the profits of the giant 'agribusiness' companies who swallow up vast areas of land, including thousands of small-scale farms every year. There is nothing sustainable about a high-energy, high-chemical, globalized corporate web: the energy required to farm in this way far exceeds the natural capacity of the soil or water to provide food. The myth of 'sustainable' industrial farming is perpetuated by corporations such as Cargill – the largest grain exporter in the world – in order to show to the people of Earth that farming can only feed the mouths of the world if it is run by big business.

Try telling that to the indigenous tribes throughout the tropics, who have had their hunting grounds taken away and deforested in order to produce grain and graze cattle. Try telling that to the fishermen who have lost any chance of catching food for their families off the west coast of Africa because of the giant European pair-trawlers that blanket the oceans and scour them of life. Try telling that to the thousands who lost their lives and their homes in the Indian Ocean tsunami of 2004 that battered the coasts of east India and Sri Lanka; coasts that had previously been protected by mangroves, but are now dominated by shrimp farms as far as the eye can see.

Weaving a Fishy Web

Webs and loops fascinate scientists for all sorts of reasons. One reason is that they are potentially eternal: a loop will move round and around getting larger, smaller, faster or slower, or just staying the same. A web has things going into it, and out of it, but in the main is self-contained with each part of it being dependent in some way on the other parts. Here are a couple of examples.

Let's consider Chris, who likes to go skiing; regularly travelling from his generous suburban house in Boston, to a drop-dead gorgeous winter chalet in Aspen, Colorado. Getting there wasn't too easy a few decades ago, but the tourist industry wants people to go skiing because that's good for the companies who sell skiing holidays, so airports have been built in the most remote locations. Chris can take a plane from Boston to Denver, then another one to Aspen, with only a short taxi trip at either end. Very convenient. The problem here is that he is rather dependent on there being snow when he arrives; otherwise he may have to be content with enjoying the scenery, as well as partaking of lots of après-walk drinks. Flying, as most people know, is a sure-fire way of boosting the amount of carbon dioxide, as well as a few other greenhouse gases, in the atmosphere. Not only does it take a lot of energy to keep a hunk of metal in the air, but various chemical reactions from the aircraft's contrails, especially in the upper atmosphere, make this effect all the more significant. If you are one of the few scientists who don't believe that our greenhouse gas emissions are heating the Earth up, and you haven't got the funds from an oil company, or a car manufacturer resting in your bank account, then you might want to skip this bit: for everyone else who has realized that our emissions are heating the Earth up (even the conservative Intergovernmental Panel on Climate Change are 80%-90% sure),[11] this is what the process looks like:

1) Person takes flights from Boston to Aspen
2) Emissions from aircraft cause atmosphere to heat up
3) Higher atmospheric temperature means that snow melts quicker
4) Less snow means that less sun is reflected and more is absorbed
5) Earth heats up, causing atmosphere to heat up more
6) Return to step 3.

Stages 3 to 6 are known as a feedback loop. I admit that it is greatly simplified but the basic facts are correct, and it exhibits two things that everyone needs to understand about feedback loops: first, at least one part of the process goes round in a cycle forever, or until some end point is reached (for instance, all the snow has melted); second, many loops can be made more intense by having *inputs*, such as people continuing to fly to Aspen (steps 1 and 2), speeding up the snow melting process. Even without the additional flying, the loop 3 to 6 is a *positive* feedback loop, in that it is adding to the effect each time it goes round. A *negative* feedback loop is one that gets weaker with each cycle: if the land underneath the snow were as white as the snow itself, and the flying stopped, the loop would quickly break down and, in the absence of global warming, the snow would return.

Most people learnt about food chains at school: Fish 1 is eaten by Fish 2 which, in turn is eaten by Fish 3 and so on. In this food chain, each fish occupies a different trophic, or food, level. This can easily become a loop if, when Fish 3 dies its body decays to be eaten by Fish 1. Webs are slightly different. To make this a food *web*, there have to be more connections between the different components, ideally in more than one direction.

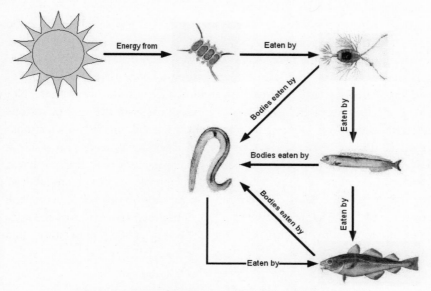

Figure 7: Simple oceanic food web showing four trophic levels.
Arrows indicate the direction of the energy (food) supply

The simplified food web in Figure 7 shows that the ultimate energy source is, as with everything on Earth, the sun. The algae, which are a type of phytoplankton (literally meaning 'drifting plant'), use photosynthesis to convert the sun's energy along with the carbon dioxide dissolved in the water to make the bodies of the algae themselves. These algae become food for any herbivores (plant eaters) patrolling the upper levels of the sea. In fact, algae are the primary source of almost all food in the deep seas that the cod and other demersal fish occupy.[12] The herbivores are eaten by carnivores, which in turn are eaten by bigger (or more ferocious) carnivores; these carnivores are more likely to be fish that occupy the deeper parts of the ocean because algae do not grow where there is no light. When the carnivores (or herbivores, for that matter) die, their bodies are consumed by a plethora of scavengers at all levels, right down to the very floor of the ocean, where scavenging is the lifestyle of choice. But even those scavengers are not free of danger, for carnivores are also partial to a tasty bottom dweller or two. If the amount of sunlight, and thus algae, going into the web reduces, the total food energy in the web reduces, and the total volume of creatures in that web also reduces.

Unlike the loop, there is no point at which I can say, "and then it repeats", because any one of a number of processes could take place next: they are extremely difficult to predict without some very special analytical skills. This is another reason why scientists like webs. Both webs and loops play a vital part in working out what will happen to biological (or ecological), atmospheric and other systems when environmental conditions change. I purposefully wrote "when", rather than "if", because environmental conditions are changing all the time; and many of those changes are of our making.

A Moment of Reflection

In September 2007 it became possible for the first time in living memory to travel by boat from the southern tip of Greenland,[13] across the sea north of Canada and then all the way along the north coasts of Russia and Scandinavia, before finally meeting your starting point again – all of this without an ice-breaker. For climatologists and anyone who has concern for the future habitation of this planet, this is a frightening occurrence. For oil and shipping companies, as well as governments wishing to impress their power on other nations, it's open season:

> In an exercise in sabre-rattling, the Canadian government has ordered two new military bases to be set up in the Arctic region and commissioned six new patrol ships. But the US is equally adamant that the passage remain free to all comers.

Angry exchanges [in 1985] prompted a 1988 co-operation deal which is now under threat. Russia, Denmark and Norway are separately involved in the scramble to exploit the Arctic's mineral riches.[14]

It doesn't take a genius to realize that every disaster is seen as a commercial opportunity by someone in the world – but it is truly breathtaking to watch the clawing and biting taking place amongst national governments, some of whom pretend to be interested in protecting the planet, in order to gain commercial advantage over each other. This scramble for material wealth (basically a high level form of 'beat your neighbour') both puts the lie to governments' claims to be co-operative, and also makes it very clear that the strongest motivation of all in the industrial world is the acquisition of wealth. Why people are so strongly motivated by wealth is something that I will explore in detail later on.

You may have spotted a feedback loop in this. If money is driving climate change, by virtue of the greenhouse gases being produced by commercial activity, and climate change is causing more commercial 'opportunities' to open up, then clearly this loop will continue to get stronger and stronger until something snaps – such as the planet no longer being able to support human beings in any great number. Alternatively something or someone may decide to drive a stake through that absurd cycle before it gets too late to stop the feedback, and it is taken out of our hands.

Albedo is something I alluded to a few pages back. I often make the mistake of wearing a particular t-shirt I like on sunny days; it is grey, but with thousands of flecks of black, and those black flecks absorb solar energy (solar radiation) very effectively, leaving me hot and bothered. The difference between black and white is simply that black absorbs every wavelength of visible light (if it is truly black it also absorbs infra-red radiation, which makes things particularly hot) and white reflects every wavelength. Blue-coloured objects only reflect blue light and absorb everything else, green objects reflect green light, and so on. The more solar radiation absorbed by an object, the more energy is being forced into it, causing it to heat up. Albedo is a measure of how much radiation is reflected by something: the higher the number, the more reflective it is.

The melting snow in Aspen reveals a darker surface than the snow itself. Fresh snow has an albedo of 0.8 to 0.9 – it reflects 80% to 90% of the radiation. Green grass has an albedo of 0.25, and soil has an albedo of about 0.2. In other words, the melting of snow increases the amount of energy taken into the ground by a factor of four. Now, compare this to what is happening in the Arctic Ocean. Bare ice, which is typically what floats on water, reflects 60% to 70% of the solar radiation falling on it, whereas open sea may reflect almost nothing, depending on the angle of the sun. This huge difference in absorption can make the difference between the temperature of the sea being below freezing – so the ice doesn't melt – or above freezing. Once the sea gets above freezing-point, that heat energy spreads out with the movement of the ocean currents, melting more and more ice, which in turn causes the sea to heat up. This is a dramatic positive feedback loop and it is happening right now.[15]

The effect of this on marine life is complex, but not really surprising. Water held at close to freezing-point can absorb about 14 milligrams of oxygen per litre, whereas at 20°C it can only hold about 9 milligrams of oxygen in the same volume.[16] The high levels of oxygen in cold polar waters compared with warm tropical waters affect the ability of the water to sustain life, but it is not easy to find out what difference this makes in practice. One study involving squid found a plausible relationship between the temperature of the sea surface and the number of squid in a shoal;[17] some studies find that higher temperatures reduce the amount of food available to predators; but other studies say that the warmer the sea, the higher the biomass. The issue seems to be that there are very complex relationships between different species of marine life at different depths of the ocean, and across different geographical areas; and when you start looking at the more complex food webs then some of these relationships break down, so it's sometimes safer not to make any assumptions at all.

This type of problem infects all studies of complex systems, and makes it very easy for sceptics to attack a bit here and a bit there while ignoring the overall picture. Greenhouse gas emissions continue to increase; their levels in the atmosphere inexorably rise, while global temperatures continue to creep up; and yet, the denials continue. Denial keeps fear at bay. Denial keeps the wheels of industry turning. Denial keeps rich people rich and powerful people powerful. I will discuss this in Part Three.

A classic example of this selective, convenient denial occurred following the release of a paper by the eminent NASA climatologist James Hansen. The paper explained that USA temperatures between 2000 and 2007 had been overstated by 0.15°C because a necessary adjustment in the climate models had not been applied.[18] Bearing in mind that the global picture was untouched by this adjustment, the reaction by the climate change sceptics was over the top, to say the least:

> As to the stuff about the hottest years . . . Well, whaddya know! Turns out that's wrong, too. Figures from NASA's Goddard Institute for Space Studies (GISS) now show the hottest year since 1880 was 1934. Nineteen-ninety-eight dropped to second, while the third hottest year was way back in 1921. Indeed, four of the 10 hottest years were in the 1930s, while only three were in the past decade.[19]

Excuse me for being picky, but this only affected the USA temperature record, which puts the commentator on rather rocky ground to start with. As for the record temperatures, the US Climatic Data Centre says: "The last eight 5-year periods [up to 2007], were the warmest 5-year periods (pentads) in the last 113 years of national records, illustrating the anomalous warmth of the last decade. The 9th warmest pentad was in the 1930s (1930-34)."[20] Six of the ten warmest years on record in the USA occurred in the last ten years. To add insult to injury (for the sceptics, that is), *every one* of the ten warmest years globally have occurred since 1995. Now, let's get back to the bigger picture.

The Bigger Picture

Part of this picture is that cod grow tremendously fast at higher temperatures.[21] At 14°C the growth of cod larvae is up to five times quicker than at 4°C. The problem with any fast-growing animal is that it requires lots of food, and a baby growing five times as fast as normal requires at least five times the normal amount of food. In a sea with unlimited food then that isn't much of a problem, but in a sea where the amount of food is also being affected by the increase in temperature that is a huge problem; especially when that baby is near the top of the food chain. If a baby's metabolism is fast but it can't get the food it needs, then it will die.

Another part of the picture, and one mentioned a while ago, is that oxygen can cause a 'squeeze' if there is not enough to match the metabolism of an animal.[22] The amount of oxygen required by an animal relates directly to the speed and efficiency of its natural processes – breathing, digestion, growth etc. – so if the amount of oxygen available is not sufficient for that animal's metabolism then its metabolism will have to slow down or the animal cannot survive. Just like when you reach the top of a steep hill and you have to stop for air, if you keep running or walking without a break then you will eventually collapse. Recent NASA data shows at least a 4°C increase in the temperature of some Arctic waters compared to the 20th-century average.[23] If we use the figures from a couple of pages back, this means that the amount of oxygen the ocean can dissolve has dropped by 10% across significant parts of the ocean.

The final part of the picture is that the amount of phytoplankton, the primary source of food for the oceans, is being badly affected by oceanic heating. This is nothing to do with the increased 'acidity' of the oceans caused by growing levels of carbon dioxide being drawn into the sea, which in turn causes the shells of zooplankton (tiny floating animals) to dissolve; instead, the warming of the ocean surface means that cold water is not descending as rapidly as it needs to in order to refresh the levels of nutrients close to the surface. Cold water is heavier than warm water, so warm water will always reach the surface eventually; but if the air above the water is warmer than the water itself, then the surface of the water is not cooled down, mixing cannot take place, and nutrients essential to the survival of phytoplankton stay where they are – out of the reach of the plankton. The impact of this is far-reaching,[24] and is bound to affect both the amount of prey available to cod, and the ability of the cod to catch their prey in the first place.

If you add this all together then you get a picture of a fish that is being, or will soon be, adversely affected by climate change: enforced faster growth causing starvation, reduced oxygen impacting the normal functions of the fish, and finally a simple lack of food. In an age where we are fishing the oceans to exhaustion because of the perceived need for high levels of cheap animal protein, this additional volley of blows could be the last straw. When the cod are gone, what will be left to replace them? Haddock, mackerel, tuna, swordfish – at what point do we decide to stop pulling tonnes of protein out of the oceans and let the natural processes get on with the job of repairing themselves?

Chapter 6

One Hundred Metres

Many years ago, and it does seem like an age, I was obsessed with geography at school. There really wasn't enough information in those early teenage years to satisfy my interest, but what there was I rapaciously gobbled up. I think it was the words that did it; new, wonderful words like Hinterland, Thalweg, Tropics, Tundra, Taiga. Taiga was my favourite, an immense word bringing to mind an ancient, tangled and wild environment that should never be set foot in. The word is Siberian, possibly Mongolian, and seems to just mean, 'wild forest'.[1] The originators of that word must have lived in such an environment all their lives and, to them, it *was* their life: their world.

The Taiga stretches across the northern hemisphere in a vast swathe of spruce, pine, larch and fir, enveloping much of northern Canada, Lapland and the entire length of the Russian nation, often taking great excursions southwards where the dry continental heart is a savage environment for lush grasslands. The Eastern Siberian Taiga alone is a continuous forest 3.9 million square kilometres (1.5 million square miles) in area that is as large as India and Pakistan combined.[2] This is worth repeating: the Eastern Siberian Taiga alone is as large as India and Pakistan combined.

In July 1908, at the heart of this vast tract a mighty explosion threw down millions of trees, scorching the ground for miles around:

> I do not remember exactly the year, but more than twenty years ago during plough-ing season, I was sitting at breakfast on the house porch at Vanavara trading post facing North. I suddenly saw that directly to the North, over Onkoul's Tunguska road, the sky split in two and fire appeared high and wide over the forest. The entire Northern side was covered with fire. At that moment I became so hot that I could-n't bear it, as if my shirt was on fire. I wanted to tear off my shirt and throw it down, but then the sky shut closed.[3]

It was not until 1921, following a decision by the then Soviet Union to become a force in the scientific world, that Leonid Kulik, a Russian mineralogist, was commissioned to find the source of the explosion. It would take him until 1927 to find the crater, along with the arboreal destruction that spread out for miles: "The huge trees of the Taiga lay flat. Pines, firs, deciduous trees; all had succumbed. The sharp outlines of the winter landscape etched it like a plate."[4] Nearly six years to find a disc of devastation perhaps 70 miles across; this surely says something about the size of the area being surveyed.

Yet this dark vastness that defines entire landmasses is now under attack from a multitude of sources: the loggers that think nothing of penetrating its mysteries to feed our ravenous appetite for timber, woodchip and paper; the changing rain and snowfall in places flooding out stable soils, and in others desiccating the land; the acid rain that still falls on the branches stripping them bare. And who would have thought that such an expanse, containing some of the largest living organisms in history – some weighing in excess of a thousand tonnes – could be brought to heel by a tiny beetle measuring just five millimetres in length?

Even the magical word Taiga is dropping out of favour, to be replaced by the term Boreal Forest – still evocative, but as with the Victorian habit of replacing the ancient Celtic names of geographical features throughout Britain with florid descriptive alternatives, when its name is changed, a place seems to lose part of its identity.

What is a Spruce Tree?

More to the point, what is a tree? In essence, a tree is a living machine that generates energy in order to feed its need to be taller than everything around it. A forest in its natural state is a set of different canopies trying to compete with each other for light, their roots reaching out for nutrients and water; all the time at the mercy of the landscape and the weather. The tallest trees are tremendously heavy, their trunks bound into columns of woody tubes that carry water upwards to the leaves where it takes its part in the photosynthetic process – the conversion of carbon dioxide and water into sugars that the tree uses to build itself; leaf, twig, root and trunk. Photosynthesis is common to all plants. As with phytoplankton, the energy used by the tree comes from the sun; and the by-product is oxygen. Along with their crucial role in building and stabilizing topsoil, providing habitats for countless species and moistening the air around them; a waste gas liberated from them through a simple chemical process gives life to every animal on Earth.

It is utterly remarkable, when you think about it, that all animals, including humans, depend on oxygen for life, in return for which they produce carbon dioxide. The carbon added to the oxygen to make this waste gas comes to animals through the consumption of (ultimately) plant matter. This plant matter took its carbon from the carbon dioxide that it absorbed from the atmosphere, which had been expelled by the animals, and in return it produced oxygen, which animals depend on for life. The cycle is so perfect; yet until green plants colonized the Earth, no animal existed – instead, the plants depended on bacteria to produce the vital carbon. For most of history the plants themselves were just microscopic blue-green algae,[5] little more than bacteria. For 85% of the span of all life on Earth a slow battle took place in which the tiniest puffs of oxygen released by the tiniest photosynthesizers fought to raise the oxygen level against the chemical processes that took the oxygen into every rock, in every crevice and every pore.[6]

But eventually the plants mastered the atmosphere and the energy that surrounded them. Now, after numerous turbulent glaciations, the forests are a hard outline of their former lush glory; the oxygen-rich world of the Carboniferous[7] which boasted insects the size of humans, with mosses and horsetails reaching twenty metres or more in height,[8] also produced the vast beds of coal that humans burn with abandon, hardly daring to care that they comprise millions of years worth of photosynthesis, and enough carbon to end our time on Earth forever. The trees do their best to remove the carbon, a great deal of the work being concentrated in the disappearing hearts of the great rainforests of the tropics. The huge Redwoods, the Douglas Firs and the Sitka Spruces – the three largest of all the northern trees – grow more sedately than those in the tropics, taking the carbon they need, storing it out of harm's way.

The Sitka Spruce is the largest of the many varieties of spruce. If left to thrive it can reach 90 metres, maybe more. The one hundred metres in the title of this chapter may contain a hint of artistic licence, but when compared to any other living things on Earth, the scale of the largest trees is such that they are in a category all of their own. Spruce trees form a group of about 35 species of tree that are part of the greater family of pines, and the order that comprises all conifers on Earth. A conifer is simply a type of plant that produces cones in which its seeds are contained. Spruce are unique amongst the conifers in that they are both evergreen – they do not shed their leaves, or rather needles, in any great quantity – and have needles that form spirals around each branch. They are extremely hardy and can be found across the globe, from the USA and Canada, to Norway, Russia, Japan and China.

The great Canadian forests are dominated by just a few species of tree: black spruce, balsam fir, white spruce, larch and white birch.[9] Of these, the two spruces and the fir are evergreen conifers, constantly renewing the fragrant, acid carpet at their bases. The larch is a rare example of a hardy, non-evergreen conifer, while the birch is a hardy deciduous tree, one of the few that can survive such testing conditions.

It is easy to forget, amongst all the mystery and vastness of the Taiga, that the majority of the northern coniferous forests have only been in existence for a short time. The last ice age only started to dissipate 20,000 years ago, and the ice was still predominant until about 10,000 years ago. It was not until the temperature and precipitation reached conditions suitable for the growth of large trees that any significant forest growth was possible, which makes it remarkable that such a massive area could be fully colonized in such a short time, and with such a richness and diversity of inhabitants. The Taiga is most definitely a product of the changing climate, but itself is now instrumental in improving the stability of the climate that we are doing our best to change.

Locked-away Carbon

Calculating the amount of carbon dioxide locked up in these wooden towers is a fine art, and depends on the age of the trees, their size, their density and, not least, the amount of carbon that would also be released from the soil if these trees were removed – soil is one major type of carbon 'reservoir', forests are another type. The Intergovernmental Panel on Climate Change have produced a detailed workbook and set of guidelines[10] for calculating the size of these reservoirs, but even they cannot tell you the precise amount of carbon in a forest: for boreal, the estimate is anything between 22 and 113 tonnes of wood per hectare. If we take somewhere in the middle, say, between 40 and 75 tonnes, then we can use this to work out how important the Canadian boreal forests are as a store for greenhouse gases. Wood in trees is about 50% carbon,[11] which gives between 20 and 37.5 tonnes of carbon per hectare; but carbon is not a greenhouse gas – it only becomes that when it combines with oxygen through burning or decomposition to make carbon dioxide. When that happens you multiply the amount of carbon by 3.6, which gives potentially between 72 and 135 tonnes of carbon dioxide per hectare of forest cut down, burned, consumed or otherwise removed.

The Canadian Boreal forest is estimated to occupy about 35% of the total landmass of Canada,[12] making it something in the region of 3.2 million square kilometres in area. If we use the IPCC figures, that means that between 23 and 43 billion tonnes of carbon dioxide is stored in just the trees of the forest. This store of carbon slowly ebbs and flows as the forest naturally changes in density, age and species mix, but as long as it remains intact, that carbon largely remains locked away from the atmosphere.

In 2005 Canada produced over 600 million tonnes of carbon dioxide from the burning of fossil fuels alone (which doesn't include any produced by deforestation),[13] so that means that if Canada were to rapidly lose all of its native Boreal forest, the equivalent of about *seventy years worth of carbon dioxide emissions* would be puffed into the atmosphere in one giant breath of heat-trapping gas.

In recent years the Canadian government has, on paper, stood by its Kyoto commitment to cut the amount of greenhouse gases it is putting into the atmosphere,[14] even if that commitment doesn't stand up in reality. Between 1990 and 2005 the amount of carbon dioxide it produced went up by 35%. This was not some temporary aberration; the quantity had been going up year after year almost as though no agreement existed at all. When it realized that it was on a hiding to nothing, and that the income from the lucrative oil sands mining in Alberta would make it one of the richest oil-producing nations on Earth, then it took decisive action – it refused to commit to any reductions in greenhouse gases at all.[15]

But we mustn't blame the whole of the Canadian government machine for this; the finger points primarily at Alberta, whose provincial website balked at the idea of showing the amount of greenhouse gases it had produced over the last few years,[16] instead showing something called 'Greenhouse Gas Intensity'. Greenhouse Gas Intensity compares the amount of carbon produced to the amount of money made – the more money made in comparison to the amount of greenhouses gases produced, the lower the Greenhouse Gas Intensity. Apparently, according to the graph shown on the website, the quantity of greenhouse gases went down by 20% between 1994 and 2004; but only when compared to the huge amount of money Alberta is making from oil production. When you consider that Alberta's Gross Domestic Product[17] increased by 3.6% per year in the same period[18] then it becomes clear that, in fact, Alberta's greenhouse gas emissions went *up* by no less than 20%. If you are going to try and lie with statistics, make sure you get rid of any contradictory evidence.

The point of all this statistical juggling is to demonstrate how powerful and potentially dangerous figures can be. It doesn't take a great deal of effort to show that the provincial government of Alberta is essentially lying about their greenhouse gas emissions. It also doesn't take a great deal of effort to show that, because Canada's overall carbon dioxide emissions have been going up by an average of 2% a year (and will almost certainly accelerate as the rush for sand- and shale-based oil gains momentum), the Boreal forests become more important as a carbon sink every year.

Unfortunately, the forests are not remaining intact. I showed in Chapter 1 that the Central African Rainforest was under extreme pressure from logging and other practices including the mining of mineral resources. The natural Canadian Boreal forest may not have the deeply rich ecological diversity of the rainforest, but nor is it a monoculture plantation of identical trees marching across the landscape in some grotesque military spectacle. The 'owners' of plantations in these forests proudly claim the planting of two trees for every one removed – look at the back of a birthday card, or a pad of paper – and they are not lying; yet they fail to explain that those two trees are part of a cash crop, substituting a complex interweaving of dependent species for a desert of quick-growing sawmill fodder.

The Canadian Government reports to the UN Food and Agricultural Organization every five years on the state of its forests, yet miraculously has stated *identical* figures in each of the previous three reports: an outstandingly precise 310,134,000 hectares.[19] This has been eagerly seized upon by the Forest Products Association of Canada who state: "If all countries of the world could eliminate or virtually eliminate deforestation as Canada has done, this would have an impact comparable to eliminating fossil fuel emissions in the United States in terms of advancing GHG mitigation efforts",[20] which would be wonderful if it were true. The FAO, in fact, refers to "the absence of information about forest plantations in Canada"[21] and goes on to state:

> Wood removals are declining in Mexico and the United States of America, while they continue to increase in Canada. This trend is reflected in economic data, with modest growth in several economic indicators in Canada and a slight decline in the other two.

Something else in the FAO report caught my eye, too. It is in a section called 'Forest Health and Vitality'. British Columbia, it seems, is undergoing its own logging frenzy, not for economic gain, but to protect against potential economic loss. "The Government of British Columbia has dramatically increased logging in an attempt to slow the spread of the beetle by removing recently infested trees and to recover value from trees already killed." If BC is indeed logging to protect its future, then somewhere else trees are having to be planted at a rate sufficient to keep up with this; which means that the age and diversity of the Boreal is taking a direct hit, and the Canadian Government are making bare-faced lies about the state of this mighty ecosystem.

There also seem to be some big problems with beetles.

Racing to the Pole

The story of the Tortoise and the Hare has a nice moral:[22] slow and steady wins the race in the end. There are a couple of flaws in the telling of the original fable, though. First, can you imagine what Aesop would have felt had it turned out that the finish line had been reached before the hare took his first nap and, in fact, the hare was just enjoying a well-earned victory bask under a tree? Second, what if both protagonists were being chased by a hungry man with a big gun? I guess the hare would feel pretty good knowing that he had a shiny gold medal *and* that he wasn't going to be turned into hare pie. Poor tortoise.

Aesop was trying to make the point that many humans have a tendency to rush into things with their eyes closed, and end up not seeing the bigger picture; which is a good analogy for how the world has ended up being on the cusp of global environmental catastrophe. It seems, though, that the more power and wealth an individual has, the more tortoise-like he becomes where issues of genuine global importance are concerned. When faced with the need to take rapid action by which such a catastrophe might be averted, then the 'tortoise' becomes rather shy. By the time he eventually slides his head out of the shell, looks around and says, "Now then, what's going on around here?", the climate is changing, and everything is sliding in a giddy, untidy mess towards the brink. Meanwhile the tortoise has decided to sit down with the other tortoises and have a good chat about it.

Some races can't be measured on a stopwatch, and have little entertainment value for enthusiastic crowds; but they are happening, whether we like it or not. Imagine a great rolling race between three heavyweight contestants: three giants of environmental change that, between them threaten to gobble up enormous areas of habitat and change the face of the Earth. Please allow me to introduce them.

Figure 8: Equipment used by Contestant One – Harvester / Feller-Buncher

Contestant One is the Industrial Logger. We met him earlier. Armed with mechanical harvesters, feller-bunchers and bulldozers for that tricky undergrowth, and backed by friendly governments, he spends his time punching great holes in the forest and stripping down habitat leaving piles of broken scrub and huge geometric areas of infertile, acid soil in his wake. You can find him all over the globe, wherever money can be made from wood. Because of Europe's centuries-old appetite for vast amounts of timber and paper – an appetite unfortunately not matched by any desire to preserve nature – only 5% of Scandinavia's forest remains in its native state, the rest being little more than plantation.[23] The 'timber frontier' is now encroaching on the Siberian Taiga: in the ten years up to 2006, the timber production of the Russian Federation rose by 41%.[24] As we have seen, the Industrial Logger has a tendency not to tell the whole truth about his activities.

Source: UK Forestry Commission

Figure 9: Contestant Two – *Dendroctonus micans*, the Spruce Bark Beetle.

Contestant Two are the Bark Beetles. Weighing in at around one gram and with a nose to tail length of 5mm, they are nonetheless true giants in terms of impact and numbers. *Dendroctonus micans*, the Spruce Bark Beetle, tunnels into the living bark of spruce trees to form galleries where their larvae feed and develop, ultimately killing the tree.[25] In Alaska alone, the beetle is spreading at a terrific rate, occupying 120,000 acres of forest in 2006, an increase of 68% over the previous year.[26] Bark beetles are very picky about what they eat, but in large areas of forest that contain a limited number of tree species that is not a problem for them. The 2006 outbreak of Mountain Pine Beetle – another type of bark beetle – in Colorado, USA, only affected lodgepole pines of a particular age, and no other trees; nevertheless 4.8 million of these trees were killed in that year, and expectations were that the entire 1,000 square mile (2,590 square kilometre) area of lodgepole pines in Colorado would be destroyed, with another 36,000 square miles further north and west in similar peril.[27]

There are a number of factors that affect the likelihood of bark beetle attack. The age of the tree is quite important: the thick bark of older trees provides some resistance, but thick bark also tends to be more fractured, allowing the beetles easier access; older trees also provide much more scope for mass breeding, given the volume of wood available. Another effect of age appears to be the amount of resin a tree is capable of producing: younger trees tend to be more adept at producing resin. Copious production of resin upon attack has been shown to be a tree's best defence against bark beetles.[28] Overall, old, large trees are more vulnerable to attack than young ones, which makes the impact of the bark beetle particularly significant in terms of scale. Resin production is something also affected by the health of a tree: the Colorado attack followed a long-term drought, leaving the trees unable to produce sufficient sap. There is also a situation where we can once again use the concept of Degree Days.

Remember that in Chapter 3 we found that the amount of time the temperature stayed above a certain threshold allowed the calculation of the speed at which a nematode could grow and reproduce. The same applies to bark beetles. According to a report from 2004: "The spruce bark beetle is strongly affected by the ambient temperature. A higher frequency of storm damage events and a higher temperature can increase the risk for a build-up of a large population."[29] High temperatures can bring out the worst in bark beetles. Storm damage is an important factor too, for a dead tree is not able to produce sap, making itself a perfect habitat for bark beetles. As the IPCC has shown time and time again, storminess is something that is bound to increase with climate change in the future, leaving larger swathes of dead trees and thus, when combined with the steadily rising temperatures of the Taiga, a wonderful springboard for bark beetle infestation to spread further and further across the land.

Contestant Three is Climate Change itself. The bark beetles are enjoying the benefits of rising temperatures – basking in the extra degree days and occupying the storm-damaged timber; but with climate change also come changes in precipitation, increasingly early snow melt, and a whole world of pain for species

adapted to very specific climatic conditions. As temperatures increase, the whole
broad band of Taiga is creeping northwards: abandoning land in the south and
occupying land to the north that was once the sole preserve of sturdy lichens and
mosses. Given the potential scale of the shift, this is one of the more sinister
impacts of climate change:

> Evidence of recent vegetation change is compelling. Aerial photographs show [that]
> along the Arctic to sub-Arctic boundary, the tree line has moved about 10 km
> northwards, and 2% of Alaskan tundra on the Seward Peninsula has been displaced
> by forest in the past 50 years.[30]

Ten kilometres in 50 years doesn't seem terrifying, but then these impacts are
the result of a mere 0.7°C increase in global temperatures, and way ahead of any
feedback loops kicking in. If you recall, the melting snow in Aspen revealed a
land surface that had a far lower albedo; it reflected less energy, and allowed the
ground to absorb more. The same albedo effect happens when coniferous trees
move into previously scrubby, snowy areas, like the Tundra – an area of almost
permanently frozen sub-soil to the north of the Taiga. It turns out that the Taiga
absorbs between three and six times as much solar energy as the Tundra,[31] creating a positive feedback loop that increases the temperature of the Earth's surface, which in turn causes a further northward shift in the Taiga. If the Taiga
remained in the south, the additional extent of forest might offset the reduction
in albedo, but as temperatures increase, droughts and outbreaks of forest fires[32]
also become more widespread, precisely where extra forest would be most beneficial.

Using methods that calculate the area of climatic zones based on temperature, Muyin Wang and James Overland have estimated that the area of Tundra
lost worldwide between 1980 and 2000 was 1.4 million square kilometres, or
20% of the total.[33] That would be bad enough in most natural habitats, but here
we are also looking down the barrel of a methane-filled gun.

*   *   *

Beneath the Tundra, deep within the permafrosts of Siberia, northern Canada
and Alaska, lie structures known as *clathrates*. These are tiny pockets of frozen
methane ensconced in the sub-soil that, due to the millions of square kilometres
of land under constantly frozen conditions, lock away vast amounts of this
potent greenhouse gas. Some estimates suggest that beneath the Siberian per-
mafrost alone there are 70 billion tonnes of methane,[34] only prevented from
escaping through the chance encounter of methane gas with innumerable

minute ice caskets. The release of such a huge amount of gas (it has at least twenty times the global warming potential of the same amount of carbon dioxide) over a period of 50 years would be enough to raise the temperature of the Earth by around 3°C,[35] causing tight, intense feedback loops rapidly sending the planet into a climatic freefall.

This, you will appreciate, is not something that should be happening.

Some authors, largely those keen on the potential for mineral exploitation and the opening up of shipping routes, are reporting the potential changes as positive; one even goes so far as to say, "the warming of the globe's climate could possibly lead to a more productive and positive natural environment than we have today."[36] I am guessing that most people with a semblance of concern for life on this planet would choke on these words: optimism is fine, providing there is something to be optimistic about – enjoying the fruits of global climate change while mass extinction takes place is little short of murderous.

In the race between the voracious industrial logger, the swarming, spreading bark beetles and the seemingly unstoppable forces of climate change, there is no winner. The Taiga will shift and will fall, but the way we view this marvellous ecosystem – as some kind of permanent clothing on the surface of the Earth – suggests to me that we still can't see the wood for the trees.

Chapter 7

Beneath and Beyond

If you were to measure every individual life form on Earth and take an average of their size, you would end up with something invisible to the naked eye, such is the domination of microbes in this world. That said, the range of sizes that known life forms take is truly impressive. This inevitably begs the question: "Is there anything else?" As far as we know, probably not – certainly not that you could count as an individual organism. But there *is* more: you just have to broaden your horizons a little.

Beneath

Despite the complex and often fragile nature of our relationships with other organisms, some humans want to rewrite life and break the evolutionary monotony they see as being a barrier to 'progress'. Individual genes occupy a space beneath even that of the diminutive virus. What is so special about genes is not that they are life itself, but they allow life to happen. They are the magical molecular ingredients that define what an organism will become: its physical appearance; its thoughts; its potential as a survivor. Modifying them – moving genes from one organism to another – is like a complete, and possibly malevolent, stranger swapping an ingredient in your favourite cake recipe for something you would never expect to find in cake. The cake may taste better, but it may also poison you.

It may seem as though these changes are being made to fulfil some altruistic desire to do good – increasing crop yields, building in resistance to insects, curing human diseases – but I am not alone in having deep suspicions. As I said earlier, the companies using, and making the money out of these ventures, won't accept liability for the potential failings of their products. The largest of the corporations involved in genetic modification are also keen to patent their 'inventions' as though it is possible to own life,[1] like the nineteenth-century slave traders who claimed to own their cargoes of imprisoned humanity.

Overriding all of this is that genetic modification is big business:

Shares of the St Louis-based agri-biotech giant [Monsanto] skyrocketed last week when the company announced it nearly tripled its fiscal first quarter earnings, which rose from $90 million in 2006 to $256 million. Sales for the period rose 36% to $2.1 billion.

The stunning results are largely due to sales of Monsanto's genetically modified seeds, which have been engineered to repel pests and be immune to herbicides.[2]

Whatever the history of genetic modification, experimenting with the stuff of life is not something that should be guided by profit. Nor must such tinkering be motivated by politics: governments trying to show that they are supporters of business, or of scientific progress. Science does not have any political leanings, nor does it judge whether one development or another constitutes 'progress'; it is simply a set of tools and methods for showing whether something is physically true or not. Science does not have all the answers, not least because not all questions can be couched in scientific terms. It is most certainly true, though, that the *misuse* of science does cause problems.

You may be familiar with the deep controversy that arises wherever genetic modification rears its head, but this may be as nothing compared with the controversy that threatens to envelop the use of Synthetic Biology. Here is a definition: see how you feel about it.

Synthetic Biology is:
a) The design and construction of new biological parts, devices and systems, and
b) The re-design of existing, natural biological systems for useful purposes.[3]

Some futuristic pipe dream, you may think. Think again: synthetic biology is real and it is being created at a university, government or corporate research laboratory near you. At this level of work biology, technology and chemistry fuse to provide the means to create the building blocks of life from scratch or make modifications to living things that would have been impossible 20 years ago. A glance at one website,[4] used by many researchers as a hub for information, reveals a host of tools, methods, protocols and systems that would be far more at home in a computer programmer's library; and essentially, that's what it is – a library of tools for reprogramming life. Fancy a new strain of *E. Coli*, yeasts with artificial chromosomes, or perhaps a faster-growing mouse cell? You can find instructions for creating these right now, on the internet. Downloading such 'recipes' from the web is perfectly legal, yet were the same website to host information assisting conventional 'terrorist'[5] activities like taking out an electrical grid infrastructure, it would almost certainly be shut down.

Proponents of cutting-edge biological research often use the 'greater good' argument to justify work that would, in isolation, seem abhorrent to anyone concerned about genetic modification or other processes that alter the nature of life. This idea that there is a necessary level of sacrifice – be that in terms of human life, that of other animals or maybe some long-held belief – required in order to achieve a greater good, is not new. The British philosophers Jeremy Bentham and John Stuart Mill developed a concept known as Utilitarianism, which essentially means 'the greatest good for the greatest number'. In fact, this is a gross oversimplification of something, on the back of which so many false claims have been made. What Mill actually wrote in his book was:

> The utilitarian morality does recognize in human beings the power of sacrificing their own greatest good for the good of others. It only refuses to admit that the sacrifice is itself a good. A sacrifice which does not increase, or tend to increase, the sum total of happiness, it considers as wasted.[6]

Essentially, any sacrifice made must be voluntary, and that sacrifice is only worthwhile if it increases the sum total of happiness, or good. By co-opting this idea in order to justify the cloning of embryos as a cure for wasting diseases, or open-skull experimentation on the brains of primates to discover the causes of Alzheimer's, the supporters of these methods seem to have ignored the need for such sacrifice to be voluntary. When considering the potential risks that arise from creating self-replicating artificial life forms, or manipulating life in such a way that its traits can be passed on to future generations, the sacrifice to be considered is one of global proportions. An editorial in *The Economist* from 2006 puts this succinctly: "No technology is risk-free, but synthetic biology has the twist that its mistakes can breed. Today the risks are not great. Nevertheless, as knowledge increases, so will the risk that something truly nasty might be unleashed."[7]

It seems to me that the 'greater good' that is so glibly spoken of by enthusiastic politicians and embedded scientific journalists, is utterly eclipsed by a Greatest Good: the need to protect the future from the actions of the present.

Beyond

Whatever scale we examine life at, each individual organism is just one component of a far greater mass: the bees in their hives and swarms, the cod in their shoals, the trees in their forests. Yet, even the greatest collections of individuals are still only parts of the thing that binds all life together in an infinitely complex dance of birth, survival, change and death. That which some call Gaia, Mother Nature or Creation may just be a vast ecosystem, but it transcends all chance of description or scientific analysis – sometimes all we can do is look on in awe. Humility is not a weakness:

> You must, in studying Nature, always consider both each single thing and the whole: nothing is inside and nothing is outside, for what is within is without. Rejoice in the true illusion, in the serious game: no living thing is a unity, it is always manifold.[8]

On July 4, 2005 the space probe Deep Impact completed its mission successfully. Launched in January 2005 the spacecraft containing the sacrificial probe made a beeline for the comet Tempel 1, describing a curved trajectory, which placed it in the path of the comet orbiting the sun between Mars and Earth. On approach the larger 'fly-by' craft released Deep Impact, which plunged into the surface of Tempel 1, causing "a brilliant and rapid release of dust that momentarily saturated the cameras onboard the [larger] spacecraft."[9] The impact crater was the size of a house, and the strength of the collision was sufficient to allow the deeper layers of the comet to be released into space for analysis by the fly-by craft. The mission was hailed a tremendous success by NASA, and widely recognized as a great achievement in the annals of space exploration.

What right do we have to affect a stellar object in this way? Which celestial judge issued humanity with the warrant by which we would be allowed to take chunks out of unearthly bodies? And how can we know that there was no life form on this comet – a life form we could not have detected prior to impact, and certainly not one that we have the moral right to kill. Humans have barely unlocked the first set of gates on the path to discovering all that the Earth has to offer; yet 'civilized' humans are now taking the devil-may-care attitude that has damaged so much, to the stars, into a place where the ideas of sustainability and balance lose their comfortable meaning.

Carl Sagan, the luminary cosmologist and philosopher, once wrote: "There are worlds on which life has never arisen. There are worlds that have been charred and ruined by cosmic catastrophes. We are fortunate: we are alive; we are powerful; the welfare of our civilization and our species is in our hands."[10] He could have also added that, with such enormous power and the ability to both create and destroy, we have a moral duty not only to curtail our destruction of the Earth, but also to ensure that, as we move beyond the confines of this planet we do not lose sight of that responsibility. Industrial Civilization makes the assumption that life on other planets, in other galaxies, will only be 'advanced' if it can communicate with us; but surely the truly advanced society is one that, above all, has attained equilibrium with its own environment. Technology is no measure of advancement; it is simply a tool that may be used by life for good or ill.

If we choose to search only for life that we consider 'advanced' by our own measure, then we are potentially ignoring the majority of life elsewhere. The Earth may be all that we are certain of that contains life, but that does not mean we should not respect that which lies beyond it: we have so far made a pretty bad job of looking after our own home. Should we be entrusted with the care of anyone else's?

Bringing It All Together

So there you have it: from the very smallest organism that might just qualify as life, to the very largest that has ever been, we have seen the richness and complexity of life operating across a vast range of scales, all of them within the thin envelope of atmosphere and ocean that provides a home for every living thing on Earth.

The tales you have read, which move from virus to bacteria, nematode to bee, cod to spruce, exclude many other life forms that have so many stories to tell; but even with these inevitable gaps, one thing is clear. At every scale we have looked at, humans are tied up in the tale – both as cause and effect, often the perpetrator of the ills that have befallen the life form, and always the victim. As you will see in Part Two, nothing is so dependent upon other forms of life as humans, the ultimate consumers. Everything we do has the potential to disrupt something, knock it off balance as we negotiate the finest of lines; yet, that line we are repeatedly stepping over, with our battery farms, our bulldozers, our trawlers and our relentless production of climate-changing gases, seems to be getting narrower.

If an organism exceeds the carrying capacity of its environment, a natural mechanism takes charge to ensure that the environment doesn't collapse entirely. Food, the essential ingredient for sustaining life and allowing it to expand, develop and evolve, becomes scarce. This is not intelligence as we would normally understand it, it is just something that takes place because the natural resources of that environment are finite – the environment can supply no more.

As food becomes scarce the organism contracts in terms of its distribution over space, the number of individuals in a certain area, or both. This allows the food source to be naturally replenished in such a way that the life form, if enough time is allowed, can once again thrive. As the organism once more expands its distribution and increases its density the food source will again start to run out. Unless a balance is achieved between the food source and the organism's consumption of that food then this process will continually take place, like a tide of plenty washing over the space that the organism occupies, and then receding, time and time again.

The steady state between natural food production and consumption is known as sustainability, and it applies to all resources being used by all life forms. If the organism refuses or fails to contract in the face of diminishing resources then the environment will reach a level of scarcity from which it may not be able to return in that organism's lifetime. Nature doesn't pull any punches – an organism that refuses to play the sustainability game will always lose. Nature will eventually recover.

Whether humanity will, is another matter.

Part Two

Why It Matters

Chapter 8

What Are We?

Life as we know it would not exist without deoxyribonucleic acid, or DNA. These long-strand molecules are essentially copying machines: they create duplicates of themselves throughout every cell of an organism. When the organism dies, if it hasn't reproduced, then the DNA will be stopped in its tracks – it will have failed.

DNA doesn't 'want' to survive – you cannot ascribe human characteristics to a chain of complex molecules – it just happens to have that function. Organisms are simply carriers for DNA, or Survival Machines.[1] Organisms may not understand why they need to reproduce (although we have no way of knowing for sure) but they all 'feel' that they must reproduce, and in order to reproduce they must be able to survive. Humans realize, at a fundamental level, that they need to reproduce, but how many realize that this impulse to reproduce (and also to survive) is simply the calling of their DNA molecules?

Some of you may be thinking that I've left an element out of here; where is the Creator? This book assumes that evolution is a fact, but in the interests of harmony I have no wish at all to give you a lecture on the rights and wrongs of evolution or religion – at least not yet. If you want a good read, then I recommend both *The Selfish Gene* and *The Ancestor's Tale* by Richard Dawkins. There, I have put my heart on my sleeve, but I need to explain myself.

Whatever you believe, knowing what humans think they are is very important. To start with, I'm going to run a few opinions past you that other people have given me.[2]

Human beings are . . .

. . . God's creation

. . . a fluke of the universe

. . . mostly harmless

. . . the most dangerous animals on the planet

. . . fallible

. . . finite

. . . an infestation upon the Earth

. . . bipedal carbon-based life forms

. . . here for a fleeting moment

. . . the pinnacle of evolution

. . . the pinnacle of creation

. . . stupid

. . . unaware of how lucky they are

. . . they just are

Without some serious mental rewiring, it is not possible for one person to simultaneously and sincerely believe all of these opinions. Some of them you may sincerely believe, and some of them you won't. With half an eye on the list above, I'm going to break the explanation of what we are into four small sections, each of which concerns a different physical aspect of humanity. First of all, we need to know where humans stand, sit, kneel or lie down compared to other forms of life.

Our Place in the Tree of Life

Taxonomy is a branch of science concerned with putting things into a certain order, and taxonomy is used to create something called the Phylogenetic Tree, of which humans form a part. Within this monstrously complicated network of trunks, branches, twigs and leaves, can be found humans; as we see in Figure 10.

Reading from the top downwards, you can see that it takes eight stages to get to modern humans. Not all species or subspecies take so many levels to get to; humans are a pretty special case, being rather central to our way of seeing things. In fact, humans would be recognizable at the level of the Family *Hominidae*, even though all living humans are undoubtedly of the same species.

As you move back through history, you discover that our connections to the rest of the animal kingdom are not really that obscure. Richard Dawkins refers to common links between different branches on the phylogenetic tree as 'concestors'.[3] We share a concestor with, first, bonobos and chimpanzees, then gorillas, orangutans and gibbons. Our common link with our closest surviving animal relation, the chimpanzee, with which we share at least 95% of our DNA, probably existed six million years ago – a blink in the eye of geological time. Ten concestors back and we connect to the rodents. Fifteen concestors, and we are at one with the duck-billed platypus. Humans and amphibians share a common ancestor at 340 million

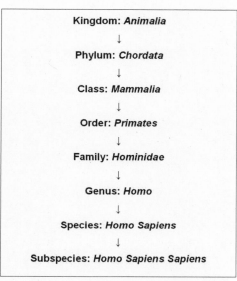

Kingdom: *Animalia*

↓

Phylum: *Chordata*

↓

Class: *Mammalia*

↓

Order: *Primates*

↓

Family: *Hominidae*

↓

Genus: *Homo*

↓

Species: *Homo Sapiens*

↓

Subspecies: *Homo Sapiens Sapiens*

Figure 10: Human Phylogenetic Tree

years BP (before present), and it was 460 million years ago – still only a tenth of the Earth's lifetime – that we split off from the same branch that we share with sharks.

The Animal Kingdom first emerged, as the jellyfish-like *Ediacara*, anything up to 2,000 million years ago[4] but, as we have seen in Part One, animals were, and are, most certainly not alone. Right up at the highest levels, we find that *Animalia* is just one of many kingdoms.

Kingdoms of Life according to ITIS[5]

Animalia: The animals, of which we are part. This kingdom is extremely diverse, but not the most diverse kingdom. It includes all insects, fish, mammals, crustaceans, molluscs, corals and worms, among other things.

Plantae: Plants. The most physically diverse kingdom of all, and probably the largest in terms of total mass. Includes all mosses, multicellular algae (in all their many hues), flowering plants, trees and grasses. Without plants humans would have no food, except for fungi.

Chromista: Possibly a kingdom of its own, formed of algae which may or may not be included in the Plant Kingdom (confusing, I know).

Fungi: A kingdom that seems simple enough but includes a vast array of different sac fungi; club fungi – including all mushrooms and toadstools; yeasts and moulds. Without fungi, nothing would decay, and there would be no soil.

Monera: Bacteria. As we saw in Part One, bacteria are everywhere and without them life on Earth would not have been able to develop. This is now usually divided into the True Bacteria and the more resilient Archaea.

Protozoa: These are the single-celled animals. They feed on bacteria and moulds, and they are food for many larger creatures, as well as being an important source of disease.

Nothing is simple in the world of taxonomy, though. Because True Bacteria and Archaea are considered to be so different from all other forms of life, they are often classified as forming two of the three Domains in which all life is included, leaving all other life forms on their own branch. Outside of these domains are viruses, as discussed in Part One; no one is really sure where they should go. If we bring together all different life forms in a single vast genetic tree, we get something like Figure 11.

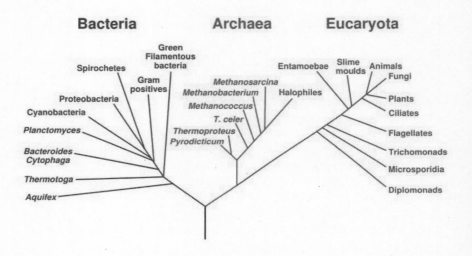

Figure 11: Domains of Life

All animals, including us, sit on one sub-branch, in the right-hand corner, next to slime moulds.[6] Go back just 500 years, though, and the common viewpoint – scientific or otherwise – was that Man was undoubtedly the dominant being on the Earth. Aristotle, that Greek bastion of self-promotion, conceived the idea that all life forms in existence were set upon a scale that reflected the 'degrees of perfection' that each was endowed with. This was extended right up to the Middle Ages in Europe to include various religious entities, at the pinnacle of which was God, the Creator.[7] Such an egocentric viewpoint, with humans just a few rungs below God, and everything else less 'perfect', is not such an uncommon view even today.

Of course, humans are just one very small (if relatively numerous) part of the Animal Kingdom. We find our place among the thousands of different species of mammals, which sit alongside the amphibians, reptiles and other animals that have backbones; but most species of animal do not have backbones. Huge numbers of animals have shell-like exoskeletons, protective shells, or no form of skeletal matter at all – we are in the minority. Incredibly, there may be as many as 20 million different animal species. Most of them may consist of only a few specimens, but others are teeming with unimaginable numbers. Ants and termites, for instance, may form between 20% and 30% of the total animal mass of some large terrestrial ecosystems.[8] In July 2007 there were 6.6 billion humans on Earth. There are very approximately 200,000 trillion termites.[9]

This is not some deliberate ploy to make you feel small and insignificant, or even mostly harmless; there is no doubt, however, that our impact on Earth – as described in Part One – is out of all proportion to our global biological significance.

How Significant Are We?

After all that you may be thinking, "If we're so small and insignificant, how come we are able to change life on Earth so much?" A fair question: if we were to base the importance of an organism upon how much potential it has for long-term survival, then you might think that *Homo sapiens sapiens* would be at the top of the pile. You would be very wrong. If you recall the way in which life forms are dependent upon each other, then one thing becomes startlingly clear: most individual life forms that we are familiar with cannot survive on their own. Insects feed off plants and other animals; fish eat plankton, weed and other sea creatures; humans can live off nothing but plant matter, but generally consume a combination of plants, animals and fungi.

But here's the catch: all of the organisms mentioned in the previous list are Heterotrophs; meaning they cannot produce enough food of their own to survive without feeding off another organism. Autotrophs, on the other hand, can make all of their food from raw materials – sun, air, rocks, dissolved minerals, volcanic gases. The vast majority of plants and algae, along with many bacteria, are autotrophs; and it is they, the organisms that can survive without any help, often in extreme conditions,[10] that first colonized this planet. Humans are often described as the 'ultimate predator' – the supreme killer which all other creatures submit to, albeit unwillingly. In energy terms, humans occupy a number of trophic (food) levels, and often make conscious decisions about which level they want to occupy: from the vegan who consumes nothing but direct plant matter, to the omnivore who may be consuming something, that consumed something, that consumed something, that consumed something else. This makes us extremely flexible, able to take advantage of a vast range of food sources, which has contributed to the success of the species. In effect we are not just the ultimate predator, but also the ultimate scavenger – fussy eaters take note. Nevertheless, humans are, as we saw throughout Part One, extremely vulnerable to changes in the ecosystems that support them.

Imagine you are sitting on a beach, facing the open ocean with nothing but miles of cream-coloured sand stretching to either side of you. Hunger strikes, and there is nothing, nothing at all, for you to eat. The sea is barren; marine life having been fished to near-extinction. The sands are dry and devoid of green matter. Reptiles that once basked in the warm sun before scuttling away to find insects have not survived whatever armageddon led to this situation. The Earth is an apparently lifeless globe of ocean and land: you will surely starve to death as the last of your kind. If only you could use the energy of the sun to convert the air and the minerals from the Earth into food. If only the tiny trace elements that sit exposed on the grains of sand could be converted into some sort of sustenance. You may have reached an evolutionary pinnacle of sorts, but you are incapable of living without the efforts or the bodies of other organisms to feed you.

If we aren't careful, the autotrophs will inherit the Earth.

The Problem of Population

In 2012 the world human population is expected to break the 7 billion mark,[11] and by around 2060 will probably reach around 10 billion. This phenomenal growth rate suggests an organism that is out of control: like bacteria that teem and multiply in an infinitely rich soup of nutrients, or a rampant tumour that must, somehow, be excised.

Demographic history tells us a very important lesson about the nature of humanity, and how our opportunistic behaviour has made us so dominant. Figure 12 shows the world population over the last 12,000 years,[12] beginning with the very approximate estimate of 1 million people in 10,000 BCE (Before Common Era)[13] and not doing much for about 9,000 years. It is not until after 1500 CE (Common Era)[14] that things begin to get going, and if you look to the far right of the graph then it is clear that the population is only really starting to go up as the year 2000 approaches.

In order to get a clearer view of our population history, you need a far more recent set of data to go on, as shown by Figure 13. Even with only 2,000 years to represent the history of human population growth, you have to examine the last tenth of the graph to see something really notable happen.

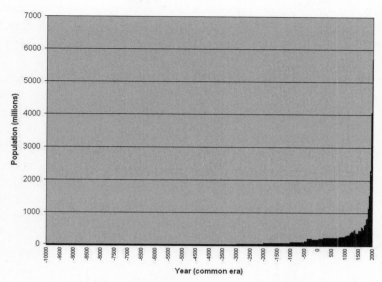

Figure 12: World Population in the last 12,000 years

In the 200 years up to the year 2005 the human population increased from just over 800 million to 6,500 million. Between 1900 and 2005 alone, the population grew from 1,550 million to the giddy heights of today's vast humanitarian swarm. According to the Optimum Population Trust,[15] the Earth *may* be able to sustainably support 4.6 billion people. Their analysis seems to be reasonable; in which case we have already overshot that 'carrying capacity' by about 50%, with the overshoot getting more critical all the time.

What is evident from the graphs is that for most of human history, the population really didn't change much at all. Up to the first great wave of animal domestication by humans, in about 10,000 BCE,[16] the population was stable at around 1 million. Domestication made it possible for humans to stay in one place and eat, instead of foraging for food – farming was born. Population growth remained fairly steady as the reach of domestication spread for the next 9,000 years or so throughout the world, but it wasn't until the emergence of the first modern civilizations in the Mediterranean basin and the Middle East that high-density human living and mass transportation allowed the population to increase more easily, where previously people had had to remain close to the source of their food. This would become very significant later on.

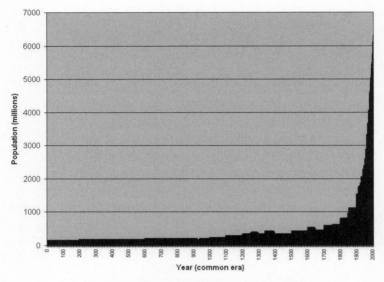

Figure 13: World Population in the last 2,000 years

Growth accelerated in the late 19th century. Up to this point the largest regional populations had been in China, India and south-east Asia, which had economically benefited from agricultural methods developed over thousands of years. The Industrial Revolution provided a source of wealth, and further inducement to multiply, for the increasing population of Europe,[17] which grew rapidly in the late 19th and early 20th century; but more than anything else it was the ability of humans to exploit and open up huge areas of land for food production which allowed the world population to keep increasing. Despite wars, the constant threat of disease, and natural disasters, humans found ways to survive – and thrive. According to the United Nations: "The rapid growth of the world population started in 1950, with reductions in mortality in the less developed regions, resulting in a . . . population of 6.1 billion in the year 2000, nearly two and a half times the population in 1950."[18]

Why has the population grown at such a dramatic rate in the last 60 years? Superficially, the answer is that people are not dying as readily as they did up to the middle of the 20th century. Infant mortality rates in most parts of the world are at the lowest since detailed records were first taken, and human life expectancy – at least in rich nations – is similarly at its highest . . . for the time being. Good nutrition along with widespread conventional medicine (including vaccinations) and sanitation are ensuring humans live through situations that, only 50 years previously, would have been almost certainly fatal. I said that this was just the superficial answer because we have created a situation where, even as we create more virulent strains of disease and – through our consumer lifestyles – subject our bodies to ever-increasing strain, we are just about winning the battle against early death. This has ensured that, *if the Earth is able to sustain us* (and that is a huge 'if'), there will be 10 billion humans crawling, walking, driving and flying around the Earth in the not too distant future.

We may think of ourselves as superlatively mobile and adaptable *today*, but it appears that between 100,000 and 10,000 BCE humans had travelled the world and occupied every continent except for Antarctica,[19] and this during a period of almost perpetual Ice Age. In that time, with a world population of less than a million, such mobility would have had little impact on the global ecosystem. As of about 1982, when we overshot the Earth's carrying capacity, our current way of living meant that the Earth was simply unable to support the number of people living on its surface without something starting to go very wrong.

Civilized Humans

The auks and the herring gulls have their cliffs; from the shallow sandstones to the precipitous overhanging crags of limestone and granite, battered by thunderous waves, but rich in plant and insect life, and close to a still plentiful sea. The pigeons, starlings and sparrows have their cliffs too; the sheer drops of sullen concrete, russet brown brick and gleaming glass that see a tide of humans below washing through the canyons on foot, and in their tireless vessels that shudder as they wait impatiently for the next green light. These cliffs and seas are no less plentiful for the birds: litter, food waste, discarded packets and canisters full of last night's leftovers – carrion à la carte. For the most part, though, the wildlife stays away.

The contrast between rural and urban living is at its clearest in the densely packed cities of India, China, Brazil and South Africa. The cities promise a life free of the hand-to-mouth squalor that is the sufferance of millions of people in denuded and polluted rural areas. The cities have job opportunities, apartments with every modern convenience and pavements of gold! In reality, the cities take people away from one world and enclose them in another – and the squalor simply piles up within the city walls.

In 2005, the UN Population Division announced that the urban population of the world would exceed the rural population within three years. Even as world population is growing, urbanization is increasing as a proportion of this rising figure.

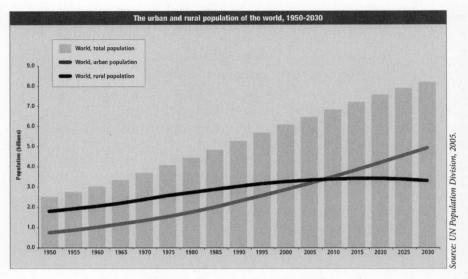

Figure 14: World Rural vs. Urban Population since 1950.

Actually, I need to rephrase the last sentence. World population is growing, because urbanization has *allowed* it to grow so quickly. Modern urban living has provided humans with a multitude of services on tap, through wires or just down the road, allowing people to get on with the important business of earning money and enjoying the fruits of their last shopping trip. It has consequently also provided what architects refer to as 'housing units', which can be crammed in left, right, centre, up and down; in tower blocks, terraces and clusters of identikit housing which keep pushing towns and cities further into the wild. Space to live? Space to multiply, certainly.

The UN report states: "During the next few decades the urban areas of the less developed regions are projected to absorb all the population growth expected worldwide. That is, global population growth is becoming a largely urban phenomenon."[20]

Urbanization is usually defined in terms of the density of human population, but there is more to it than that. An urban environment is *dominated* by humans. The domain of humans is becoming the city: a complex infrastructure of housing, commercial and public buildings, utilities and transportation, which has little or no space for those species that cannot adapt to suit the urban way of life. The 50% level of urbanization is a monumental event; it indicates the point at which global humanity has become not only culturally, but physically associated with the dominance of cities. This is what it means to be 'civilized'.

With close to 7 billion people on Earth, the kind of subsistence behaviour[21] that supported just a few people thousands of years ago, and still supports pockets of humanity in some areas, doesn't seem possible – there doesn't seem to be enough land or wildlife to go round. Surely city dwelling, with its emphasis on high density, high efficiency living is the only way to support even the 4.6 billion people that WWF and the Optimum Population Trust say may be sustainable, isn't it? One way of answering that question is to consider how much land a person needs to grow their own food and obtain the other basic requirements for life, such as shelter and clothing.

An interesting analysis was carried out by Andy Collier in 2007, who estimated that a family of four would need around 0.5 acres (0.2 ha) to be fully self-sufficient as a family unit.[22] For seven billion people, this works out as 3.5 million square kilometres, or 2.4% of the Earth's land surface. Even if we triple this to allow for building, clothing and heating materials, it is still a mere 7% of the entire Earth's land surface – a tiny proportion of the land area that humanity is directly affecting at the current time. However, we do not live off the land, we live largely in a civilized culture.

It takes a radical thinker like Derrick Jensen to put that into perspective: "Cities, the defining feature of civilization, have always relied on taking resources from the surrounding countryside, meaning, first, that no city has ever been or ever will be sustainable on its own, and second, that in order to continue their ceaseless expansion cities must ceaselessly expand the areas they must ceaselessly hyper-exploit."[23] He goes on to explain the psychology behind city living; a state of mind that allows urban dwellers to lose the connection with the areas that supply them with resources – much like the increasing number of people who don't understand how their food is made, or why it is not necessarily a good thing for a European or an American to have sacks full of plastic toys for Christmas. The city dweller – the civilized human – is cut off from his life support system. The food, clothes, building materials, even the energy, may as well come from another world.

There is a sad sense of inevitability to all of this, in that we have probably got where we are simply because of who we are. We are humans, we have become more numerous than the Earth can apparently cope with, but there is no turning back because evolution has taken us somewhere that we feel is the pinnacle of existence.

Chapter 9

Who Are We?

When my wife and I decided to have children our first instinct was to try to have one child and see where things went after that. Fortunately for us our first child was healthy, so we decided to have one more – and only one more, regardless of anything that happened afterwards. By only having two children we are, in effect, contributing to the reduction in global population, because the 'replacement fertility' in our part of the world is around 2.1 children per couple.[1] We could have decided to have just one child or none at all and, based on the previous chapter, you would think that would be the natural choice for a committed environmentalist; but I am also a human being, with human instincts.

Being a human means I am, like all organisms, susceptible to the demands of my DNA. It also means that I have conscious awareness of the need to survive – for humans, and probably few other life forms, biological urges are not the be-all and end-all. If an organism has the mental capacity to understand that it needs to survive and reproduce, then it may also have the mental capacity to make its own choices. Humans can choose whether to reproduce and, *in extremis*, whether to live or die. They can also choose a lot more besides.

You are probably reading this thinking that I have just stated the obvious and, in fact, you could choose to stop reading this altogether and go and watch some police chases on TV. This book, or police chases: hardly a life-or-death decision really, although I would stress that invoking your right to choose and closing this book for good could deprive you of a good read, and maybe even a life-changing experience. The point is, you have that choice, and it is a conscious one. Even if that choice is not yours – for instance, someone walking up to you and taking the book away – someone, somewhere along the line made a conscious decision.

The conflict between choice and necessity rarely comes up in our lives now. True necessity, which invokes survival instincts, is usually encapsulated in a series of conscious decisions about when to eat, what to drink, where to live, which job to take and even whether to have children or not. In the latter case, such choice is not particularly modern; there are references to the use of contraception and abortion from as far back as 1500 BCE;[2] but who is to say that such practices are not far older? It seems clear that the division between choice and necessity can be found wherever survival is at issue; so, where infant mortality is high, and life expectancy low, contraception is not particularly relevant, and where the only means of earning a living is to work down a mine or on a farm, then career choices go out of the window. On a personal level, I have chosen to become a vegetarian for a number of reasons – the desire not to kill animals and the understanding that such a diet is more environmentally sound among them – but if I was a nomadic Inuit or a Kalahari Bushman, then dietary choice would only be possible if there was a surplus of the necessary nutrients to keep me alive. If I had to eat meat to survive, then my vegetarianism would take second place to my hunger.

Not Just Physical

Our ability to choose, and the choices that we subsequently make are expressions of the way in which our minds are constructed. Each experience we have, each emotion that triggers a response within us, each time our senses are awakened, has an effect on our future decisions. The stimulation of our physical and mental being reinforces connections between different areas of our brain; a flavour which evokes a vivid childhood memory, or a sound which takes us to another place or another time, are examples we can all relate to. Some connections in our brain, though, are only made obvious when we have to make use of our instincts.

An instinct is any thought or action operating at a level 'below' our conscious awareness. This is sometimes referred to as gut feeling or gut reaction; the inference being that what has occurred has bypassed our conscious mind. But instincts are not reflexes (actions which operate without the direct involvement of our brain); they are the result of something far more cerebral, albeit unconscious. When I hear a person making a racist comment, my instinct is one of distaste; I do not make a conscious decision to feel like that, it happens before I have a chance to think about it. Of course, I have to process the comment in some way to decide whether the words spoken amount to something I could call 'racist', but the instant that this becomes clear, the instinctive gut feeling of distaste occurs.

Now here is an interesting irony. The most widely known modern proponent of instinctive behaviour, Malcolm Gladwell, who wrote the book *Blink*, is shown on the inside front cover of that book. I had enthusiastically read and enjoyed *The Tipping Point* (more of this later), which did not have an author photograph in the paperback version; but, almost certainly because I am a white male brought up in a culture of predominantly white-male dominance, I was later surprised to see that the author was of mixed race. Rather like the double-take story of the surgeon – assumed by most readers to be male – who will not operate on *her* daughter, our cultural influences define how we react: what decisions we make in the face of information. I find racism disgusting, but my cultural filters still made the author of *The Tipping Point* white by default.

In fact, it is almost impossible to entirely ignore your cultural filters. A groundbreaking television advertisement for *The Guardian* newspaper that ran a few years ago showed this very clearly.[3] The UK has a rich history of recreational violence: the sort that used to take place on the beaches of Margate, Brighton and Southend-on-Sea between various groups of people in the summer sun. In the 1970s the 'tribes' most commonly involved were the various groups of skinheads, who would fight tooth and nail, before retreating to the local pubs for a celebratory drink. The skinhead was, and still is, a symbol of white supremacy in many parts of the world; and also of many other types of behaviour often associated with the fringes of society. The *Guardian* advertisement showed a heavily built skinhead racing towards a man in a pork-pie hat and suit, from various angles. The thought in my mind, and those of most people who saw the film, was that the man in the suit was about to be attacked. The crunch came in the last ten seconds, which showed the scene from an entirely different angle: the skinhead was, in fact, saving the other man from being crushed by a falling pallet of bricks. Cultural history has a huge part to play in defining the way we think.

The extent to which our decisions – conscious or instinctive – are coloured by our experiences is a key to understanding whether, and to what extent, people are likely to be influenced by news and other information about environmental damage. A study carried out at the University of Oulu, Finland[4] found that when looking at the way in which information is perceived across different cultures, a huge range of factors had to be taken into consideration, including: the 'nature' of people and their beliefs; a person's relationship with the external environment; the way in which that person communicates; and whether a person identifies with the past, present or future, and to what extent. The study found that technology only went part of the way to bridging cultural gaps – far more important in overcoming cultural differences was simply the ability to understand those differences. In short, in order to influence, you first have to get inside people's minds.

Whether people understand what is going on in their own minds is another matter.

The 17th century philosopher Gottfried Leibniz believed – possibly in a moment of weakness – that our minds are controlled by independent beings known as homunculi, which literally means 'little men'. Such images crop up throughout history, usually in a light-hearted manner, but few people would admit to having such serious beliefs now. However, ask someone to explain who they are – what are they in *themselves* – and they would probably struggle to give you a convincing answer.

I spent a long time reading philosophy books, from Plato to Mill, from Machiavelli to Kant, and finally to a philosopher that few people have heard of – Derek Parfit. Halfway through Parfit's *Reasons and Persons* I stopped. I had reams of notes. Here is a sample of my thoughts:

> Let's suppose that when we sleep, our memories (for which read the specific states of all the neurons in our brains) are transferred to another person. Our brain – that which we inhabited prior to sleep – is destroyed. Do we wake up in the brain / body of the other person?

> Well, for a start, in order to transfer these memories to another person, we have to fundamentally change the state of many, if not all, neurons in that person's brain. This will effectively, on most views, destroy the continuity of that person. But do they become us?

> At first glance the answer would seem to be yes, our mental state has been transferred, so we are bound to wake up in the other brain / body.

> But what happens if our original brain is not destroyed – would there be two of us? And if so, could we be simultaneously aware of waking up in both of these people.

It's not the kind of thing to give you a good night's sleep, and that's one reason why I gave up reading philosophy. My studies allowed me to make a conclusion about what we are, in ourselves – at least to my own satisfaction: "We are the result of the interaction of our accumulated memories with the awareness and control of our physical being and its surroundings." This is obviously a gross oversimplification, but it gets round the idea of having little men cropping up in my brain pulling levers and pushing buttons; after all, who is controlling the homunculi?

The other reason I gave up philosophy was that I realized it was fruitless discussing the metaphysical nature of things when all around me a physical battle for the future of the planet was going on. I wasn't going to cut carbon emissions by contemplating the inside of my head. One thing was clear already, though: just by applying a little bit more self-awareness, some of the things that we hold so dear show themselves up to be completely absurd!

The Importance of Being Happy

It seems that beyond the desire to live and (in most cases) reproduce, we desire one other thing that sometimes outweighs even the instructions of our DNA – happiness. At a physical level, happiness comes from our senses being stimulated in just the right way, whether by touch, smell, sight, sound or taste; to give us the feelings that we associate with 'being happy'. We can also 'think ourselves happy' in various ways – such as recalling happy times, ridding ourselves of worrying thoughts and so on – which are the enduring results of previous pleasant sensory activity.

It is no accident that we remember the things that make us physically happy; our memories are vital for ensuring we avoid 'bad' things and seek out 'good' things. The roots of this are almost certainly evolutionary. Sex (and thus DNA replication) would not happen as often if we did not enjoy it; we would not know which foods were safe to eat if we did not receive positive smell and taste stimulation from them; children would be less likely to remain in the safe care of their parents if they did not feel happy with them. John Rawls, the American philosopher, spoke of happiness being a combination of "carrying through a rational plan and being confident that it will succeed."[5] This is an almost perfect analogue for survival. Given this definition, happiness must be a good thing.

Darrin McMahon, author of *Happiness: A History*, said in a recent speech: "No matter how hard we try to fix its meaning, the word and concept will always come to us . . . as the ultimate human end, the final place of rest, the solution and salvation to human dissatisfaction, the answer to the riddle of existence."[6] Not surprising then, that so many aspects of humanity revolve around the need to attain happiness, and that so many activities, regardless of their outcome – short- or long-term, small- or large-scale, constructive or destructive – offer the great prize of 'happiness'.

* * *

Retail Therapy is essentially shopping to make you feel better. Elated, in fact, if the looks on the faces of those being sold goods on almost every television and press advertisement are anything to go by. Have you ever seen an unhappy look on the face of a purchaser in an advertisement?

retail therapy   *n.* the practice of shopping in order to make oneself feel more cheerful.[7]

Results for each Google search query:[8]
'retail therapy' = 1,250,000 results
'retail therapy' + 'happy' = 334,000 results
'retail therapy' + 'bargains' = 160,000 results
'retail therapy' + 'low prices' = 30,500 results
'retail therapy' + 'addiction' = 43,700 results

There is an awful lot of symbolism in the above results. First, the heavy appearance of the phrase 'retail therapy' in the first place, and its inclusion in almost every major dictionary, implies the acceptance of shopping as something that makes people feel happy. The association of the phrase with 'happy' is not surprising – this is part of the common use of the phrase – but the association with 'bargains' and 'low prices' is more significant. About 15% of all uses of the phrase 'retail therapy' come with the word 'bargains': the phrase is being used to sell products!

None of this is likely to be startling to anyone who has spent time under the influence of advertising, be it through the mass media or at the point of sale. We are hardly going to buy something that is not absolutely essential to us without having a positive feeling about it. I remember being glued to the television during the times I was allowed to watch it as a boy in the 1970s, and now carry with me jingles and catch phrases that associated happiness with goods: "The sunshine taste of Kellogg's Corn Flakes", "Have a cracking Christmas at Woolworths", "I'd like to buy the world a Coke, and keep it company".

Businesses now realize, though, that the simple message of happiness put across from the earliest days of television advertising is not enough to tempt shoppers to use their particular outlet or product in the face of increasing competition, so must be licking their lips as the rebranding of shopping as a core leisure activity takes hold. I found the following itinerary advertised on an American self-drive tour website.[9]

CALGARY - BANFF/LAKE LOUISE - JASPER - EDMONTON
Day 1-2. Experience Calgary.
Day 3-4. Travel to Banff and Lake Louise area and enjoy the delights of the spectacular scenery that abound.
Day 5-6. Continue North and visit the Athabasca Glacier, Maligne Lake and Jasper National Park area.
Day 7-8. Travel East to Edmonton for some last-minute shopping at the West Edmonton Mall (arguably the largest shopping Mall in North America) before flying home.

Days 7 and 8, which have shopping as the main activity, contrast sharply with the previous days of exploring spectacular scenery and regions of geographic interest. You would be hard pushed indeed to find any tourist location that does not boast some form of shop in any part of the Western world, and increasingly countries like Thailand and India are using retail as a magnet to attract tourists in addition to, and sometimes instead of, culture and heritage. A 1999 survey of New South Wales, Australia, visitors found that shopping was by far the most popular pastime for international visitors, with 82% of all respondents stating this as a preference.[10] The next most popular response was "Go to the beach" at 60%. The Visit Britain website offers shopping as a main heading for its itineraries, attractions and events sections. Leisure activities are those that people choose to carry out for the purposes of enjoyment. Shopping has become a key part of that enjoyment. My own trip (by train and bus) to north Wales in the summer of 2007 brought this strikingly home. The railway platform, which famously bears the name of the longest place name in Europe, was empty; the new shopping mall and car park next to the railway station were packed with tourists buying souvenirs.

Some forms of happiness are more subtle, but no less intrinsic to our lives.

*   *   *

In early 2007 I wrote an article called 'Did You Have A Good Life',[11] contrasting a rich, successful man called Alan with a poor, seemingly unsuccessful man called James. Alan 'speaks' of his material success:

> "Sit yourself down; it's a nice sofa, isn't it? Cream leather, with invisible stitching, and mahogany inlays. I would have had walnut, but it doesn't match the wall unit, but the leather matches the car interior very well; I upgraded to the new Range Rover Sport three months ago, after I heard about the latest tumour. We thought, 'What the hell? The life insurance will cover that, and the Lexus.' I don't want Jean going without; she's used to this way of life, and I'm not going to deny her that after I'm gone."

> "I've had a really good life, when you think about it. Look around – have you seen a better parquet than the one in the sitting-room? And when I look out of the window, I know that most of that is mine. It's a great feeling. No, I've got no regrets – life's for living, isn't it?"

Alan thinks he is happy. He really thinks that a good life is something that can be bought with hard cash. James, on the other hand, feels his life has been a failure:

"Oh, hello. Sorry, I didn't see you there. Sorry about the mess, I've been trying to keep the place tidy, but haven't got the energy lately. If you're going past Oxfam this afternoon could you pop in and see if they need any help? That's really kind; I hate to let them down. Do you want a tea? There are some bags in the jar by the kettle; mind the boxes, I've asked Julie to pack up some of my old clothes for the recycling – I don't think I'll be needing them any more."

"The airport are trying to get planning permission to extend the runway, and they want to move a bit of the cemetery. Progress, I suppose, but they want to move Linda's plot, and I can't stand the thought of that. Why can't they just leave things alone? I mustn't complain too much, but sometimes life feels so unfair – some people have it so much better."

James' dialogue continues with a couple of sentences that I think say more about happiness than anything else I have written:

"We had our honeymoon at the seaside, at the same hotel we stayed at for years after – it wasn't too posh, but we liked it. We loved getting the train; didn't seem any point driving as we'd only be stuck in a traffic jam."

James doesn't think he has had a good life, but within these two sentences is a joy that is entirely missing from Alan's words. Alan's apparent happiness rests on the acquisition of material wealth, the appreciation of this wealth by people within his social circle and, no doubt, the jealousy of those who had not achieved the levels of consumption that Alan has attained. His happiness ultimately comes at the expense of other people and the natural environment from which the resources that fuelled his consumption were taken. Alan's happiness is purely selfish – yet it seems that is what most people within Industrial Civilization are striving for.

Whose life would you rather have had?

Selfish Beings?

It's tempting to think that our natural state of mind, and being, is selfishness; we are hard-wired for survival, and an element of selfishness must be in us all. Survival, though, is not what I mean by selfishness. For humans to survive there will inevitably be some knock-on effect within another part of the food / ecological web that we occupy, but that doesn't have to be at the expense of another human. It is perfectly possible for one human to survive without causing another human to die, even if it seems that some politicians' careers depend on being in denial over that position. In fact, in a sustainable world our survival need not be at the expense of any part of the global ecosystem; at least not so the affected part cannot adjust to take account of our activities. For instance, the use of wood from a Canadian spruce forest is perfectly all right, so long as its removal does not cause a net loss of the natural biodiversity within that habitat.

True selfishness happens when the veneer between survival and excess is breached. My use of the odd tree from a Canadian spruce forest may be sustainable on its own, but the use of that forest by seven billion other people is not going to leave very much forest at all. In a way, then, my use of just one tree in a forest is selfish behaviour, because I cannot assume to have sole use of that resource amongst humans, or any other organism that depends on that forest for its own survival. As we saw in Chapter 8, humans are currently behaving in a selfish manner – the biosphere simply cannot support our current net activities as a species – but that does not mean that we are individually selfish. An interested observer would probably, if viewing humans as a single entity from afar, tar us all with the same brush: "Selfish humans! Do they really want to destroy their planet?"

In the 1950s, the explorer Laurens van der Post experienced something that sheds light on the difference between the absolute selfishness of taking more from the Earth than you give back, and the Western view of selfishness, which seems to value 'civility' higher than anything else. Following a game hunt in South Africa, for which a number of San Bushmen had been paid to assist the white hunters, one of the party noticed that the San did not thank them for their gifts, thinking it rude. Thom Hartmann takes up the story:

> One of van der Post's assistants, a hunter who'd never encountered Bushmen before, commented that they seemed ungrateful and uncaring. Ben, one of the other men in the group who understood Bushman culture, responded that to give another human food and water is only good manners and is routine behaviour among the Bushmen. If the white men had been starving on a long trek and the Bushmen had found them, they would immediately share their food and water, even if it endangered their own survival. And they wouldn't expect thanks in response.[12]

It is only when you get up close do you realize that selfishness is not some innate, unlearned human behaviour: it is actually something almost totally alien to pre-industrial humanity.

The respect that Native Americans give to their food resources is widely documented. Professor Erna Guntha, an anthropologist at the University of Washington, wrote extensively about the First Salmon Ceremony, which was (and is) performed by many tribes along the north Pacific coast of North America to cel-ebrate the return of the spawning salmon to their ancient runs. She writes: "None of the tribes who catch the salmon practice agriculture, but depend largely on fish. In most streams [the] spring salmon run comes in prodigious numbers, and is awaited with great eagerness. It presents an occasion for expressing the attitude of veneration which is held throughout the area toward the salmon."[13] This veneration for the salmon is a reflection of the tribes' need to ensure they return year after year; the ceremony may not have an effect on the salmon numbers, but if nothing else it reinforces in the celebrants' minds the need for salmon runs to be looked after in perpetuity. When the explorers Lewis and Clark came across the salmon runs in 1803, millions of wild salmon thrived in the clean, open runs, despite around 10,000 years of continued use[14] by at least 1.8 million tribespeople.[15] Selfishness, when it came to salmon, would have been catastrophic for the Native Americans.[16] As it was, by 1872, following four decades of European disease and relentless slaughter, the Native American pop-ulation had been reduced to less than 240,000.[17]

It appears that such unselfish, sustainable behaviour, when it comes to the use of natural resources, is typical, and no doubt essential, for the few remaining hunter-gatherer tribes around the world. Marshall Sahlins studied this behav-iour for many years in Africa and Australia. Although hunter-gatherer activity requires a large area of uncultivated land through which the tribe can move in their quest for food, they still consume less energy per person per year than any other group of human beings.[18] It is not just food that is used sparingly, though. Because personal belongings are a burden, they simply do not manufacture nor acquire anything that is not essential to the hunter-gatherer way of life. Rodney Frey, Professor of American Indian Studies[19] at the University of Idaho, made a comparison of the energy requirements of different societies.[20] His results are startling, to say the least:

Hunter-gatherer society: the equivalent of *5,000 kilocalories** are needed daily per capita (2,000 kilocalories food energy and 3,000 kcal firewood energy).

Horticultural society (domesticated plants harvested by hand from gardens): the equivalent of *12,000 kilocalories* are required (4,000 kilocalories food, 4,000 kcal firewood and 4,000 kcal domesticated animals).

Agricultural society: the equivalent of *26,000 kilocalories* are needed daily (7,000 kilocalories food, 6,000 kcal firewood, 12,000 kcal domesticated animals and 1,000 kcal coal).

---

* A kilocalorie is the same as a dietary calorie.

Industrial society: the equivalent of *77,000 kilocalories* are required per capita per day (24,000 kilocalories food, 7,000 kcal firewood, 32,000 kcal domesticated animals, and 14,000 kcal coal).

Technological society: the equivalent of *from 230,000 to 273,000 kilocalories* are needed per individual each day (91,000 kilocalories food, 10,000 kcal firewood, 33,000 kcal domesticated animals, 63,000 kcal coal and 33,000 kcal electricity).[21]

It becomes clear, the more that you look at our way of life in the distant past (and the ways of life of some people who still manage to eke out a subsistence living from their disappearing natural habitats) that selfishness helps no one, not even the protagonist, when it comes to survival.

But not only is selfish behaviour ecologically unsustainable, it is also logically unsustainable. The term Prisoners' Dilemma is used to describe a situation where two people have the choice whether to behave selfishly or not. Nigel Warburton describes it like this: "Imagine that you and your partner in crime have been caught, but not red-handed; you are being interrogated in separate cells. You don't know what your partner has or hasn't owned up to. The situation is this: if neither of you confesses, then both of you go free. At first thought this seems the best course of action. However, the catch is that if you remain silent and your partner confesses and thereby incriminates you, he will be rewarded for his collaboration and set free."[22]

Confessing and then turning 'Queen's Evidence', thus giving your partner a hefty time in jail, is selfish behaviour which seems to be beneficial for you. However, if your partner also turns Queen's Evidence, you will both receive time in jail. It may be that later on evidence will appear to incriminate either of you without a confession being required – and the act of committing a crime may be selfish in itself – but acting selfishly in order to gain a pardon is not actually in your own best interest. Putting this in an environmental context: you may think it perfectly acceptable to help yourself to another fish from the river, so that the angler on the other bank has to work harder for tomorrow's dinner, but suppose the angler on the other bank has the same idea? A river may be able to support the voracious appetites of two, ten or a hundred anglers for a short while, but eventually an over-fished river becomes an empty river; and an empty river can feed no one at all.

Chapter 10

Why Does It Matter?

I don't know about you, but I have a problem with death. It's there, at the end of the journey, waiting to take us all, and there is nothing you can do about it except hope that the act of submission is as painless as possible. Come to think of it, though, maybe even that doesn't matter; maybe it's better to go out kicking and screaming in agony, having given Death something to think about on your way out.

It's a romantic vision of sorts. We like romantic visions of death to take the sting out of our inevitable fate: from Ingmar Bergman's stark, obstinate chess player challenging Death to a final match, to the diaphanous, flower-strewn Ophelia being drawn along to her doom by the lazy river in Millais' celebrated painting; death is something we have represented in as many ways as we have emotions.

Figure 15: Just one of the myriad different ways we treat the dead.

Not only do our representations of death vary widely; the way we treat the dead reflects so many things about the cultures we live in. In France, bodies are routinely cremated – a practice that is becoming more popular in almost every industrial nation. In the USA, on the other hand, bodies are encased in the finest wood, and then entombed in concrete caskets, as though somehow death is not the end and we must ensure finality reigns. In Neolithic Europe, high status bodies were set into individual burial mounds along with objects symbolizing their lives, whereas the majority of people were buried in shared mounds or barrows, prior to which bodies were "left in the open air and progressively cleaned of all flesh by the wind and the birds, leaving the bones ready for the burial."[1]

Whether this 'excarnation' makes you feel queasy probably depends on whether you view the body as the essence of a person's existence, or as merely a carrier for the soul. Both views are as ancient as humans, and neither can be proven as false, such is the nature of faith. Religions exist to help people know the unknowable, to think about the unthinkable, to believe the unbelievable: I mean that last one sincerely – faith allows you to believe in whatever you want to believe. It is extremely difficult to know how many people on Earth profess to follow or adhere to a formal religion, as each person's definition of 'follow' or 'adhere' may be different; but one semi-reliable source gives the figure as being about 5.5 billion.[2] That is an awful lot of people who believe in us having something more than a physical existence on Earth; an awful lot of people who want more than mere birth, life and death.

For most people, life is largely a set of repetitive tasks, interspersed by occasional ups and downs. The seemingly monotonous path we tread while on Earth is surely the essence of life itself, though, otherwise we would have people thinking about ending their lives as soon as they understood that there was a better, more fulfilling existence beyond our mortal coils. But rules have been set: life is a test; it is what we will be judged on in the hereafter; it is a stage in the everlasting progression towards a final place in eternity. Maybe the rules exist because we don't actually want to die. Maybe life is all there is.

The Three Selfviews

Whatever your spiritual viewpoint, while we are on this Earth we find ourselves in a web of differing cultural viewpoints and attitudes; social, economic and political systems; physical and mental interactions with the world around us; all of which end up giving us something we call a 'worldview'. Fundamental to this worldview is how we envisage our place on Earth, in both a temporal and spatial sense; and how we, as humans, relate to that sense of time and space. Knowing what your special type of worldview is – I'm going to refer to it as your 'selfview' – is one of the most important things you will ever know: it is nothing less than a template on which all of your actions are based.

Selfview One
Humans are a vital component of life on Earth. They have a special place in the pantheon of all life such that they must be treated with special reverence. They are a supreme organism that must never fail. They have the right to dominion over all other life and as such hold the future of all life in their hands.

Selfview Two
Humans are part of life on Earth. They are no more special or important than any other organism. They exist to play their part within the web of life and as such, like the vast majority of organisms, are relatively short-term players. They have no more right to decide the path of the biosphere than any other organism.

Selfview Three
Humans are naturally of little relevance to the rest of life. They are a scourge upon the Earth. The Earth would be better off without them, and therefore they have less right than any other organism to exist. They must be willing subjects to the actions of all other organisms.

An interesting range of views, and all the more odd for being equally extreme. Given that these Selfviews run from the truly despotic to the humble self-loathing, you would think that the middle ground would be acceptable to the majority of people; but to me, and maybe to you, it feels no less extreme than the other two. How can a middle-ground view be extreme? The answer lies in the questions.

Ask yourself the following four questions, and make sure you are completely honest with your answers:

Question One:
What do you feel is humans' physical place within and in relation to the rest of life on Earth?

Question Two:
Are humans more important than, as important as, or less important than other life on Earth, and to what extent?

Question Three:
What is, or should be, the time span of humans' existence on Earth – or any other place?

Question Four:
What, if any, right do humans have to determine the course of life for anything else on Earth?

How did you do? I have absolutely no idea what you had as your answers, obviously, but I'd like you to look back at the three Selfviews and decide where, if anywhere, you fit now. I suppose you want to know what I, as the person writing this book, had as my answers, but I'm not going to tell you yet – all that will become clear during the course of this chapter. I will say this, though: there are more ways to skin a cat than you might suppose.

The Three Tests

I want to simplify the three Selfviews, so that they can be evaluated more easily. The Selfviews are, in the order previously written: Humans Are Vital; Humans Are Relevant; Humans Are Irrelevant. There are three tests that now need to be applied to each of those Selfviews: the Ecology Test, the Cultural Test and the Personal Test. This may seem a bit analytical and long-winded, but it will rapidly become clear why this has to be done.

The Ecology Test is a way of objectively understanding the physical importance of humans within the biosphere. The whole of Part One and much of Chapter 8 looked at this in detail, so the results shouldn't be too hard to predict, should they?

The Cultural Test takes a wider look at humans in terms of how we, as a species, view ourselves; this was discussed in Chapter 9. The culture you live in will have a huge bearing on the outcome of this test, so I'm going to give you a few different viewpoints so we can work this out between ourselves, regardless of your own cultural beliefs.

The Personal Test finally looks at our relevance from an individual point of view. The outcome of this test is highly personal, but surprisingly there seems to be just one, which relates to this question: If a tree makes a sound when it falls in the forest, does it matter if no one is there to hear it?

The Ecology Test

As we saw in Part One, small changes to the world's ecology, to even the most minute organisms, can have a devastating impact on the ability of humans to survive. The problem with being Top Predator is that you are bound to the actions of everything below you. To a certain extent you can control this, as has been attempted with the use of agriculture and animal domestication; but nature always finds a way to come back and bite you: bluetongue disease, potato blight, boll weevil, avian flu are four examples – those that have made the news – but there are far more lurking in the well of life.

Humans can ingest just about anything that other heterotrophs (organisms that cannot make their own food) are able to. One outcome of this is that ecologically it is not that difficult for humans to adopt less damaging lifestyles: not eating endangered species; not eating anything that damages habitats; not eating animals; not eating anything produced by animals; not eating anything that causes the death of a plant. Yes, if you want to live a truly sustainable lifestyle then you don't even have to kill plants: Fruitarianism – a diet consisting entirely of food 'given' by plants without killing them – isn't exactly widespread, but it's very ecologically sound. The Ecology Test, however, judges how ecologically important humans *currently* are to the rest of life. It is a test not of mere significance – we are obviously significant by the mere fact that humans are having a colossal impact on the natural world – but a test of whether humans make a positive contribution to the global ecology.

There is a school of thought, mentioned earlier, that says humans are fundamental to life. The thinkers that place humans at the top of the tree of life (which, incidentally, feels like a pretty precarious place to be in such a large tree) take what is known as an Anthropocentric viewpoint: we are at the centre, head, top – whatever shape this thing happens to be – of creation, which logically makes us vital to life itself. I have to point the blame for this squarely in the direction of those religious leaders who extolled (and sadly, some still do) this viewpoint in the face of so much contrary evidence. Yet, as Shannon Burkes writes: "The relative importance of humans in the cosmic hierarchy is made clear in the divine speeches at the end [of the Old Testament], which fail to mention any human significance in creation, and instead exalt Behemoth, 'the first of the great acts of God,' (Job 40:15) and Leviathan, 'on earth it has no equal' (Job 41:34)."[3] Always check your references before you quote from them.

A similar school of thought, less polemical but seemingly more ingrained in our culture, sees the world as the outcome of human intervention: i.e. 'it is what it is, so it must be so.' Let me explain. Because humans have had such an impact on, for instance, the landscape of the planet, that landscape must, therefore, be natural: it is natural because it is the result of human agency, because humans are part of life. It makes some sense when you think about it. William Wordsworth in his *Guide through the District of the Lakes* asks the reader to try to imagine the landscape without any human intervention:

> He will form to himself an image of the tides visiting and revisiting the friths, the main sea dashing against the bolder shore, the rivers pursuing their course to be lost

in the mighty mass of waters. He may see or hear in fancy the winds sweeping over the lakes, or piping with a loud voice among the mountain peaks and, lastly, may think of the primaeval woods shedding and renewing their leaves with no human eye to notice, or human heart to regret or welcome the change.[4]

The world that Wordsworth inhabited was one of grand romanticism, of the sanctity of human design and invention, and one in which the aspects of the natural world that mattered most were those which pleased the human eye. The age that valued aesthetics has a legacy in the groups of people that oppose wind farms on the basis of lack of attractiveness, and wish to preserve a sense of order in the countryside rather than let nature have its way. If only the rest of life could talk.

"There's been so much death out there. Who gave the humans the right to decide who's a weed and who's not? They say they're doing it for the crops but even the crops have started to complain. They don't like being sprayed and regimented – there's no variety any more."[5]

We have but one viewpoint, that of the human. The rest of life only has a voice in modern cultures when humans choose to offer it; and even then any 'rights' we grant other species are couched in our terms alone. The anthropocentric viewpoint is only relevant to *our* ecology. To get an idea of the difference humans make to the rest of life, you have to imagine a world without us.

You can take two approaches to a world without humans: one of them in a world where humans once dwelt such as we are now, in the same numbers and with the same impact; a second in a world in which humans never existed at all. To understand the first world you must suddenly take humans away: don't even leave those who live relatively sustainable lives – exterminate us all from the face of the Earth. Who would miss us? Pets maybe – I can envisage a smattering of mournful, solitary Greyfriars Bobbys lying at the bedsides of their former owners, pining away – but even the most devoted companions would eventually be forced into following their instincts by the drives of thirst, hunger and the need for a mate. Animals in cages would starve, after resorting to cannibalism. The same goes for farmed fish in concrete pens and synthetic nets, but the fish in ponds in gardens throughout the world would – as mine started to many years ago – live happily on weed, insects and other wildlife. Farm animals in fields would break down fences and roam wild: flimsy electrical tape being no impediment after humans stopped producing the source of those little jolts.

Bob Holmes took *New Scientist* readers on a stark ride into a world in which humans once existed, ending: "It will only take a few tens of thousands of years at most before almost every trace of our present dominance has vanished completely. Alien visitors coming to Earth 100,000 years hence will find no obvious signs that an advanced [sic] civilization ever lived here."[6] The toxic impact of humans in the industrial age lingers for a while, continuing to heat up the Earth for decades before this trend finds a natural balance; while the chemicals gradually break down through a host of natural processes, eventually dissipating to harmless levels. This may take aeons, and some substances may never completely go away. What is particularly interesting is the rapidity with which our *visual* impact breaks down in the face of Nature. Without the constant attention given to mowing, cutting, shaping, beating down, ploughing, realigning and reclaiming the Earth's surface, the planet will once again take on the softness that is the mark of life forms that intimately depend upon, rather than push back and defend against, each other.

The second world, one in which humans never existed, would resemble the world 100,000 years after humans had left: a mere forty-six thousandth of the lifespan of the Earth. Life would go on, all forms of life except for those we purposefully created for our own ends: the synthetic hybrids; the chimaeras; the genetically modified organisms that ravage the plains of Canada and Argentina; the farmed salmon that threaten to dominate the gene pool each time a marine wall breaks down. And what of the dodo, the passenger pigeon, the Yangtze River dolphin, the unknowable numbers of species that lived and then were snuffed out by our agency – often without us ever realizing we were doing it? Imagine a world in which humans had never caused a single extinction: this could only be a world in which humans had never existed.

We don't come out well on the Ecology Test: the rest of life would be better off without us. It seems that we are irrelevant.

The Cultural Test

I was listening to the news on the radio the other day; it was an article about the UK armed forces in Afghanistan losing soldiers because of a lack of decent armoured vehicles. The phrase that struck me was the same one that some other writers have picked up on, 'Our armed forces'. I don't remember being asked permission for my armed forces to fight in Afghanistan, nor did I realize that I even had any armed forces that I could ask to fight on my behalf.[7] It turns out that my sister has some armed forces too, and my best friend, and my neighbours who go everywhere by car.

We all have to share the same armed forces, of course – well, at least if you are in the same country as me. But then who are those other people in Afghanistan, the NATO lot? And there are lots of United Nations forces trying to sort out problems in West Africa. Are they all mine? Which ones belong to me? I'm getting confused. The problem with trying to ascertain which culture you belong to is that there seem to be so many different ones to choose from. I could easily put myself in the following social / racial / religious etc. groups:

Earth dweller

European

White

Non-religious

British

English

All pretty standard stuff, and none of them contradictory – or are they? Britain is a Christian nation, according to various religious people I hear on the radio. I can be an Earth dweller and White, for sure, but does this recognition of my global position mean I've opted out of any regional or national geographical identity? In fact your cultural identity is a mix of just about anything you want it to be: football team, favourite brand of cola, sexual orientation, hair colour.

However you position yourself amongst others, though, you probably feel you belong in one of the few dominant cultures on the planet, and almost certainly the one you have been born into. Someone born in North America, Europe, Australasia, certain states in Asia, South Africa and many other parts of the world, would have been dominated from birth by a culture that is predominantly Christian (at all points along the belief spectrum) and which is centred on the acquisition of money and property through the production of goods. This culture has a tendency towards high-consumption, high-pollution, the private ownership of land and property, representative democracy,[8] the English language, and a relatively free press and media. This culture is usually known by a combination of the words 'industrial', 'Western' and 'capitalist', though there are many other names for it. There are variations on the predominant features, especially in the use of language, but in general that's about the size of it.

Many other people (or rather their governments and especially their business leaders) aspire to be like those in the industrial capitalist West. Religions provide some resistance, especially where the church and state are closely linked – Iran, Nigeria and Pakistan are examples – but even where religious belief is strong, like in the USA or Italy, the high-consumption, high-pollution norms seem to do fine, or even thrive, on such beliefs.

Huge population centres, like those of India and China – accounting for nearly 2.5 billion people between them – have their own cultural systems which originate from a combination of theistic and secular beliefs; but the whole-hearted embrace of capitalism by both nations, if not that of the appearance of a democracy or a free press, suggests that other truly distinct cultures are more of the exception rather than the norm. I don't think I would be insulting many people by making an assumption that the majority of people reading this fall within the same basic culture that I was brought up in. If you were not, then you may come out of this test better than the people who have the majority of financial wealth on this planet.

Figure 16: How many do you recognize?

One way of getting towards the level of objectivity needed for the Cultural Test is by looking at the dominant 'symbols' of a culture, and working out what they say about the people within it. That can be complicated, but also very enlightening.

I put together the montage of logos you can see in Figure 16 because it seems to me that if you can bring together many of the symbols of a culture you can create something that actually resembles that culture. When I went about choosing the logos, I selected those that I thought most people would be able to recognize throughout the entire Western industrial capitalist culture: most of them are commercial, which is not surprising considering the importance of commerce in almost every aspect of the culture; some of them are media organizations, like the BBC, CNN and MTV, which reflects the importance of the media in defining cultural inputs from day to day; very few are non-commercial – the Red Cross / Red Crescent, the Star of David, the Christian Cross and the WWF panda amongst them. There are lots missing, of course, but overall I think the montage fairly represents the priorities of this culture.

The message that this gives to me is that much of humanity has become a commercial entity. No longer are we about subsistence, despite the rich, fulfilling life that – as you have seen – it can entail. There is apparently far more to life than this: we enjoy listening to music; watching TV; buying toys, clothes, cars and computers; eating fast food; flying to far-off places and, when it suits us, giving a little money to charity. We even pray, for others and ourselves: for longer lives, for healthier lives, for the dead, for the living, to make us wealthy, to make us happy. Some of us pray for a healthier natural environment; some of us try to create a healthier natural environment. When it comes down to it, though, it's really all about taking what we want, so long as we can afford it.

Humans are Vital; Humans are Relevant; Humans are Irrelevant: which is it to be? The predominant culture is one that certainly puts humans at the centre of things, so it's clear that humans cannot be irrelevant, but does this culture really suggest humans are vital? In this culture, wars are started and countries are invaded, within and beyond its cultural boundaries. In this culture, only some people have access to universal health care, and commercial pressure is encouraging those countries that do have it to privatize their health provision. In this culture, heavy metals are released into the water and air; organophosphates and other long-lived chemicals toxic to humans are widely used in poorly controlled conditions; corporations lobby to prevent the control of cancer-causing substances. In this culture humans are warming the Earth as a by-product of the commercialism that dominates those cultural symbols. The implication is that some humans are vital to this culture, but not the majority.

One more way of judging the cultural importance of humanity is to look at the aspirations of humans: what it is they want to achieve in the long run. It is certainly not a universal truth that all humans aspire to something beyond living their lives in a regular way: what can you possibly aspire to if your life is deeply fulfilling? In Western cultures, on the other hand, aspirations to greatness have driven technological and social development to places where, without the desire for greatness, they would never have reached – for better or worse. In Western educational systems, and also those of many other modern cultures, it is assumed that people want to 'become' something, such as a lawyer, doctor or hairdresser, before they have even reached their teenage years. Presumably many people's aspirations are going to be cut tragically short due to the kinds of activities I mentioned above; but there must be more than just commerce if humans really are Vital.

Michio Kaku, author of *Parallel Worlds*, is a highly respected cosmologist who dabbles in philosophy. He views humans as having enormous potential for good, even beyond the lifespan of the Earth, but has severe doubts about our current efforts to realize that potential. Beyond carrying out useful work and giving or receiving love – two vital ingredients (he says) in ensuring humans are fulfilled – he sees two other key factors that, in my mind, make the difference between whether humans are Vital or just Relevant: "First, to fulfil whatever talents we are born with. However blessed we are by fate with different abilities and strengths, we should try to develop them to the fullest rather than allow them to atrophy and decay.

"Second, we should try to leave the world a better place than when we entered it. As individuals, we can make a difference, whether it is to probe the secrets of Nature, to clean up the environment and work for peace and social justice, or to nurture the inquisitive, vibrant spirit of the young by being a mentor and a guide."[9]

Does this culture fulfil all of Michio Kaku's requirements? If so, then I can, without hesitation, pronounce humans as being Vital. But it's not true, is it? The culture does not truly care for the environment; it does not give equal opportunity for all to fulfil the range of their talents; it does not provide widespread provision for nurturing mentors and guides. This culture as a whole does not even value love in any obvious capacity: certainly nowhere near as much as it values economic work. The 2005 European Working Conditions Survey[10] found that an average of 83% of workers were either 'very satisfied' or 'satisfied' with their working conditions. Interestingly, when asked about job opportunities to learn and grow (i.e. the job mentors and guides them), only 54% of respondents agreed that this was a factor in job satisfaction. An awful lot of people don't see work as a means of self-improvement: perhaps there is a message there.

Is it just serendipity that the New Economics Foundation's 'Happy Planet Index' (HPI)[11] has managed to take into account almost every one of the above factors and package them into a convenient measure of how much a culture (in the shape of individual nations) views humanity as a going concern? Possibly not. Unsurprisingly we have returned to happiness as the key factor in judging the well being of humanity. Neither is it entirely surprising that the Happy Planet Map shows that the countries most dominated by the Western industrial capitalist culture – the USA, Australia, Canada, Western Europe – score as badly as those countries suffering from abject poverty or political repression. In fact, despite our being told that happiness is something you can buy in a shop, China comes out better than any of these other areas: political repression aside, the people of China still manage (at the moment) to be 'planet happier' than much of the rest of the world.

What I especially like about the HPI is that a culture that is environmentally destructive will, on balance, comes out worse than a culture that is not. You cannot value humans if you are making the environmental conditions they live in unbearable. According to the 2007 list, Vanuatu, Columbia and Costa Rica come out on top, closely followed by Dominica and Panama. To find the countries that are most closely associated with the predominant culture you need to go all the way down to Austria, at 61. The UK is at 108, sandwiched between Laos and Libya; the USA is at 150, admittedly brought down with a tremendous bump by its massive environmental impact.

In some cultures humans are considered to be no more than Relevant, largely because the rest of life is considered to be just as important. In other cultures humans are considered to be transcendent – right at the top of existence – yet such cultures also manage to treat the natural environment with sufficient care so as not to grievously damage it. The predominant culture, in which exists the majority of financially wealthy nations, and which is having an increasing influence on billions more people, seems to put humans right at the centre of things; but somehow it has conspired to treat the majority of humans as not really important at all. As far as Industrial Civilization – the dominant culture – is concerned, humans were never going to be judged as vital. I'm afraid it was a bit of a fix: we are merely Relevant.

The Personal Test

How would you feel if you were dead? If ever there was a 'non-question' then this is surely it. But, it's still worth asking – critical to ask, in fact, because unless we know how we feel about our death then we cannot possibly know the answer to the next question: Does it matter to *us* if we are not here?

Imagine that you are to undergo an operation,[12] one that will lead to a great deal of discomfort for a few days requiring heavy doses of morphine in order to make the pain bearable. Unless you are the kind of person who thrives on pain – and there are such people – then the chances are that you will need some support from others, a range of distractions and quite a lot of tea or coffee leading up to the operation. Once the operation is complete then, as I have said, there is pain; but eventually the pain goes and you are better off for the procedure that has been carried out.

If you look back on that operation you may feel a pang of emotion, maybe even a phantom memory of pain, but you won't actually feel the pain as it was; nor will you 'look back' to the event in the same way that you were forced to look forward to it. Time travels forwards and so we do too. The human body has various tricks that it can pull to ensure we are in tune with the incessant movement of time: one of them is hormonal, and every new mother will have experienced this trick under normal circumstances. When a woman is giving birth, large amounts of various hormones are released into the bloodstream. One of these hormones is called oxytocin, and it is this hormone that prepares the mother-to-be for both the second stage of childbirth – the delivery itself – and the essential task of breastfeeding. During the most strenuous and painful stages an odd thing happens: the pituitary gland, that sits just behind the forehead, releases further chemicals known as endorphins. The result is a decrease in pain perception, quite naturally. The rising level of endorphins also contributes to a shift from a thinking, rational mindset to a more instinctive one. Endorphins create a dream-like state, which appears to help women in the tasks required for giving birth.[13]

Natural birth (without artificial chemicals) may be a question of taste, but there is little doubt that the natural chemicals the human body is able to produce make childbirth a more bearable process. Now here is the really clever part: the endorphin rush not only reduces pain, but it also acts to suppress the memory of that pain, and many other aspects of the birth itself. This effect is not unique to childbirth; in fact there are countless documented cases of people who have undergone grievous injuries, immense tests of stamina and traumatic incidents who just can't remember the pain of these events.

Why would this be beneficial? If you think about the kinds of situations during which pain-reducing endorphins are released, then it becomes clear that pain memory would not be helpful in most cases. Undoubtedly the visual and other sensory aspects of an event may remain vivid – I still feel tense inside when I recall the time I sliced the edge off my left index finger with a Stanley knife when cutting a piece of card – but the pain does not. I have no memory at all of the pain, so while I would be more careful with a sharp blade in the future, based on my memories of the event, I could not tell you how much that knife incident hurt. With childbirth it is critical for the DNA to be able to replicate, so the evolutionary process that has led to endorphins being released ensures that a woman can remember many of the sights, smells and sounds of previous births but, crucially, cannot remember the pain that would otherwise discourage her from trying for another baby. It seems that we have evolved to only remember the parts of the past that it is worth remembering.

Another trick that humans have developed – working out how you would test for this in any other organism is challenging, to say the least – is our ability to treat the future as more important than the past.

Time is a concept that philosophers, and more recently scientists, have struggled with for millennia. There is an organization called the International Society for the Study of Time that presumably talks about nothing but time, and has been doing so for over 40 years with seemingly little agreement. I love this quote from the Internet Encyclopedia of Philosophy: "Time has been studied by philosophers and scientists for 2,500 years, and thanks to this attention it is *much better understood today*. Nevertheless, many issues remain to be resolved. Here is a short list of the most important ones . . . what time actually is; whether time exists when nothing is changing; what kinds of time travel are possible . . whether the future and past are real . . ."[14] and so on. Maybe the author has had his irony gland removed, or maybe he forgot to read what he had just written, but it is pretty obvious that time is something that we understand very poorly.

We do know that time is distinct from space in as much as you can travel forwards and backwards in space, but you cannot travel backwards in time: the notional 'fourth dimension' tag given to time is merely a convenience based on the fact that humans are three-dimensional beings. If we were two-dimensional then (a) we would treat the third dimension differently from the way we do as three-dimensional beings and (b) laying gas, sewage and water pipes to houses would be an absolute nightmare! Maybe if we were four- (or five-, or six-) dimensional beings then time travel would be a breeze, but only relative to beings that exist in fewer dimensions.

Not being able to move backwards in time may seem like a bind, but anyone who has watched *Doctor Who* or *Back To The Future* will understand why it's probably a good thing that we can't go back in time and alter the course of events – regardless of my overwhelming desire to go back to 1980 and present to every student what we now know about climate change. My younger daughter became very upset when she realized that, if my wife and I had never been born, or had never met, or had never decided to go to Dover one New Year's Day, she would never have been born: such thoughts are of no practical use, and rarely trouble the adult mind. The fact that we are always moving forwards through time, eating up our future as it becomes our present and then our past, means that it would be completely pointless for us to have evolved a fear of the past. I fear the future – I would not be writing this book if that were not the case – but I am only *aware* of what has happened in the past. The aforementioned painful operation, once it has occurred, merely becomes a memory of something that only happened in the past.

The point of all this discussion about time is to give you another perspective on top of the spatial one that you read about in Chapter 8. We should not only see ourselves as relatively insignificant when it comes to knowing our place in the Tree of Life; we also need to put the past into perspective. By all means we can learn from it, reflect on it and enjoy the memories it has given us, but what matters to us will not happen in the past – it will happen in the future.

Ask yourself the question again: *Does it matter to us if we are not here?*

Remember the discussion about selfishness in Chapter 9? The conclusion of this was that selfishness is unsustainable, and that we must take account of other things in order to ensure that our behaviour does not lead to unsustainability. Sustainability is not just about the use of natural resources; it is about the use of our lives.

If we do not survive, then our DNA will not survive, therefore our DNA will have failed in its role as replicators of information. If you are thinking that we can deny our genetic information, then go ahead, do something fatal – take a knife, or a rope or some non-prescription drugs and deny your DNA their inbuilt destiny. It's not something that anyone would carry out lightly, nor is it something that happens very often. Suicide, although relatively more common amongst older men, is not a leading cause of death on a global scale. The World Health Organization estimates that suicide accounts for less than 2% of all deaths, 90% of whom have been diagnosed with a psychological condition, which would increase the likelihood of the sufferer taking his or her own life.[15]

It is worrying to note, though, that the global rate of suicide has been steadily on the increase, up by 40% amongst females, and 60% amongst males since 1950. Economic pressure and social fragmentation, in a culture in which the words, "There is no such thing as society"[16] have become iconic, have no small part to play in this trend.[17] Studies in a wide range of cultures have consistently found a close negative relationship between the personal value people place on material wealth, and their psychological health:[18] depression appears to be less common amongst people who don't live their lives in the pursuit of wealth.

The role that religion plays in the question of suicide is fascinating. It would be tempting to think that a religious belief that has as part of its articles of faith the existence of an afterlife would be rife with followers eager to take the next step towards a divine future. It is significant, as I hinted earlier at the beginning of this chapter, that all of the world's major religions treat suicide as a mortal sin or its equivalent, which draws the conclusion that the founders of such doctrines were not too keen on their followers taking a shortcut to eternity. Was this a conscious (or super-conscious) decision to maintain the natural desire to preserve life? Certainly the presence of willing volunteers in 'suicide bomb' attacks is testament to the power of religious belief to overcome the natural desire to survive, both for the perpetrator and the victims: were it not for certain types of religious indoctrination, such attacks would be far less common.

The rarity of suicide overall, and the prevalence of psychological problems amongst those who do commit suicide makes a very strong case for humans as being natural survivors. If this were not the case then humans would have died out long ago through natural processes, much like any other organism that, through a lack of viable healthy adaptable DNA, no longer exists.

More than just our natural tendency to survive, though, is the manifestation of that survival instinct in the way we think. Consider the question: What would you risk your life to save? My initial instinct is to say 'my family', then 'me', then, with a little more thought, 'the Earth in general' and 'my friends'. Remove the Earth from the equation and you have the kind of answer that most people give.

In fact, all three typical responses are directly related to the natural instinct for survival. We instinctively want to protect our families in order to secure the continuation of our DNA through blood relatives and the people they depend upon to survive. We want to protect ourselves in order to protect our own DNA, and the opportunity for that to be further replicated. We want to protect our friends because they too are human beings, but not only that, we have consciously chosen our closest friends because of what they have in common with us – they are almost like family.

It might seem crass to bring all of this down to genes and DNA, but it makes perfect sense when you think about it. When a male spider mates with a female it has to adopt various strategies to ensure that it will not be eaten or killed prior to inseminating its mate; its utmost priority is to ensure its DNA gets passed on to the next generation of spiders. Male redback spiders, that are doomed to die following mating, have developed a method of carrying out 'dual insemination' – a remarkable adaptation that counters the female's ability to choose between the sperm of different mates.[19] The even more remarkable thing is that the adaptation does not ensure that the male spider himself survives, in fact the extended mating time makes death even more likely: the spider is simply ensuring that his DNA has the best possible chance of surviving. This is the way of nature, and we are simply following nature's rules.

The Ecology Test showed that humans, however successful in evolutionary terms, are irrelevant to the continuation of the Earth's ecosystem. The Cultural Test showed that although the dominant culture on the planet puts humans above all else, it is not treating humans as though we were vital – we are merely relevant. The Personal Test has given another outcome entirely: humans are the ultimate expression of all we hold dear, *and nothing is more important to us.*

* * *

The outcome of both the Ecology Test and the Cultural Test could change dramatically, depending on how we treat both the Earth and ourselves. We could choose to live lives that are fully sustainable and give all other species on Earth the ability to exist according to the rules of nature, rather than the toxic rules we have drawn up. We could choose to live in a culture that values humans as individuals, treats them equally and does not threaten our very existence through its destructive activities. But we can't choose what we are: we are simply humans who want to survive.

In the end, when all is said and done, what really matters is what matters to us.

Part Three

Making The Connection

Chapter 11

Why Connect?

In January 2008, the amount of carbon dioxide in our atmosphere touched 385 parts per million.[1] That same month, Dr James Hansen of the Goddard Space Institute in New York gave a short presentation to the Royal College of Physicians in London:[2] in it he stated that, based on historical data comparing atmospheric carbon to global temperatures, the maximum safe level for carbon dioxide in the atmosphere was 350 parts per million – beyond this, the Earth's natural systems would change irreversibly. As I type these words, the volume of CO_2 mixed with the air in the chilly back room I am sitting in exceeds this safe limit by 10%. I am inhaling something that is already capable of removing the Greenland ice cap and raising the level of the ocean by seven metres.[3] Seven metres? I go to a website that shows what this would mean to the world's coastal regions,[4] click on the drop-down arrow and select '+7m'.

The website knows which country I live in: much of the fertile growing land in eastern England is under water along with half of the Netherlands. I scroll the map down and zoom out a little: most of Europe is safe at the moment. Across the Atlantic the Mississippi Delta is flooded – the recovering towns and cities of southern Louisiana have taken their last breath. The playgrounds of the Florida Keys and Ocean City are gone, along with great swathes of the eastern seaboard. I scroll eastwards. South-east Asia is hit terribly: Shanghai and Hong Kong are just small islands in a sea of floodwater; Bangladesh sees permanent floods beyond the imagination of even those who experienced the catastrophe of 1970. And this is just the calm, tidal ocean, without storm surges and hurricanes; quite unlike the tempestuous one we can look forward to in the next 50 years, even with the carbon dioxide levels in the atmosphere unchanged, at just 385 parts per million.

Carbon dioxide accounts for about 65% of all anthropogenic global heating that is taking place[5] (the word anthropogenic just means 'made by humans'). Carbon dioxide is especially significant, not only because it is responsible for a large portion of the unnatural Greenhouse Effect but also because it is the one gas whose level is continuing to rise while the others – such as methane and nitrous oxide – are relatively controlled, for the moment.[6] The lack of carbon control is everywhere: from the belching SUVs and power-hungry air conditioners of high-tech USA, to the teeming coal-fired power stations of newly commercial China and India; from the fuming peat left burning after the Indonesian forests were scorched, to the reeking oil sands of Canada. Oil, wood, coal and gas are being ignited across the world to feed a growing appetite for more of everything. More technology; more heat; more cold; more meat; more money; more greed; more profit; more speed; more vacations; more need.

More deserts.
More flooding.
More storms.
Less ice.
Less food.
Less life.

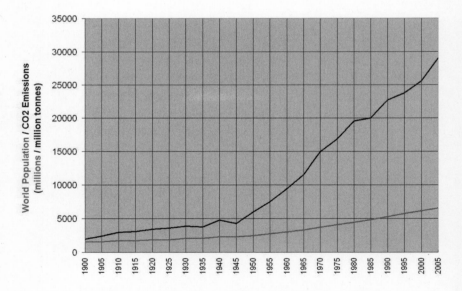

Figure 17: World Population vs. World Carbon Dioxide Emissions

In 1900 the world population stood at about 1.5 billion people, about the same as the current population of India, Bangladesh and Pakistan combined. In the same year, historical statistics show that the amount of carbon dioxide being produced by fossil fuel burning was 1.9 billion tonnes,[7] or just under a third of what the USA put into the atmosphere in 2004. By the beginning of the Second World War, the population had risen considerably, to 2.3 billion, an increase of over 50%; by the same year global carbon dioxide production was around 4.7 billion tonnes. The war took the edge off industrial production in the West so that, by 1945, emissions had fallen by nearly 11%, but it had taken a global event that directly caused 50 million deaths for civilization to reduce carbon dioxide production by just a tenth.

The upturn in population growth that I described in Chapter 8 has its significance in the way it took human numbers from a relatively modest 2.5 billion people in 1950, up to 6.5 billion in 2005; an increase of 160% in just 55 years. Over that same period of time carbon emissions grew from six billion tonnes to 29 billion tonnes, a leap of extraordinary proportions: no less than 380%, or nearly two and half times the rate of population growth. This was achieved even with almost an entire decade of carbon stability in the 1980s.

From the first graph it is evident that population growth and carbon dioxide emissions do have something in common, but the increase in human numbers doesn't go anywhere near explaining where all the carbon is coming from. Once I had fed in some economic figures from the World Trade Organization[8] and produced Figure 18 (on the next page), though, something was startlingly clear: carbon emissions and trade are dancing to the same tune.

The graph, which illustrates the period between 1950 and 2005, has sprouted another line – the dotted one – showing how trade between different countries boomed over a period of 55 years. Trade is affected by a great number of things, but the most important of them is whether there is a market for something or not: if there is a market then a producer can sell things to a consumer. The market for something will eventually become saturated unless the producer can find ways of making the consumer interested in buying more of a product, but it is often easier to open up new markets for the same thing, which is one reason why trade has rocketed since 1985. I'm getting ahead of myself, though – what is important here is the uncanny similarity between the shapes of the Emissions line and the Trade line.

The post-war boom in the industrial West, with its acceleration in the use of consumer goods – such as televisions, vacuum cleaners and refrigerators – the rise of the 'car culture' and an upsurge in the number of new houses, pushed global carbon emissions up by 250% in just 25 years. Coal was the fuel of choice for electricity generation, and massive oil discoveries in the Middle East during the 1950s and 1960s, including seven of the largest oil fields ever found,[9] meant that cheap fuel, almost literally, drove consumption through the roof. The oil crisis, in the 1970s, and two major economic recessions in the 1980s pushed emissions growth down a little, but still it sped ahead of population growth. Between

1950 and 1985 annual carbon emissions increased at double the rate of population growth. Bearing in mind that they had been almost neck-and-neck in 1900,
this is phenomenal growth by anyone's standards.

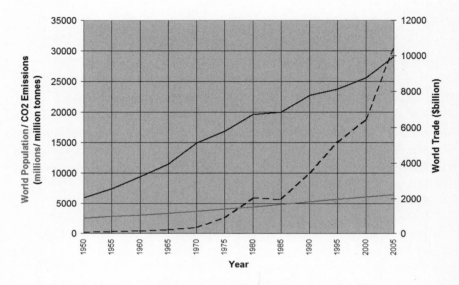

Figure 18: World Population vs. World Carbon Dioxide Emissions
vs. World Trade

Between 1950 and 1970, international trade (imports and exports) grew from
$60 billion to a still relatively modest $317 billion: growth of 413% in 20 years is
impressive, but nothing compared with later on. International trade started to
climb rapidly after 1975 – because the graph only shows trade between *different*
nations, the freeing up of international markets during the 1970s is particularly
visible, as is the massive global recession in the 1980s, and the explosive growth
in the international trade of consumer goods since 2000. These variations in
world trade[10] between 1975 and the present day are closely matched by changes
in carbon dioxide emissions – with the notable exception of the early-1990s,
when the smokestacks of much of Europe stopped belching following the collapse of the Soviet Bloc, and the emergence of natural gas as a cleaner generator
of electricity. This blip was not to last long.

Despite promises by many governments and businesses to control their emissions, the slope is steepening. This inflationary jump is primarily the result of
manufacturing being shifted from rich nations in which labour is relatively well
paid, to poorer nations – in which workers are generally paid a pittance – that gen-

erate electricity by far dirtier means. The fruits of this transfer of labour are then laboriously transported back to the rich nations that buy the goods, thus producing even more carbon dioxide.[11] This is compounded by another lucrative export: the industrial West's love affair with cars, household consumer goods and a meat-rich diet is no longer the preserve of rich nations – it is increasingly seen as something that all people have the right to be a part of. The fact that this behaviour fattens the wallets of business leaders in the West is not entirely coincidental.

*   *   *

The connection between trade and carbon emissions, worrisome as it is, is just one of many social, political and economic connections that we encounter on an almost daily basis,[12] often without realizing it; but there is a far more important connection that we now need to consider – one that is the subject of the rest of this chapter and the one after that. It is so important that I'm going to simply refer to it as The Connection.

The Connection

Do you have a spare shoe you can look at? Any shoe, it doesn't really matter as long as it fastens using laces. If you are wearing one then that will be fine. If you need to fetch the shoe then please get it now – I won't go anywhere.

Okay?

Now look carefully at the lace – undo it if it has a knot or a bow – find the right-hand end and hold it in your hand. This end is you: a human being, no different from any other human being on Earth, whatever culture you live in, whatever race you may be or language you may speak. Now find the left-hand end, and hold on to that as well. This end is everything else in the world: from the smallest atom of carbon, to the microbes, the worms, the bees, the fish, the trees, the forests, the oceans and the atmosphere that you are breathing in.

Two ends of a piece of string, so close together: one totally dependent on the other. If you have read this far, you will know by now which end is most dependent on the other. The webs and chains that lock lives together in a symbiotic embrace exist in order that life on this planet can be as complex and varied as it is. Humans would be nothing at all without the ancient history of interconnections that have been made between different species. Most of the strands have let go, fallen beside the four-billion-year path for others to replace them and take the strain; but the new strands still hold on, for if they didn't, then humanity would fall like a sack of rocks into a deep well.

Splash! As easy as that.

That we should care about our descent into the icy well water and our untimely extinction is beyond doubt. We are survival machines and we exist to continue our species – there is no greater motivation than the simple urge to stay alive, and for that reason it is simply not possible to be human and not care about our fate. *It follows that it is simply not possible to be a free-thinking human being and not care about what is happening to the planet that we depend on.*

Take another look at the shoelace. Follow each end downwards as the woven strands move in and out of the holes, intersecting, touching each other and finally meeting at the end. The two ends always were together. From the origins of life our fate has been intimately tied up with the fate of the rest of our Earthly companions, and there is nothing you can do about it.

* * *

Would you risk your life to save a tree along the street you live in; would you put yourself between the trunk of a plant and a chainsaw, axe or machete – however slender that plant may be – in order to preserve it for another day? If it were woodland near to your home, or even a forest at the other side of the world that was imminently threatened with removal, would you then endanger your life to protect it?

A British environmental activist (here referred to as 'A') whom I have known for years was narrowly saved from death by an Oxfordshire police officer. It's ironic that the reason the police officer had to stem the blood gushing from an artery was that the artery was severed while 'A' was trying to escape from a police cell. 'A' desperately wanted to escape in order to return to the scene of his 'crime' so he could once again hold up tree-felling work; felling work that was taking place in order that a power company could fill a thriving lake with the spoil from a coal-fired power station. My friend thought little of his fate, except that the trees must be saved. His attempts to stop the trees being cut down were deemed illegal, and so he was arrested and sent to the police cell in which he nearly died. Despite his brush with death, he has since told me that he would do it again: "I would try and save life again, risking my own life, because all life is worth saving."[13]

In societies where the fate of species other than humans is regarded as incidental, it is tempting to label such behaviour 'extreme', or even 'psychotic'. Certainly my friend was labelled both an extremist and a 'tree-hugger', and punished for his actions. The term 'tree-hugging' is often used as a disparaging term to describe environmentalists, like my friend, who greatly value the distinct and irreplaceable service that trees carry out for the biosphere. In fact, by definition, to be a tree-hugger is to be someone who would place themselves at the mercy of whatever humanity might exist in the mind of a person determined to destroy the tree which is being embraced. The Garhwal Hills of northern India contain a number of tribes whose lives have changed little in 1,500 years, and probably far longer.[14] They also contain the origins of the Chipko Andolan (literally, 'hug the trees') movement. In 1973, following decades of successive removal and partitioning of the forests by both the British and the Indian governments – forests that the indigenous people depended on for their well-being – the patience of the Garhwali finally ran out: the villagers had been refused permission to cut twelve trees in order to make tools while, simultaneously, a sporting goods company was granted permission to cut far more trees from the same forest to make tennis racquets.

The women of the village, in particular, started protecting the trees with their own bodies, trying to grab the axes of the loggers: risking their lives at the hands of those who had been charged to remove the trees that the Garhwali so badly needed to be managed responsibly and sustainably. A state officer, who was under the impression that the government owned the trees, not some upstart tribal women, attempted to confront the protesters:

> It was time to settle the matter once and for all. He and his entourage went into the forest to lay down the law, but instead witnessed a sight that was both fascinating and disarming: hundreds of women, more than he could count, milling about among the trees, singing songs and chanting, many with infants strapped to their waists and children at their feet. Realizing that to lay down the law would require some kind of brutal offensive against all of the women and children in the area, he left chastised and embarrassed.[15]

Do you feel that the actions of the Garhwali women in India were any less, or more extreme than those of the British environmentalist? Again, it would be tempting to suggest that the Chipko Andolan were taking unnecessary risks in order to save some trees, but their lives depended on the forests remaining intact; to provide a sustainable source of wood for cooking, heating and toolmaking; to stabilize the ground and prevent mudslides in the mountainous terrain; to ensure that the waters remained fresh and constantly available. Most people would agree that some kind of activism would be justified – but would you risk your life to maintain a way of life in the face of creeping development, and the promise of a more modern lifestyle: the kind that the British environmentalist has no choice but to lead?

The Garhwali people have a village-based culture; farming and using the land around the villages in the most sustainable manner they can. If they had not treated the land in such a way, their distinctive way of life would have been wiped out long ago. Because of their similarity to some more recent cultures, the Garhwali are able to make minor adaptations to their lives, without greatly affecting their cultural integrity; but there are limitations, and large, enforced changes would, as with so many other societies before them, cause irreversible damage.

The tribal people of West Papua live in a manner that is entirely alien to most of modern humanity. According to Bernard Nietschmann: "The people of West Papua are different in all respects from their rulers in [Indonesia]: language, religions, identity, histories, systems of land ownership and resource use, cultures and allegiance."[16] Imagine, for a moment, living in such a way that you had no concept of outside rules, beliefs and culture; when, suddenly, the land you have nurtured for centuries with delicate care is ripped away from you to be handed to a corporation intent on mining it for metals, leaving the land in tatters and thousands of tonnes of toxic spoil leaching poison into the ground. This is precisely what happened in the years following 1967 under the despotic leadership of President Suharto of Indonesia (who also forcibly took control of the country following a military coup in 1965). Two large mining companies from 'democratic' nations – Freeport, based in the USA, and Rio Tinto Zinc, a UK / Australian conglomerate – were handed the mineral rights for a large part of West Papua in return for generous donations to the Suharto regime. Despite Suharto's bloodthirsty behaviour across his empire, including responsibility for the slaughter of half a million Indonesians in 1965, the CEO of Freeport, James Roberts, called Suharto "a compassionate man".[17]

The native West Papuans have never had the land returned to them, primarily because there is no profit to be made in giving a peaceful, nature-respecting people stewardship of a region under which there are rich mineral resources to be plundered. Since the 1970s the situation has if anything worsened, with the rise in illegal deforestation for the lucrative export of tropical hardwood, pulpwood with which to make paper, and the palm oil from monoculture plantations which goes into such Western essentials as chocolate-chip cookies, hair conditioner and potato crisps. Such activities – illegal or otherwise – are actively condoned by the new democratic government and, despite the best efforts of United Nations and human rights workers, intimidation is rife:

> The Special Representative is also concerned about complaints that defenders from West Papua working for the preservation of the environment and the right over land and natural resources (deforestation and illegal logging) frequently receive threats from private actors with powerful economic interests but are granted no protection by the police. . . . This climate of fear has reportedly worsened since the incident of Abepura in March 2006, where five members of the

security forces were killed after clashes with protesters demanding the closure of the gold and copper mine, PT Freeport. Lawyers and human rights defenders involved with the trial received death threats.[18]

Tree hugging in such an isolated and tightly controlled landscape of fear cuts no ice with private security firms or the Indonesian government. In a place where the media rarely takes an interest, and the public are debarred, who is to know whether the defenders are just being killed by the military or private security guards? It is clear from regular observations that, where the indigenous people have clashed with developers, the developers have always won in the long run.[19] This puts indigenous people in a terrible dilemma: do they continue to fight for the return of land that their entire existence depends upon; or do they enlist the help of outside agencies or, even more controversially, rely on the compassion of the businesses actually responsible for the land-grab in the first place? Such compromises almost always lead, as mentioned before, to irreversible cultural change. Their lives are on the line, whichever way they turn. What would you do in their situation?

Figure 19: Fishing tribesman from Baliem Valley, West Papua

Defending something that is central to your life is not 'psychotic' behaviour, nor is it 'extreme'; it is simply human nature. A man who tries to take my life from me by suffocation, by forcibly holding his hands over my mouth and nose, is immediately locked in his own life-or-death struggle, for I would fight to the death to retain my own life – as any sane person would. The connection between the assailant's hands and my own fate is immediate: there is no doubt that the two are connected in this particular situation. In a slightly less direct sense, the total loss of your food source, shelter or any other means of sustaining yourself clarifies the connection between the thing that you depend upon and your desire to survive. I don't need to tell you this; take these things away and it becomes obvious.

As I said in Part Two, the City Dweller is cut off from his life support system. In a world where more than 50% of humanity lives in cities, this is an ever more vital observation: as far as any hunter-gatherer, or indeed any person producing their own food is concerned, you may as well have your source of nutrition completely taken away from you if you have no sight or knowledge of its origin. As you pick your ready-meal or bottle of Coke off the shelf of your local supermarket (if that is where you shop, or what you buy), do you have any concept of where those items come from? Certainly, the mere fact of having a ready-meal made from numerous different and obscure ingredients immediately distances consumers from the food they are eating; and where on Earth *do* those ingredients come from? Two studies carried out in 2001 found that the distance average food items in the USA and the UK had been transported from 'farm to fork' had risen by a factor of two and five times respectively in just two decades.[20] Average figures for common foodstuffs ranged from 2,500 to 4,000 kilometres – these are average figures, nothing like the longest distances that some foods travel.

The vast distances involved just to bring a head of broccoli or a pint of milk to your table – sometimes between very similar types of country, and sometimes (and usually in this direction) from poor to rich countries – place a psychological barrier between the person eating the food and the place where that food was grown. Not only that, but the means of production, whether for food or any other product of the industrial economy, has been divided up in such a way that the different parties involved in that production can barely conceive what the impact of their particular niche is on the environment. As Curtis White puts it: "The violence that we know as environmental destruction is possible only because of a complex economic, administrative, and social machinery through which people are separated from responsibility for their misdeeds. We say, 'I was only doing my job' at the paper mill, the industrial incinerator, the logging camp, the coal-fired power plant, on the farm, on the stock exchange, or simply in front of the PC in the corporate carrel. The division of labour . . . hides from workers the real consequences of their work."[21] Not surprisingly, concern for the damage caused to the natural environment in which the food was produced – be that deforestation for beef cattle or soybeans in Brazil, removal of mangroves for shrimp farming in India, or the ploughing up of wildflower meadows to grow rapeseed in the English countryside – is muted in industrial nations, at best. To me, it is this lack of concern that is psychotic, not the other way round.

* * *

In April 2008, James Speth, Professor of Environmental Policy at Yale University made the following sober – and startling – remarks:

> All we have to do to destroy the planet's climate and its biota and leave a ruined world to our children and grandchildren is to just keep on where we're going today, just keep releasing greenhouse gases at current rates, just keep degrading and homogenizing and destroying our biological resources, just continue releasing toxic chemicals at current rates, and by the latter part of this century, the world won't be fit to live in.[22]

When you consider the type of changes that are taking place as a result of human agency, across the complete range of scales in which life operates; and that many, if not all of those changes, will impinge upon your ability to survive, do you feel connected with those life forms?

For hundreds of millennia, humans connected tightly to the land and the life forms their survival depended upon, because that was how it had to be. Failure to connect was not an option; if you didn't know how plants grew, how animals bred, how rivers ran, how the seasons and the weather changed, then you did not survive. In some parts of the world – the Native American tribal lands of West Coast USA, the dense forests of West Papua, the deep valleys and jagged mountains of northern India – these connections remain, and cling on despite the best efforts of those who seek to gain more from the land than 'mere' survival. This connection has ebbed away from the majority of humanity, in many cases to the extent that people feel nothing for anything humans have not created themselves. But we cannot eat concrete; we cannot breathe television; we cannot drink money.

Are You Ready?

The Connection is a very personal thing. It can manifest itself as a whole range of emotions, all of which link people with their surroundings and the things they depend upon for their continued survival. That odd surge in the gut as you look up into the branches of a tree; that frisson of excitement that comes from enveloping yourself in the sea; that strange feeling that you have something in common with the animal looking you in the eye: they are all symptoms of The Connection. It is nothing great and mysterious; it is simply the necessary instinct that ensures we do not damage the ability of the natural environment to keep us alive. *Failure to connect is the reason humanity is pulling the plug on its life-support machine.*

Connection is, by necessity, a two-stage process: first, we must connect because we have to, because if we don't, then we will die out; second, we have an innate need to connect because it is part of who we are. The whole of this chapter has been devoted to the first stage – the clear imperative that we must connect the two ends of the lace together – what we are and what we are doing. This is a learning process, and for people in the early throes of Westernization, then Connecting may be as easy as falling off a lifestyle: it is simply a case of reconnecting with a way of life that existed not so long ago, and which still manages to survive in pockets tragically being squeezed out by the rush to become part of a consumer culture. For many others, the majority of people in the industrial West who identify most strongly with a hyper-consuming way of life, learning how to reconnect out of necessity is a struggle: most of us have never experienced anything but the disconnected lives we inhabit.

The second stage of Connection just is. Like the invisible join between the two ends of the lace, we have always been connected, we just need to recognize how natural and comfortable it is to be this way. If you feel you are ready to reconnect, or just want to see what it is like to take the plunge from your world to the real world, then read on.

Chapter Twelve

How to Connect

Each one of us is different. As our fingerprints make us unique, the ways we can connect reveal the many different states of mind that make us individuals. Connection doesn't require some mystical transference of wisdom from master to student; it doesn't demand that you sit in a darkened room for hours; it doesn't even need peace and quiet, for every second of every day through every sensory link we make with the world, myriad connections are taking place. The key is to capture that information and recognize it for what it is, not ignore it as just one more rogue signal amongst the noise of life. With a little help and guidance, everyone can make their own connection.

K's Connection

Seagulls: that's what takes me there. The repeating bright, sharp calls, over and over again, calling to each other and calling to the sky – that takes me somewhere else. There must have been some perfect moment, some idyllic situation in the past when everything fitted together flawlessly, and burnt the connection between myself and the coast into my consciousness: maybe it was the endless, sun-washed days in the summer of 1976, when I could walk from our guest house to the beach and play until the sun disappeared behind the cliffs, and then play some more in the fading light. Memories help unlock those connections for me.

I find the coast is what draws me back to nature; makes me understand the endless play between the sea – the immense volume of life-filled water from which everything first came – and the land on which humans, and immeasurable quantities of life, now thrive. The coast is the interface between the two: a place of constant change and disruption; its contents turned over by the tides and the waves; eroded by the sea, the rain and the wind; moved relentlessly along the shoreline – always in motion, intimately connecting one thing with another. The coast, with its sensory wash, allows me to throw off so many of the distractions and worries of modern life, leaving behind something much simpler.

It is August. A concrete sea wall is behind me, scooped deeply inwards and then thrown back out in a curve designed to deflect the beating of the winter waves. Traffic moans, the pitch shifts as each vehicle moves from one ear to the other – towards, then away – in an irregular, artificial beat. Footsteps above me, and a shadow flits across my head, then one more, making elongated human patterns on the sand. I close my eyes and shiver as a breeze ruffles my clothes, taking with it a patina of sand grains that gently patter down onto my arms. The sun warms my back and my head, and I relax onto the undulating surface of the beach.

Shoosh…shhhh! Shoosh…shhhh! The sea sweeps in and out across the gentle slope at the edge of the water; the lightest of sounds – white noise. Then a disturbance: a seagull takes off from its perch on the sea wall and another shadow crosses my face, the sunlight flickers off for a moment, then back as it wheels towards the sea taking its incessant song with it. More birds join it – a chorus of plaintive cries as they jostle for space in the open sky, swooping and crying, swooping and crying, effortlessly merging with the high shouts of children that mimic their sounds. Running, thump . . . thump . . . thump . . . thump and joyous cries from friends who push into the water, turning the glossy surface into foam, and immersing themselves in the ocean; shouting in harmony with the seagulls that continue their avian music.

I feel the sand on my back, between my shoulder blades and ruffling my neck – hot from the morning sun – the grains falling and rising with my breathing; tumbling into gullies beneath me. The redness on my eyelids gradually turns to black: I am growing drowsy and the sounds of the seagulls, the laughing children and the metronomic sea wash, merge into a sound of restfulness. I could stay here forever.

J's Connection

As the songwriter David Hughes suggested, being a poet, "you're working all the hours that God sends, your soul never sleeps, your heart never mends."[1] This was never truer than in the case of John Clare, a man for whom nature and love were his twin muses; and Connection with either or both was a golden thread running through all of his work.

Despite – or perhaps because of – his poor education, and lowly social position as a farm labourer, Clare managed to express a connection with the rest of nature that few people, before or since, ever achieved. "There is a sense of organic harmony between poet and nature discoverable in the bulk of Clare's work. Clare was a happy poet; there is more happiness in his poetry than in most others. This was no mere animal contentment of body and senses, but a quiet ecstasy . . . Such happiness is not to be had except at a price."[2] For John Clare, the price he paid was resentment by his peers, and a mental turmoil that had far more to do with a lack of respect shown by the people who exploited him and threw him back when his commercial potential was spent, than his submission to the simplicity and perfection of the nature he loved.

> These tiny loiterers on the barley's beard,
> And happy units of a numerous herd
> Of playfellows, the laughing Summer brings,
> Mocking the sunshine on their glittering wings,
> How merrily they creep, and run, and fly!
> No kin they bear to labour's drudgery,
> Smoothing the velvet of pale hedge-rose;
> And where they fly for dinner no one knows –
> The dew-drops feed them not – they love the shine
> Of noon, whose suns may bring them golden wine.[3]

It is a testament to the man that, despite the demands of the newly emerging industrial economy, Clare stands almost alone in just wanting to express his feelings for the natural world that surrounded him. The poetry is flawed, often dreamy to the point of indulgence, but never short of wonderfully descriptive detail: "This querying attention to detail epitomises Clare's poetry: he is looking into the nest, seeing it for what it is, and simultaneously seeing it in words. Even in the finished poem, you can glimpse the notes he made while peering between the branches, and hear him struggling to do justice to these embryonic nightingales, which will one day fuel Keatsian fantasies, but which are for now simply brown-green eggs."[4]

> How subtle is the bird! She started out,
> And raised a plaintive note of danger nigh,
> Ere we were past the brambles; and now, near
> Her nest, she sudden stops – as choking fear,
> That might betray her home. So even now
> We'll leave it as we found it: safety's guard
> Of pathless solitudes shall keep it still.
> See there! she's sitting on the old oak bough,
> Mute in her fears; our presence doth retard
> Her joys, and doubt turns every rapture chill.
> Sing on, sweet bird![5]

S's Connection

S. lives on a small lightly-wooded, elongated triangle of land in the east of England. His bedroom is built from a mixture of discarded wooden pallets, plastic sheeting and a few bits of timber he bought himself. The few items of electrical equipment he has – a phone, radio and torch – are charged from a solar panel that is propped up in front of this small structure. He splits his time between domestic duties (chopping wood for the burner, cooking, cleaning) in the communal area, which itself was constructed from donated items and waste materials; growing food in the shared allotment a couple of miles from the site; campaigning for the protection of the area onto which he moved, in order to save it from a new road; and discovering what it means to be connected to something special. All of this is a far cry from his previous career as an engineer for a large motor manufacturer.

Connection happened by accident: "It was a process that evolved over the time that we were here, and that's something that can only happen with time, effort and people really, so I feel more connected to the camp, connected to a degree to the people around me at the moment – and there are various people living here – so, it was a result of other things. If you go looking for it, you wouldn't necessarily find it; it's a very experience-based thing."[6] He reflects on the type of people that he meets at similar protest camps – society's cast-offs, in a way – and suspects that rejection, whether by family or society at large, makes the act of connecting a little easier: "It's interesting that it's almost like you fall out of the mainstream culture and I guess for me, and I've thought about this, it probably goes back and starts for me with being a mixed-race kid growing up in the '70s here, and you get subjected to racism and you're made to feel different, and the one time when it's really important to feel a part of things, and connected, you don't get that opportunity." For S., connection is as much with other people as with the wider natural world.

> Whether you go looking for it, or whether you happen to come across it – this connection – it takes time, and that's why I wanted to do this [interview] here, and particularly sitting under this tree, because it's about having that sense of place and feeling more complete and feeling more whole, and it sounds really pretentious, but it's the only way I can describe it.
>
> It's like the feeling I get if I walk into the allotment site, or if I go to a cemetery of all places; it's that feeling of peace, of stillness, that sense of tranquillity which you don't get the opportunity to experience so much in modern life. It's about stopping; it's about slowing down, and it's about feeling rooted – and as stressed as you might be and as hectic as things might get, you know when you go to that place, when you stand by that tree, you light the burner, it all just goes out the window when you realize that all the things that are constructed by society ultimately are

pretty meaningless; it's all very . . . transitory, it's a passing through, and people don't make the most of the moment, living in the now. I think that is forced upon you here – I always feel more grounded in this place than I do elsewhere, and when I've been around and working in London and doing other things, it just feels alien, it feels bizarre, it feels wrong: when I'm here, as bad as things might be . . . you know?

There's a sense of stillness, a sense of safety, a sense of feeling more complete. You can go away, it can be hectic, but you can come back and it's all right, it's always there . . . it's something you can dip in and out of. Like going somewhere quiet, I guess for some people it would be like the stillness on top of a mountain or walking along an empty beach, it's that sort of feeling; but it's not something you would just have for two weeks of the year when you go on holiday because the rest of your life's all fucked up, because you've got to work doing a job you hate. It's more readily available, but you've got to make the trade.

Your Connection

I'm going to have to make an assumption about you. I am assuming that you live in a fairly technological society, or at least one where technology plays a major part in the lives of the majority of people. I think that may be right for most people reading this. If you are living the kind of life where technology is unimportant to you, then you almost certainly have a good connection to wild nature – another assumption, but a nice one to make, I hope you'll agree. The point of this assumption is so that I can guide you through an exercise that is relevant to the majority of people reading this book. If you find it's not relevant to you, persevere and it may suddenly pick you up along the way – you'll see what I mean when you read it. Of course, if you already feel you are well connected then you don't need to take part: but I still recommend you read the text, even if only as an interested bystander.

Shall we start?

* * *

I want you to take yourself to a place where you can hardly hear yourself think, where the lights are bright and ever-changing, where space is a luxury and green is just a picture on a magazine or the paint on the walls. This place is indoors – away from the wind, the sun, the rain; away from animal life and plant life: not even a potted fern sits in the corner. You are encased in a synthetic environment: air-conditioned and artificially heated; chairs and tables made of plastic; and the noise! The humming of machinery; the sound of ringtones and cellphone keypads; the television calling out sports results. Voices merge into the noise, barely intelligible; faces are illuminated by the screens of computers, gaming machines or TV sets; smells are processed chemical odours – microwave meals, air fresheners, artificial reality. You need to relax: stress hurts. Too much pressure; so little time; a web of activity linking deeper and deeper and ever more complex as you struggle to process each signal, while another ten whizz through your head and out into the ether. This is a place called Civilization. It is where you live.

Come to your senses. All of them: not just the five we are told we have, but the countless senses that are tiny variations on those familiar ones, and those senses we hold inside us – that gut feeling that tells us when something is wrong; the sense that knows when we are standing upright, and where our hands are even when we can't see them; the sense that time is passing too quickly and we need to slow down. Take a breath and slow down: let the sharp sounds become gradually muffled as though you are lying back into a bath, your ears being immersed in the warm, deep water. You can hear the beating of your heart and the indeterminate rushing sounds as your body carries on its work unabated. The high-pitched bleeping of each electrical device becomes sparse and muted; the television announcer is cut off; the humming motors and roaring engines sputter out as they are enveloped by stillness. You tap your fingers and feel the vibrations coming up through your arms. The outside world is silenced.

Take another breath; taste the air; smell it. Smell and taste are direct paths to our digestive system, but are far more besides: they trigger memories; they identify friend and foe; they give us some of our deepest pleasures. There is no space for them now. You smell nothing – just the moist closeness of the densest fog: the droplets of water coat every hair and every passage with a neutral, distilled cleanliness. A cold, fresh stream of water washes your tongue and mouth, removing every trace of flavour. You are left with total blandness – sensitive to the smallest molecule of scent or taste.

The sharp edges and hard surfaces that dug into you, pushed you and shaped you are softening. A cushion of air seeps around you: warm, perfectly warm, like a second skin that lifts away any sensation of touch. Imagine the feeling as you wake up with no sensation in your arm – push this to your whole body, your chest, your head, down your trunk and through your legs all the way to your toes. Don't be scared, don't move: you are perfectly safe. All around you are the sights of your former life: switch them off now.

Blink! The lights in the ceiling are extinguished. Sweep your eyes across the walls, and as you pass by each appliance think, 'off'. Your passing eyes turn out motors, electrical circuits, gas flames. Do you feel comfortable? You have the ability to take this all out and plunge this place into a powerless state: not a single watt of electricity is consumed, not a single therm of gas is burnt. Notice everything that had to be manufactured at the expense of something else: every brick; every droplet of oil turned into plastic windows, chairs, ink; every pane of glass. Now take these things away – see them disappear as the people stand with only each other for company. Their phones, their iPods, their clothing – simply disappear. Do you still feel comfortable? Nothing exists except for you and the people around you: do you want them to go? You can wave your hand and they will be gone, if that's what you want. Let's say goodbye, and leave you alone with only yourself and the cushion of your senses for company.

Now, stop all the clocks. Listen to your own rhythms, not the schedules being forced upon you. Leave the working day behind; take a siesta, sleep when you are tired – wake when you are refreshed. As the sun sets, slow down and turn in: relax and let your body tell you when to drop off. In the morning you can wake with the sunrise: but for now you can rest all you like.

What do you want now? You can bring back anything you like: just say the word and it can all come back. You can have a crowd of people, electrical power and appliances, bright lights, plastic chairs, a cacophony of sound – is that what you want? Don't do it yet; instead, just think of something simple that you crave: a walk in the fresh air with trees above your head and the sweep of a valley before you; a crackling fire pouring heat into the air around you as you sit with a good book or a pack of cards, illuminated by the flickering of the burning wood and a couple of candles; the company of friends, sharing a joke or stories of good times past, and times to come – talking, being together and savouring each other's company; your children, grandchildren or parents, enjoying a perfect day with you – something you will remember for the rest of your life.

*   *   *

Yesterday was Sunday. I spent a lively few hours in the garden; tidying this and that, cutting brambles and pruning the razor-sharp pyracantha that seemed to say to its trailing neighbour, "So, you think you're tough, do you?" Pyracantha is a challenge, but it provides food for the birds throughout the winter – they don't seem to mind the thorns. After two weeks of on-and-off rain the ground spickled and bubbled with each footstep, but now the sun was out and the warmth was exquisite.

With the tools locked away I found myself drifting: my recognition of bird-song is lamentable, but somewhere in the concoction of delicate sounds the evening chorus threw up there was the unmistakable descending trill of a chaffinch, ending its call with a jumble of notes as though it had so much to say and not enough time. This was too good to keep to myself. At the back door I invited my children outside; they put on mud-soaked trainers and walked with me to the little 'meadow' I look after at the end of the garden – just a small patch of perfection. We stood and listened, and together we connected.

Chapter Thirteen

Why Can't We Connect?

The effect of being exposed to the world after a period of enforced sensory deprivation is intense; vivid colours, sharp, deep odours, rich sound textures – like being reborn, or taking your first gasps of air having been underwater for far too long. For a while you can enjoy being connected with the world . . . until you are forcibly held down and the mask of deprivation is slipped on you again.

Things would never be the same for the thousands of people who had their connected lives taken from them during the Clearances: a systematic and economically motivated period of Scottish history that began in the middle of the 18th century. Prior to the events that overcame huge swathes of Scotland, displacing and ravaging its inhabitants, the majority of people lived in communal townships, or *bailes* of up to a hundred individuals. Sometimes they were forced to scratch a living during bad weather; sometimes the men had to drop their tools and fight in Clan battles;[1] but in the main, this *runrig* form of life was peaceful and – by the mere fact of being totally dependent on the forces and materials provided by it – very close to nature. In the eyes of the newly industrializing upper and middle classes of Britain, and the government which they had total authority over, this was an unacceptable situation: the cities needed food and raw materials, and the Highlands had to be 'improved'.

> Immediately after May term day [in 1812], and about two months after they had received summonses of removal, a commencement was made to pull down and set fire to the houses over their heads! The able-bodied men were away at their cattle or otherwise engaged at a distance; so that the old people, women and children began to try to preserve the timber, which they were entitled to consider as their own. But the devastators proceeded with the greatest celerity, demolishing all before them, and when they had overthrown the houses in a large tract of land, they ultimately set fire to the wreck. Timber, furniture, and every other article that could not be instantly removed was consumed by fire or otherwise utterly destroyed.[2]

We are in a constant state of enforced sensory deprivation; kept in that state in order that we can be willing participants of Industrial Civilization. If we connect with the real world permanently, then the spell will be broken: we will no longer be 'viewers', 'customers', 'consumers', 'voters', 'citizens', we will just be us. Remember: *failure to connect is the reason humanity is pulling the plug on its life-support machine.*

Who are these people that want to keep us disconnected, and why are they doing it? I will address this later on, but first of all let's look at the various methods, processes and techniques that are being actively used, right now, to keep us disconnected: the Tools of Disconnection . . .

How to Keep People Disconnected

One: Reward Us for Being Good Consumers

The rewards of life are manifold: love, a feeling of belonging, happiness and pleasure, a sense of well-being from having done good things – all of these are rewards in themselves, and ultimately, as I showed in Part Two, such rewards are the reason we do things, for better or worse. Beyond the biological need to reproduce, our main aim, as a human being, is to gain rewards such as those mentioned above. It seems obvious, then, why people try to earn money or take part in lotteries, or even carry out robberies – so that they can use this money to buy things that give them a sense of well-being.

Which, of course – as I also showed in Part Two – is a complete fallacy.

The 'happiness' that comes from holding a new piece of technical wizardry in your hands is something created by the system that needs you to feel happy in buying that piece of technical wizardry; because if you didn't feel happy then you wouldn't want to buy it. The sad fact is that there are few real rewards to be had from following the consumer dream, apart from the initial flush of excitement that raises our endorphin levels – the same hormones that make childbirth more bearable – and thus leave you with a chemically-induced sense of happiness or well-being. This then leads you to associate buying things (or taking part in other artificial 'experiences' for that matter) with good times, so you do it again, and again, and again. If all this sounds like a circular argument, that is precisely the point I am making – you, the consumer, are stuck in a positive feedback loop which is growing increasingly urgent: "Buy now, while stocks last!" "Hurry, closing down sale!" "Limited edition!" "Special offer!" And all the while the economy keeps growing, and the amount of carbon dioxide being thrown into the atmosphere keeps going up.

Victor Lebow, a leading retail analyst, encapsulated the desires of the consumer economy – the economy that most of us are a part of – in a startlingly candid manner, and one that is so much more relevant today than it was back in 1955:

Our enormously productive economy demands that we make consumption our way of life, that we convert the buying and use of goods into rituals, that we seek our spiritual satisfactions, our ego satisfactions, in consumption. The measure of social status, of social acceptance, or prestige, is now to be found in our consumption patterns. The very meaning and significance of our lives is today expressed in consumption terms. The greater the pressures upon the individual to conform to safe and accepted social standards, the more does he tend to express his aspirations and his individuality in terms of what he wears, drives, eats . . . these commodities and services must be offered to the consumer with a special urgency. We require not only 'forced draft' consumption, but 'expensive' consumption as well. We need things consumed, burned up, worn out, replaced and discarded at an ever-increasing pace.[3]

Our reward for being good consumers is the ability to consume more, and feed the economy so it can keep growing. That's it. And yet, we keep doing it because we continue to believe it makes us happier, more content, and better people.

Two: Make Us Feel Good for Doing Trivial Things

Last year I reduced the amount of energy I consume in my home by around a quarter: that made me feel good because I knew that by doing this I had reduced the amount of carbon dioxide I put into the atmosphere. I had to do the 'feeling good' for myself because no one else was going to do it. No, what I would have had to have done in order to be told I was a good person was lots of recycling: certainly my local council like to tell residents that they are good people because they are recycling more than they were last year, but when I called them up to ask whether they would tell people to stop buying goods, so that the council would have to collect less rubbish overall, I was met with cold silence. The reason was simple: if you buy less stuff then you will stop the economy growing; whereas, you can recycle with abandon while still buying more and more things. In fact, the more you buy, the more you will be able to recycle – result!

'Doing Your Bit', is the clarion call for a new light-green generation. We can all do our bit and make a positive difference for the environment – apparently. Turn your thermostat down (for heating) or up (for air conditioning) a degree; change a conventional light-bulb for a compact fluorescent one; buy organic vegetables rather than non-organic . . . take a deep breath; I want you to read this list produced by the car manufacturer Lexus:[4]

When remodelling, consider sustainable materials like bamboo flooring.

Instead of sending someone cut flowers, give them a plant.

When redecorating, use latex paint instead of one that's oil-based.

Keep your tyres properly inflated. You'll get better gas mileage.

Next time you have a dinner party, use cloth napkins.

Don't toss out your old cellphone; donate it to a charity.

Keep a canvas bag in your car so you'll have it handy when you go grocery shopping.

. . . and so on. None of these things is bad, as such, but they are trivial: nowhere in the list do Lexus suggest that you should get rid of your car, or even drive less, which is not surprising because the idea of the list is to make the Lexus owner feel good about their purchase. The internet abounds with lists like this; some produced by businesses, some by local authorities and governments, some by well-meaning environmental organizations that are naively regurgitating the same ideas as the businesses and the politicians. The whole point of praising people for carrying out trivial activities, however worthy they may be, is so that those people carry on living in almost exactly the same manner as they did before: you have to expend only a little effort in order to feel better, while the businesses and politicians that depend on a vibrant economy for their existence can continue to carry on operating in almost exactly the same manner as *they* did before.

Three: Give Us Selected Freedom

What is meant by freedom? The most obvious answer would seem to be, 'the right to live your life in whatever way you choose, whilst not interfering with the right of anyone else to live in the way that they choose.' This is fraught with problems, not least because – taken to extremes – you would have to account for the impact of all of your actions, however trivial, on everyone else.

In fact, freedom is one of those things that has to be taken in perspective. Going all the way back to Chapter 7, we see the idea of the Greatest Good coming into play – the idea that we should strive towards something that benefits the greatest number of people in the most effective way – alongside a number of rights that no human should do without: clean air, fresh water, shelter, food and a basic level of mental and physical stimulation. No one can reasonably deny anyone those rights. The sum of the Greatest Good along with these basic human rights actually leads to a mutual respect and care for the natural environment. The millions of people breathing in the rancid, choking air of Mexico City, Beijing, and countless other towns and cities around the world have had their rights curtailed; as have those people who drink polluted, toxic water; as have those people who had their native food sources taken away from them by mining companies; as have those people whose homes were destroyed to clear space for agriculture and commercial expansion. This is not freedom.

What we are actually given are those 'freedoms' selected in order to ensure minimum disruption to the continued business of making money: voting is a perfect example. I am often struck by the sheer brilliance of the phrase, "If voting changed anything, it would be illegal." This is often attributed to the social reformer and anarchist Emma Goldman, who may not have said these exact words, but most certainly railed against the pretence that voting was something worth doing; and in doing so made herself extremely unpopular amongst those who were fighting at the time for the right of women to vote. As I write, the Zimbabwean dictator Robert Mugabe is still refusing to reveal the outcome of the presidential election after two weeks of waiting. The opposition leader, Morgan Tsvangirai, won the election, which is why the result is being withheld, and there is nothing the voting public can do about it within the laws that Robert Mugabe put in place – they have cast their votes, they have expressed their democratic right, and a dictator remains. Think about your options in the country in which you live – how much change can you really make by casting a vote, while all the time the millions of people around you cast theirs?

> Forget the politicians – they're an irrelevance. The politicians are put there to give
> you the idea that you have freedom of choice. You don't. You have no choice.[5]

The next Presidential election in the USA will be won by either a Democrat or a Republican, and nothing will change beyond a little tinkering around the edges and the type of rhetoric being spouted by the new President. It is sobering to note that before George W. Bush came to power, Al Gore – joint Nobel Peace Prize winner, and the poster boy for the new light-green generation – had already terminally weakened the Kyoto Protocol that Bush subsequently refused to sign. As Vice-President, Al Gore realized that not including poor countries in the Protocol would be a vote loser, and thus ensured – through his influence on the negotiating table – that rich countries would be able to, by trading their emissions with poor countries, buy their way out of any potential punishment when the emissions were added up.[6] Funny, the difference a bit of power makes to people.

So, go and protest, make some noise, wave some banners, sign a petition: just make sure you stay within the law. I mean it – protest of some form or another is permitted in most nations, but the severity and the type of protest allowed depends on the legislation that is in place; both standing legislation and the widely used 'state of emergency' which, in fact is simply an extension of the existing laws. As the Zimbabweans ponder their electoral fate, the Mugabe regime has imposed 'emergency' laws to prevent any form of gathering that may threaten the government. What the Mugabe regime knows only too well is that in Zimbabwe, as with many other African, South American and Asian states, protest often takes an entirely different form from the kind that the people of the industrial West have become accustomed too. The Mugabe regime knows that real protest is capable of overthrowing governments; whereas in the USA, for instance, it almost goes without saying that protest will lead to nothing more than a warm feeling in the hearts of those taking part:

> One will find hundreds, sometimes thousands, assembled in an orderly fashion, listening to selected speakers calling for an end to this or that aspect of lethal state activity, carrying signs 'demanding' the same thing . . . and – typically – the whole thing is quietly disbanded with exhortations to the assembled to 'keep working' on the matter and to please sign a petition.

> Throughout the whole charade it will be noticed that the state is represented by a uniformed police presence keeping a discreet distance and not interfering with the activities. And why should they? The organizers will have gone through 'proper channels' to obtain permits. Surrounding the larger mass of demonstrators can be seen others . . . their function is to ensure the demonstrators remain 'responsible,' not deviating from the state-sanctioned plan of protest.[7]

Laughable, isn't it, that such a well-controlled event – and this is the way every official rally I have ever been on works – should be considered a 'protest' by the organizers? The laws in each country are tailored to suit the appetite of the population for change: a country full of people that want to fight for change needs to be kept tightly controlled; a country full of catatonic, drip-fed consumers can march all it likes, be given a well-controlled soapbox on TV – and the voltage on the tasers can be turned right down.

That is, unless someone decides to break the law.

Four: Pretend We Have a Choice

When you accept the label of 'consumer', you accept that you have become a financial object, willing to be manipulated by whatever marketing tricks abound. Consumer choice would be far better entitled 'Conchoice', a term describing the true level of choice that individuals are provided with, should they find themselves within the consumer culture. Benjamin R. Barber puts it like this: "The apparent widening of individual *consumer* choices actually shrinks the field of *social* choices. . . . For example, the American's freedom to choose among scores of automobile brands was secured by sacrificing the liberty to choose between private and public transportation. This politics of commodity . . . offers the feel of freedom while diminishing the range of options and the power to affect the larger world."[8] The individual is being conned: there *is* no choice.

Step outside the business districts of most cities in the Western world, and your ability to move around is dramatically curtailed. I tried to advise an ecologist friend of mine how to travel the 1,300 miles to Boston from a town in Iowa without using car or aircraft – it was just about possible using a combination of suburban and cross-country buses, along with three different trains running on three different rail networks and a couple of taxi journeys along the way. Her journey would have taken around 31 hours, not including the waits between the various legs of her journey. Her 'choice', in reality, was no choice at all: a car to the airport, and a plane to Boston – about seven hours in all.

America is a very large country, but even in small countries the way people travel is limited by whatever economic policies the government of the time decide best serve the thinking of the time. The 1960s nearly dealt the railway system in Britain a fatal blow: had the recommendations of Dr Richard Beeching – a transport adviser working for the British government – been fully carried through, the UK would have been left with just 3,000 miles of trunk route rather than the 12,000 miles that exists today.

As it was, a third of the stations and a third of the track were shut down in the space of two years. It turns out that Doctor Beeching was only doing what he was told, for as Charles Loft writes: "[Transport Minister] Ernest Marples was a self-made man who owned a road-construction company. He was required to sell his stake in the business on becoming Minister of Transport in October 1959, but was slow to do so. . . It was easy to attribute ulterior motives to the Minister's apparent enthusiasm for closures, particularly as he also presided over a shift in investment from rail to road. . . . With both road freight and the motor-car industry now essential sectors of the British economy, with restrictions on motoring a political impossibility and congestion a growing problem, the case for more and better roads seemed clear."[9] There is little doubt that the British government, under severe pressure from the car industry, had tried – and partially succeeded – to kill off the railways, and entirely remove one genuine choice.

Look at the way you are currently living: you can 'choose' between plasma, LCD, cathode ray tube or Internet TV, but not having a television is inconceivable to most people in the consumer culture; you can 'choose' between shopping at Walmart, Aldi, Tesco, Carrefour or any other supermarket, but not using a supermarket is impossible for hundreds of millions of people who need to buy food and have no way of growing it themselves. Some 'choices' are even more blatantly false:

An off-camera interviewer asks a woman, "What would you rather have: a car or a cleaner environment?"

The woman pauses, seemingly thoughtfully, before at last saying, "I can't imagine me without my car. Of course I'd rather have a clean environment, but I think that that compromise is very hard to make where we are."

The ad ends with a voiceover saying what BP is doing to make the world a better place.

How would the ad run if we changed the question to, "What would you rather have, a planet that is not being made filthy and in fact destroyed by automobiles and other effects of civilization, or your car?"[10]

How much of your life was simply picked off the shelves of the Conchoice Mall, and how much of it came out of a conscious decision to live in that particular way?

Five: Sell Us a Dream

On 1 April 2007, the Brazilian city of São Paulo officially became billboard-free. The tide of advertising that had swamped every physical dimension of the city had become intolerable, even to the local authorities; such was the scale of the problem. The law that demanded the removal of all billboards was – incredibly – passed by a huge majority, with the only 'no' voter being an advertising executive on the council. People are happy, except the advertisers, who made their position clear after the law was proposed:

Border, the Brazilian Association of Advertisers, was up in arms over the move. In a statement released on 2 October, the date on which law PL 379/06 was formally approved by the city council, Border called the new laws "unreal, ineffective and fascist". It pointed to the tens of thousands of small businesses that would have to bear the burden of altering their shop fronts under regulations "unknown in their virulence in any other city in the world".[11]

We're all smart enough to see through the rhetoric of these comments: "unreal, ineffective and fascist" are perfect descriptors for the synthetic, disconnected, material world that advertising has forced upon humanity – a world that is swamped with branding, corporate 'messages', sponsorship, flyers, free sheets, pop-ups and numerous other forms of corporate propaganda. São Paolo may have lost its billboards, but the advertisers can still feed their messages to the public through newspapers, magazines, television, radio; even schools, into which corporations don't so much sneak advertising, as blatantly trumpet the goodness of their products and services. Almost every school in the UK collects Tesco's and Sainsbury's supermarket tokens, through which they can acquire computers and books. Every token handed over by every child is a graphic advertisement for competing brands that want their cut of the family shopping budget, and the future loyalty of the children who carry these little pieces of paper into the classroom. North America has it far worse: "It is never enough to tag the schools with a few logos. Having gained a foothold, the brand managers are now doing what they have done in music, sports and journalism outside the schools: trying to overwhelm their host. They are fighting for their brands to become not the add-on but the subject of education."[12] As you have seen, the individual is not offered real choice in this culture of consumption – simply 'Conchoice'. The real choice has already been lost in favour of corporations that have sold entire populations down the commercial river: the individual's ultimate dream is no longer a response to "what can I achieve in my life?" but "what can I buy?"

This goes back further than you can imagine. Long before mass advertising and competition between corporations, commerce was the prime motivator in the foreign policies of the imperial powers of Europe and, later on, the USA. The events in Haiti over the last 500 years reflect this perfectly. Like countless tribal peoples prior to European settlement, the Taíno[13] people lived a connected life – connected with the land, the sea and the sky that drove much of their mythology. Then Christopher Columbus landed at Hispaniola in 1492 – the island that would become Haiti and the Dominican Republic – and irreversibly changed things:

> It took no time at all for the [people] who first greeted Christopher Columbus to be all but erased from the face of the earth. . . . Less than 30 years after Columbus' three ocean-crossing ships dropped anchor off the island of Hispaniola, the Taíno would be destroyed by Spanish weaponry, forced labour and European diseases.[14]

Those that survived lived at the behest of the invaders, and somehow managed to hold on to a semblance of their ancestry. The commercial advantage such a fertile environment provided to invaders in terms of crops, slave labour (both local and imported) and trading routes made Haiti the subject of continued negotiation and conflict ever since; but it was the specific words that were used with reference to Haiti that reveal so much. In 1833, in relation to the Haitian people but, no doubt, a view that could be applied across the entire British Empire, a British parliamentarian observed: "To make them labour, and give them a taste for luxuries and comforts, they must be gradually taught to desire those objects which could be attained by human labour. There was a regular progress from the possession of necessaries to the desire of luxuries; and what once were luxuries, gradually came . . . to be necessaries. This was the sort of progress the negroes had to go through, and this was the sort of education to which they ought to be subject in their period of probation."[15] In a striking parallel to this, Arthur Millspaugh, an adviser to the occupying USA government wrote in 1929: "The peasants, living lives which to us seem indolent and shift-less, are envariably [sic] carefree and contented; but, if they are to be citizens of an independent self-governing nation, they must acquire . . . a new set of wants."[16] In other words: the commercial Americanization of a culture.

Quite what the people of Haiti did to deserve such a long period of turmoil, especially considering their 'carefree and contented' existence in the past, is difficult to understand at first glance. The more you look at the history of commerce, though – the ravenous British East India Company; the endemic slavery to feed the coffee, cotton and sugar industries; the limitless ambition of Coca-Cola and McDonalds – the more you realize that this is just par for the course. The reason you are surrounded by logos, adverts and brands, and the reason entire cultures are being cut up into bite-sized pieces and swallowed is because commerce needs to constantly sell a dream of a new reality in order to survive.

Six: Exploit Our Trust

If I were to tell you to hit someone, just because I wanted them hurt, you would almost certainly refuse, and probably report me to the authorities for suggesting such a thing – and quite right, too. If I were to don a white coat, welcome you into a laboratory and explain that you were to take part in an experiment, and that the person on the other side of the screen who you were about to apply extremely painful electric shocks too was a willing volunteer, you would probably say, "Thanks, but no thanks." Or would you?

The groundbreaking experimental work of Stanley Milgram[17] simply reinforced what he already knew – that individuals, when exposed to an authority figure in a pressure situation will obey the authority figure far more readily, and to a greater extent, than would have been possible in other circumstances. The reason Milgram already knew the power of authority – although he was, himself, surprised at the level of obedience in his experiments – was historical. In 1961, when the experiments were first conducted, World War II was fresh in the minds of every adult living in the parts of the world where the conflict had taken place. The hierarchy of authority within the Axis Forces had been carefully designed to ensure maximum obedience: from Hitler, the master orator and 'saviour' of the German people; through to the SS guards and local enforcers operating on behalf of the Third Reich; the weight of power upon ordinary citizens and soldiers was irresistible. But, even given such a level of authority, it is still shocking to read of the ease in which people were coerced to carry out appalling acts:

Judicial interrogations of some 125 of the [reserve police battalion] men indicated that, while no one had to participate . . . the great majority stayed in ranks and later killed whoever was brought to them out of loyalty to those ranks, and to maintain their standing in their units. Thus the men chose to become murderers rather than look bad in the eyes of the other men.

Over time, as the battalion participated in more and more mass murders, it became far more relaxed and efficient in its deadly operations. These ordinary men got used to killing thousands of people at close range as part of their day's work. By the time their part of the 'Final Solution' was completed in Poland, the battalion had shot at least 38,000 Jews to death.[18]

You might think that you would behave differently to these ordinary people caught up in the rigors of war, and that you would refuse to obey the requests of those in authority. In fact, only about 20% of those ordered to kill Jewish prisoners, without fear of repercussions if they refused, did refuse.[19] The chances are that if you were put in this same situation, you would not refuse and would, yourself, become a murderer. It is a chilling thought that the simple act of being in a controlled situation where there is a hierarchy of authority pushing down on them can turn people into something that would otherwise be unthinkable to them – but that is the power of authority. In effect, it is our good nature, our trust of other people that allows us to be manipulated in such a dramatic way; and not even the threat of certain death can change that.

The daily grind of work exposes billions of people to some form of authority, but only in a minority of cases do people ever think to question the tasks they are given. To be sure, many of the people carrying out their work are in a very difficult situation: however mundane and soul-destroying, the completion of these tasks is simply the only way they can envisage earning the money necessary to buy food to keep themselves alive. The sweatshops of south-east Asia and Central America starkly bear testament to that reality. There are people, though, who carry out work that is utterly destructive; yet because of the deep disconnection between what that person is doing and the impact of that work on the environment, and humanity in general, they continue to do it – and authority serves to deepen that disconnection.

The person operating the feller-buncher in Chapter 6 knows quite clearly that he is removing trees, destroying habitat and leaving behind bare earth which will be washed away in the next rainstorm. He also knows – despite the efforts of those who have tried to suppress this information – that the removal of trees contributes to the greenhouse effect, which is heating up the planet and threatening to bring on a catastrophic cycle of events at all scales of life. He knows all these things, and yet he continues to do his work.[20] The CEO of the forestry company – say Georgia-Pacific, Kimberly-Clark or Asian Pulp and Paper – knows the impact of his company's activities; as do the directors, upon whom the pressure to meet financial targets is imposed by their CEO; as do the managers, upon whom the pressure to improve output is imposed by their directors; as do the operators of the feller-bunchers, who have been clearly told that they are doing an important job, and they have to process a set tonnage of timber every day, otherwise the contract will be lost. The hierarchy imposes authority, and the destruction continues.

As you will see later, the threat of financial loss is most definitely a factor in the continuation of highly destructive activities; but, as Stanley Milgram demonstrated all those years ago, we don't really need those threats: we just do what we are told.

Seven: Lie to Us

It seems so obvious, especially after reading to this point, that in order to thrive as a species, humanity is dependent on a fully functioning, healthy and diverse global ecology. When you turn on the television news, listen to the radio or read a newspaper, the state of the global ecology is shown clearly as improving or deteriorating in quality overall, with x number of species having evolved or become extinct, and certain trophic levels becoming more or less dominant. Or rather, this is what we should be seeing and hearing: instead, we learn about the state of the global *economy*, whether the markets are rising or falling; how many jobs have been gained or lost; which companies are taking over others, and which sectors of the economy are thriving or failing. The economy is king; the ecology is a footnote.

It is impossible to create something out of nothing. National economies or, in microcosm, the finances of individual companies, cannot grow unless they take something from somewhere else: this can either be in the form of market share from other nations or companies, or by creating product from a resource like oil, metal ore, limestone (for cement) or the ecological complexity of a natural habitat, such as an ancient forest.[21] The global economy cannot take market share from another planet; it can only grow by using additional resources taken from this planet.

Taken like that, it is obvious that economic growth is ultimately unsustainable – especially given the narrow, capital-based definition used to define the term 'economy' in the industrial world – yet, we continue to be fobbed off by the message that we must have economic growth in order to progress or develop as humans. Of course, if we judge development or progress in terms of the number of televisions, computers and cars we have, the size of home we have or the amount of energy we use, then economic growth most certainly does lead to a more 'developed' human race. If we judge development or progress on rather more esoteric (and, quite frankly, more important) measures such as clean water and air, physical and mental health, freedom of expression, and having a future that our descendants will be able to thrive in, then economic growth is failing on almost all of these counts. Humans in every place touched by the rank hand of industrialization are told that development based upon economic growth is good. When you think about it, though, the only true form of development is that which moves us into balance with our natural environment – in effect a reversal of what we are now doing. You do not have to be financially prosperous for your water to be clean – you just need a basic level of hygiene, sensible water management techniques and, most of all, a lack of toxic muck being poured into the water supply by industrial processes.

Economic growth as a necessity is the biggest lie that humanity has ever been sold; yet we are lapping it up because the lie is repeated day after day by every information source we are unfortunate enough to be subjected to.

*　*　*

In a rather wonderful chapter of his book *Heat*, George Monbiot describes how the vested interests of climate change – the corporations, agencies and individuals whose existence depends on producing greenhouse gases – have colluded for decades to ensure the public, you and me, are kept confused and ill-informed. The methods now used for denying that humans are changing the climate are the same methods used by the tobacco industry throughout the late decades of the 20th century:[22] corporate funded articles and press releases that specialize in misinformation and pseudo-science; artificially created grassroots coalitions known as 'Astroturfs'; a host of media representatives funded by industry; and an unhealthy dose of 'greenwash',[23] specifically designed to make companies look environmentally sustainable when they are nothing of the sort. This is a pet hate of mine, so much so that, at the start of 2008, I set up an anti-greenwashing website called The Unsuitablog. In one article, regarding the mining company BHP Billiton, I wrote:

> Like all destructive companies, BHP Billiton are engaging in some striking greenwash: in fact they have just agreed a new Climate Change Policy, which is not surprising considering their operations emit nearly 52 million tonnes of carbon dioxide equivalent into the atmosphere every year (that's about the same as Denmark – yes, the entire country!) It's a pity they have entirely failed to commit to any reductions in greenhouse gases at all. Exactly what kind of Climate Change Policy is this?[24]

Corporations, in particular, take advantage of the innate trust we have in authority figures, often hiring scientists (in the spirit of Stanley Milgram's electric shock experiments) to speak to the media, apparently on their own behalf, while in fact ensuring that the information put across is precisely the information the corporations want the public to hear. The damage that has been caused by the continuous stream of lies and denial is impossible to quantify: certainly it has put back public awareness of the climate situation by a decade, at least. When you consider that most environmental damage has been caused in countries whose governments support the biggest lie of all – the 'need' for economic growth – it is clear that the greenwashing corporations are in very good company indeed.

Eight: Scare Us

We live in times of fear: fear of the impact of terrorism on our ability to live in safety; fear of the effects of economic collapse on our future financial security; fear of what strangers and paedophiles might do to our children. Some of us are even afraid of the effects of climate change. Industrial Civilization instils us with a succession of fears not only because we may be genuinely afraid of a particular thing happening, but also because we live in a state of comparative ignorance. Few people have a good understanding of the nature of risk: for instance, a person might tell you that she drives her child to school in order to protect him or her from 'stranger danger', but in doing so she is exposing the child to the far greater risk of being the potential victim of a vehicle crash. This is simple ignorance: the type of fear I want to describe preys on our poor understanding of risk, and is propagated on purpose in order to keep us in check.

Anyone who grew up in the United States in the 1950s will be familiar with the fear of communism, and the many lists that Senator McCarthy threatened to release in order to expose those people who were threatening the stability of the USA with their left-leaning political ideals. What most people in the United States don't realize, is that 'McCarthyism', as the specific attitude came to be known as, had as much to do with communism as the type of politics being espoused in the Soviet Union had to do with genuine communism. A certain suspension of belief is required when you consider that last sentence – especially if you grew up in either the USA or the USSR during the Cold War – because it completely denies two articles of faith that were in place at the time. Firstly, Senator McCarthy, along with the entire state hierarchy (with a couple of exceptions), helped to spin a web of fear in order to encourage patriotism amongst the American people, and ensure everyone was kept 'on side'. The author Bill Bryson, who grew up in 1950s America, writes:

Thanks to our overweening preoccupation with Communism at home and abroad America became the first nation in modern history to build a war economy in peacetime. Defence spending in the Fifties ranged between $40 billion and $53 billion a year – or more than the total government spending on everything at the dawn of the decade.[25]

History repeats itself, as always; so it was that 50 years later George Bush Jr., along with his cadre of high-ranking political colleagues (all of whom had financial interests in either the arms industry, the oil industry or both) used the threat of global terrorism on the USA to ease through military spending bills totalling more than $3 trillion dollars since September 2001. The 2008 Pentagon budget alone was a shade under $600 billion – nearly a thousand times the amount of money spent on diplomatic relations.[26] It was the threat of terrorism that ensured Americans meekly accepted the Patriot Act, and its even more intrusive successor, Patriot Act II. It was the threat of terrorism that ensured that the torture of hundreds of innocent people in Guantanamo Bay, and thousands more in Iraq and Afghanistan was tolerated by the majority of people in Western Industrial Civilization. It was the threat of terrorism that ensured that, since 2001, every conference of the richest industrial nations had 'national security' at, or near, the top of its agenda – pushing climate-change prevention conveniently down the list. Since September 11, 2001, not a single American has died on US soil as a result of a terrorist attack; yet, in that same period at least 300,000 people in the USA have died as a result of motor vehicle incidents.[27] How many times do you hear your political leaders urging you to be afraid of cars?

The second denial of an article of faith I make is that the USSR under Stalin, Khrushchev and Brezhnev, was never a communist country. Communism implies 'commune' and 'community' – it does not imply centralized control of all assets with an elite minority benefiting greatly from the labours of the poor majority. But, just like in the USA and every other industrialized nation since the start of the Agricultural Revolution, the Soviet Union practised a deliberately bastardized form of communism designed to funnel economic wealth to a rich and powerful minority. As with the USA, the people of the Soviet Union were kept in a state of fear by their government. This excerpt from a 1941 Marxist document illustrates what had already happened to the Communist Dream:

> The Soviet Union can be best understood as a great trade union fallen into the hands of corrupt and degenerate leaders. Our struggle against Stalinism is a struggle within the labor movement. The Soviet Union is a Workers' State . . . degenerated because of Stalinist rule.[28]

Essentially, two governments were creating a state of fear within their respective borders in order to control the people, and that state of fear was an almost total fabrication of the truth. The Cold War was simply two imperialist, hierarchical states trying to gain global power by force. If only the majority of people in those states had known that at the time.

* * *

However, fear doesn't only have to be an extension of a real, if muted, threat. Cast your mind back to the Tree Huggers of northern India and the native West Papuans, who were prepared to challenge government and business in order to protect their ways of life. It is now standard practice amongst certain vested interests to refer to such people as 'eco-terrorists' or the 'green mafia': anything that creates a sense of fear is a vital weapon in ensuring that the public at large see environmental action as a negative thing. For many business-friendly politicians, the doyen of 'green mafia' writing is Michael Crichton, whose dramatic, but ultimately fictional book about eco-terrorism, *State Of Fear*, launched a thousand spin-offs and a great many newly converted climate sceptics. In fact, the eco-terrorism argument goes far deeper than the books of fiction writers – however much they manage to scare people. Senator James Inhofe, former chairman of the US Senate Committee on Environment and Public Works is a self-confessed climate-change sceptic who used the fear agenda in the most direct way possible – by comparing environmentalists to Nazis:

"It kind of reminds . . . I could use the Third Reich, the big lie," Inhofe said.

"You say something over and over and over and over again, and people will believe it, and that's their strategy."[29]

Which, of course, is exactly how governments all around the world advance the message that economic growth is necessary; along with the message that people of different colours, religions or political beliefs are a constant threat to the security of the people those governments rule over. In Brazil, such ideas flow freely from the keyboards of many journalists and politicians. A plan by WWF – one of the most conservative of the big environmental NGOs[30] – to set up a large wildlife reserve in the Amazon rainforest was met with typical contempt:

"This is a new form of colonialism, an open conspiracy in which economic and financial interests act through nongovernmental organizations," said Lorenzo Carrasco, editor and co-author of *The Green Mafia*, a widely circulated anti-environmentalist polemic. "It is evident these interests want to block the development of Brazil and the Amazon region by creating and controlling these reserves, which are full of minerals and other valuable natural resources."[31]

When you don't have the fear of Communism or terrorism to fall back on, then it's time to roll out those old staples, 'preventing development' and 'blocking economic growth'. There is most certainly a pattern emerging here. Sadly, though, we have to now leave behind the mere threat of loss and move on to the reality – the execution, as it were – and we don't even have to change countries to find the first example.

Nine: Abuse Us

Just another day in the Brazilian Amazon rainforest: the dank, humid air hangs like lianas, the moisture dripping from leaf to branch and down onto the shady litter-strewn soil; insects feed on plant matter, and themselves are preyed upon by birds – the tumult of the deep dense forest being heard for miles; chainsaws buzz and scream as they carve up massive trunks, leaving behind acid, infertile soil that may never again be fertilized by the tree canopy; Dorothy Stang, an American nun, defending the same area of forest she had defended for 20 years, is shot six times – murdered in cold blood by a hit man hired by a cattle rancher, determined to ensure that this swathe of forest can be cleared and grazed for a healthy profit.

The men directly responsible for Dorothy Stang's murder in 2005 were eventually prosecuted and sentenced, but it took another two years for the cattle rancher who 'owned' (or rather, took from the native inhabitants) the land, to be prosecuted. In fact, despite nearly 800 people having been killed in the heavily forested Para region of Brazil in land disputes, only four people have ever been convicted: "Intimidation by loggers and land-grabbers, corrupt local authorities and a lack of law enforcement resources mean that many of these cases go uninvestigated and unsolved. Meanwhile, the decimation of the Amazon continues at alarmingly high rates."[32] What you will never see is the conviction of anyone higher up the ladder than the rancher – the chain of responsibility ends where it connects to those who have a significant part to play in the global economy: these people will never be held to account. The simple fact is that corporate leaders invest in wholesale human misery and, where required, they will initiate and then ignore the slaughter that is invariably the outcome of their activities – euphemistically known as 'turning a blind eye'. This slaughter is not necessarily the pernicious, gradual type either – the roasting of the planet, or the toxification of the land and the oceans – some forms of corporate slaughter are very much in the open and visible to all. These most visible forms of corporate slaughter have almost always been state-sanctioned.

The British colonial slave trade, and the use of slaves as a form of cheap (free) labour, which persisted throughout the 18th and 19th century in order to provide a ready supply of exotic foods for the public and vast financial rewards for the companies involved, was readily sanctioned and overseen by the British government. The brutality of the West Indian plantations, which were the source of the British companies' riches (and not just companies, for the Church of England were the landowners of one of the most notorious plantations, at Codrington in Barbados),[33] led to a death toll that we would now call genocide:

> When slavery ended in the United States, less than half a million slaves had grown to a population of four million. When it ended in the British West Indies, total slave imports of well over two million left a surviving slave population of only about 670,000. . . . The Caribbean was a slaughterhouse.[34]

If you are under any illusions that such corporate and state-sanctioned atrocities are no more, think again. The mining companies' destruction of the native West Papuans' forest – their means of survival – was, as discussed in Chapter 11, ably assisted by the Suharto government of Indonesia. The continued, senseless slaughter of thousands of Sudanese in the oil-rich Darfur region is regarded by both the Sudanese government (who are gaining tremendous wealth from oil sales) and the Chinese government (who have an insatiable thirst for oil) as an unavoidable consequence of economic activity.[35] Arms companies throughout the USA have benefited tremendously from the purchase of billions of dollars worth of weapons by the US military for the second Gulf War in Iraq – which, incidentally, tops up the GDP of the country in which the weapons are manufactured. The war has been responsible for at least 80,000 civilian deaths since 2003.[36]

Such abuse of people and power may seem, on the surface, to be unrelated to the environmental disconnection that humanity has had foisted upon it; but this would be ignoring the subtext. The driver for this abuse is primarily to gain wealth for a privileged few. The unwritten reason for using abusive tactics, as with using fear, is to ease people into a state of denial. Denial of a situation, however terrifying, is the standard human response to prolonged abuse of all types; whether parent-child abuse, employer-employee abuse or state-civilian abuse. Riane Eisler, president of the Center for Partnership Studies in the USA, writes:

> In a top-down, authoritarian family that relies on fear and force, children often learn to be in denial about their parents' behaviour since they depend on them for survival. This makes it easy to later be in denial about 'strong' leaders who abuse power, and to identify with them. People's willingness to countenance the erosion

of democratic safeguards . . . and their support for the pre-emptive Iraq War, even though it was justified by false information, are also largely due to early habits of obedience to authority figures coupled with denial that 'strong' leaders can be wrong.[37]

The various tools and methods used in order to disconnect us from the real world and accept the way that the world is being run on our behalf – the way that the planet is being trashed for economic gain – accumulate over time, from birth to death, to create an almost insurmountable personal barrier. We willingly disconnect because, eventually, we see it as the only option.

That said, there is one final method that I need to tell you about: one that almost everyone on Earth is a party to, and one that feels so natural to accept that it couldn't possibly be to our disadvantage – or so you would think.

Ten: Give Us Hope

Not all hope is bad. There is the simple type; the benign wish or blessing, that shows you care: "I hope you have a good day", "Hope to see you again soon", "I hope you pass your exam." In isolation, and as merely a gesture, then this kind of hope can make someone feel wanted and rather special. This kind of hope is nice – it is harmless.[38]

There is a second kind of hope that is not harmless; it is the kind of hope that implies more than benign wishes. This kind of hope is, essentially, prayer – religious or otherwise. Religious prayer, we all know about and, as we saw in Chapter 10, a large proportion of the world's population uses prayer of one sort or another. Even when not religious, 'secular prayer' bears all of the hallmarks of its religious namesake, and carries the same dangers that are faced when someone's future is entrusted to it.

Like it or not, there appears to be no empirical evidence to show that prayer works. The Religious Tolerance website[39] has carefully broken down the methods and results in, and reaction to, all of the recent major studies carried out on the effectiveness of prayer; and the conclusion you have to reach is that prayer alone simply does not have any recordable effect. The reactions that this kind of statement invokes are often furious, but also more specifically along the lines that God must not be tested. As one theologian put it: "You're going to do your best to limit the prayer some people get so that you can measure the benefits for those who receive a lot of prayer? Do you think that's how God intended prayer to be used?"[40]

So that appears to be that. Except that when you look deeper into the research, you find something very interesting. A widely cited and carefully controlled study into the relative effects of prayer on post-operative coronary recovery found no significant difference in recovery rates between those who received prayer unknowingly and those who did not receive prayer at all.[41] But here's the interesting bit: the group of patients who knowingly received prayer had a 15% to 20% *worse* recovery rate than the other two groups. Some commentators suggested this was because of the increased pressure of knowing you were expected to respond to prayer, but I believe the cause to be down to something different.

Hope.

When you hope for something to happen – not the benign good wishes, but the deep, heartfelt hope that aches for an outcome of your choosing – then something happens to you: your motivation to work for the desired outcome actually decreases. Like the detached worker who can't accept their responsibility for the destructive outcome of the process they are part of, by entrusting an outcome to the ethereal entity that is 'hope' then you are passing on responsibility to something that is out of your control. This is what you are doing when you pray: you pass on the responsibility for the outcome of your prayers, meditations and deepest wishes to an external force.

A positive state of mind is often a vital attribute in recovering from illness, whether mental or physical, and also other conditions such as addiction. Quite how this works is uncertain, but more studies than not show that maintaining positivity is beneficial. Knowing that someone cares about you enough to pray for you is one thing, though; thinking that the job of getting you better has passed from you to something you have no control over is another thing entirely.

* * *

Every day, in all sorts of ways, we hand over the responsibility of our actions to other parties. We entrust religious leaders to act as proxy supreme beings, to give us blessings and pray for the delivery of our souls and, as is becoming more common, the protection of the natural environment. We entrust politicians to justly run districts, states, countries, the whole planet, on our behalf, and deliver whatever is in their jurisdiction from whatever evils we have asked them to deal with. We ask the heads of corporations to use profits wisely, to provide fair wages, allow union representation and listen to their staff and respond appropriately – we ask them not to destroy the planet. We ask environmental organizations to look after the planet on our behalf, to lobby fiercely and petition prudently, to give us a world worth living in.

We are guilty of a mass dereliction of responsibility.

When we vote, we hope the politicians will do the right thing after they have been elected. When we buy a product from a company, we hope that company are acting in the best interests of everyone and everything they impact. When we sign a petition, go on a protest march or write a letter, we hope that it will change things for the better. But it is never that simple.

Voters vote for different things: your hope that a politician will increase pollution controls will be running counter to the hope of another voter that pollution controls will be weakened. Your entrustment of a company that they will act ethically runs contrary to the basic needs of a shareholder in that same company, who demands an increase in profits, which requires poorer labour standards, increased use of natural resources, corner-cutting and cost-slashing across the board. Your petition or protest march may give you hope that something will change, when in fact you have simply channelled your anger and concern into a symbolic action that threatens not a single media executive, company director or head of state. You innocently believed that right would out simply because you placed your demands on the wings of hope.

> When we stop hoping for external assistance, when we stop hoping that the awful situation we're in will somehow resolve itself, when we stop hoping the situation will somehow not get worse, then we are finally free – truly free – to honestly start working to thoroughly resolve it. When hope dies, action begins.[42]

* * *

The Highland Clearances were just part of the Agricultural Revolution – the starting point for the disconnection which the newly dominant Western culture turned into an art form. From this point onwards a gash was opened between people and the real world that has been growing wider and wider ever since. This was, and is, entirely intentional. It is now time to identify the culprits and try to explain why they are doing what they do.

Who Is Responsible?

It is far easier to blame others for something than to blame ourselves. There is something alluring in pinning the woes of our situation on forces that are 'out there' – stupendous, unreachable forces that chart our every move and guide our hands to do their bidding. Somewhere, in the minds of the disenchanted, there is a room in which the most powerful people in the world sit and decide the fate of entire continents, political systems, religions and the Earth itself.

And, yes, there are rooms in which far-reaching decisions are made by extremely wealthy and powerful people: The G8, The Bilderberg Group, The

World Economic Forum, NATO, The United Nations Security Council, The World Trade Organization . . . but they aren't in charge. They are just fulfilling an obligation to something far more powerful: the belief that this is the way it has to be. You won't get anywhere near the people on the top tables of these groups, anyway, because they are being protected by those who believe that they must be protected; who would probably give their lives to keep the system in good health. But they aren't in charge either. They are just fulfilling an obligation to the belief that this is the way it has to be. And even if you do get near, and manage to dispatch the protectors and the protected, it won't change things, because the people in the shops, the people in their cars, the people in their offices, the people at home watching the news on the television and the people protesting on the streets are simply fulfilling an obligation to the belief that *this is the way it has to be.*

Hopeless, isn't it?

But, of course, *you're* not going to hope, are you? Hope is one of the ways in which we are disconnected from the real world, just like everyone caught up in this accursed culture – "The Culture of Maximum Harm", as Daniel Quinn accurately describes it.[43] The ten Tools of Disconnection I have spent pages of exhaustive analysis showing you, are real. They are, more or less, the essence of Industrial Civilization: they are what make it what it is. We all accept this because we cannot think of anything else – because we are so disconnected from the real world and attached to this way of being that any other way of life seems impossible.

But stop! Can you imagine what would happen if you walked up to a group of people outside this culture and said, "This is how you are going to live from now on: instead of looking after the land, water and air on which you utterly depend – without which you will die – you are going to wreck it. Instead of taking only what you need to survive, you are going to take far more – stockpile it and call it wealth. Instead of enjoying the lives you have, the interaction you have with the world and the rich, intense stimulation that it provides you with, you are going to withdraw from it, provide yourselves with artificial stimulation and pay others – with the wealth you have accumulated – to entertain you. Instead of being happy with what you have, you are going to live in a state of constant anxiety and restlessness, craving more and more things that you are told are necessary. Instead of thinking for yourselves, you are going to be told how to think, and you will learn to see this as the only way to think."

Can you imagine what the response would be?

We are in the terminal stages of the greatest addiction humanity has ever seen. We live in a constant disconnected haze; drip-fed a cocktail of proto-choice, dreams, lies, fear, abuse and hope. We are users of this culture, and it makes us feel good – until we need another dose. We are also players in this culture. Whatever your social status, whatever your 'class', whatever your level of wealth or influence, you are likely to be taking part in the process of disconnection just because of the job you do or position you hold.

I'm going to repeat the Tools of Disconnection, adding just a few example roles to each: if you are in one of these roles, or anything remotely similar, then you are probably a party to that method, whether you like it or not.

- One: Reward Us For Being Good Consumers – store managers, marketing executives, investment bankers;

- Two: Make Us Feel Good For Doing Trivial Things – local politicians, writers, therapists;

- Three: Give Us Selected Freedom – national politicians, judges, dictators;

- Four: Pretend We Have A Choice – vehicle salespeople, travel agents, shop assistants;

- Five: Sell Us A Dream – advertisers, educators, missionaries;

- Six: Exploit Our Trust – scientists, military officers, office managers;

- Seven: Lie To Us – economists, government ministers, public relations officers;

- Eight: Scare Us – journalists, broadcasters, customs officers;

- Nine: Abuse Us – soldiers, police officers, property developers;

- Ten: Give Us Hope – religious and spiritual leaders, company directors, environmentalists.

There is a whole web of integrated and interdependent interests whose primary goal is to ensure that every single member of this culture, including themselves, is kept dosed up with the same heady, addictive cocktail. So completely are the different interests immersed in their roles that it is no longer possible to establish individual responsibility. This web of interests is, to put it simply, the system itself:

> It is not merely individuals acting in accord with their perceived needs and acquired desires, but the global treadmill of production itself that has become the main culprit in the ecocidal endgame. This treadmill has been churning for some time, creating a predicament that is at odds with the ecological health of this planet.[44]

Of course, there are some who would appear to benefit far more than others.

The 'Elites', the people who have more influence and more material and financial wealth than the rest of us, have played the system as far as it is possible to play it. History shows the influence of these Elites stretching across oceans – commanding armies, shipping fleets and masses of slaves in a giant imperial game of Risk. One false move and entire empires could collapse: and so they did, through carelessness or the greater power of other empires, commanded by their own elites. What is unique about this new civilization – the most pervasive in history – is that pure power is no longer desirable: with power comes tremendous responsibility, and tremendous risk. What is far more desirable now is wealth. Wealth can be accumulated; it can provide status symbols; it can provide a lifestyle that completely cuts the holder off from any disruptive influences – as if that is a desirable state to be in. This adoration of wealth propagates from the top to the bottom, by influence, generating a mad clamour for a particular lifestyle: 'I can be like him! I can have a big car; a big house; fly to exotic places and eat exotic food – and even if I can't, I can aspire to live such a life (such a lie). I can surround myself with goods and read about the rich and famous, while imagining what it would be like.'

We buy into the trappings of this lifestyle because it makes us feel as though we are taking a step up the ladder. What also happens is that the profit that is generated from our purchases and activities goes back upwards, giving a little cut to everyone involved; right up to the Elites, who can create for themselves an even more luxuriant, disconnected lifestyle.

* * *

Unless you are born into it, sheer wealth does not come easily: it takes time to build up capital, and most often a great deal of effort; in fact, it almost always requires the holder to also be in a position of power, whether that be as the head of a media organization, an oil company, an agricultural conglomerate, a retail chain, or as the despotic leader of a nation. The truly powerful are the wealthy; and the truly wealthy are the powerful.

The problem for them, and for us, is that humans are simply not evolved to cope with such power and wealth – we have evolved as connected beings who must work together, and with nature, in order to survive. Co-operation is an essential part of life: a plethora of ancient tribes survived for many thousands of years because of the close co-operation of their members and, of course, their close connection to nature. Unlike civilizations that have come and gone in sudden urgent spikes of activity, ancient tribal societies gradually developed to reach a state of balance with their environments – they were not intending to go anywhere soon. Were it not for the activities of those people, at all levels of Industrial

Civilization, who have helped to displace, disenfranchise, infect and slaughter tribal people, then we would still have many of these ancient tribes; but, sadly, there are precious few remaining.

Despite the close level of co-operation within tribes, loose hierarchies and leaders do exist – leadership is essential for a wide range of tasks. Unlike Industrial Civilization, leadership is always based on ability:

> Among the most primitive societies, i.e. the hunters and the food gatherers, authority is exercised by the person who is generally regarded as being competent for the task. What qualities this competence rests on depends much on the specific circumstances; generally they would include experience, wisdom, generosity, skill, 'presence', courage. No permanent authority exists in most of these tribes, but an authority emerges in the case of need. When the qualities on which the authority rests disappear or weaken, the authority itself ends.[45]

This is known as a meritocracy: you earn your place in society by virtue of your usefulness to the group as a whole – you are not born into any position of privilege; you cannot fight or buy your way to the top. Furthermore, as Daniel Quinn writes: "Tribes have leaders, and sometimes very strong leaders, but leadership carries little or nothing in the way of special benefits that are denied to other members of the tribe."[46] Our ancestral background has not prepared the Elites for their position in society: nothing can prepare the human mind for the incredible rush of power that comes to those at the very top. The outcome is megalomania; terrible, pathological megalomania that makes those people feel that this really is the life; the only kind of life we should aspire to, and so others must think like them: "You are not going to think for yourselves; you are going to be told how to think, and you will learn to see this as the only way to think."

I feel sorry for them.

Is that such a bizarre statement to make? Well, let's put it this way: there are leaders; they do have immense wealth and power over large parts of humanity and – through their leadership and the way they manipulate the system to their own ends – over the fate of the Earth; but they are still following the same toxic dream as the rest of us. We are all playing our part in the toxic dream. It seems terribly simplistic to say, "Society is to blame", but it does eventually come down to that. The Industrial Civilization we live in has taken on a life of its own, and we are all swimming around in its effluent trying to grab hold of whatever solids are floating by. Those at the top merely sit on a larger pile of excrement than the rest of us – disconnected and completely at odds with the way we need to live in order to give us a future.

A friend wrote to me recently. She said: "When I watch documentaries or read books about indigenous tribes, I can see the ancient wisdom in their eyes, the experiences of life with the land etched on their faces, and I envy them their beautiful fulfilled lives – and mourn the lost lives we will never live: growing up free and learning from our elders the real skills of life; not algebra or humanities, but how to live with the land." I don't know if we *deserve* another chance, but I think that if there is a way of reclaiming those lost lives then it has to be worth a try.

The Beginning

If, by now, I haven't managed to convince you that Industrial Civilization has to end then you are probably not ready to be part of the solution. Most people who have been brought up in this Culture of Maximum Harm still believe that this is the only way to live – the forces that have *stopped* you thinking for yourself and making the connection between the fate of this planet (on the brink of catastrophe) and the primary motivation for being human (to survive) are immensely powerful.

But, if you do want to take up the challenge, and ensure the survival of those you care about, then read on: there is a lot to do, and a great adventure to be had. . . .

Part Four

How to Survive

Chapter Fourteen

You Are the System

We're nearly ready to do something monumental, but not quite.

I used to manage IT systems for a key component of the global economy (it makes me feel a bit gloomy that I knowingly helped prop up Industrial Civilization for a while, but more of that later) and whenever a major piece of work was due to be carried out I would first analyse all of the stages of the task, finding out where problems might occur; I would then assemble a team of people to help iron out any of these flaws and identify any other potential problems I might have missed. There were always one or two small things I missed, right up to the day of execution; and usually things that we had to deal with 'on the fly': no plan is perfect. That said, if a great deal of effort went into the planning process, the work was likely to be far more successful than just plunging into it, hoping that everything would go fine.

So, here's the plan: first, I want to go over a few key points, just so they are absolutely clear in your mind, no question; second, I want to go through the approach I have taken, in creating what I think is an effective solution. The reason for this transparent thinking is mainly because I don't want you going into this as an unwilling partner. So many so-called environmental 'solutions' assume that the reader / watcher / listener will blindly obey whatever tasks are set before them, leading to an outcome where the burnished sun sets over the shimmering sea, and we all march off into Utopia arm-in-arm.

It doesn't happen that way.

I'm not saying the outcome won't be far better than what we have today (it can hardly be worse) but I am in no mood for half-measures and want something that actually does the job of fixing the problems we face; not putting little green sticking-plasters over the expanding cracks. What I am going to propose is radical, fundamental and frightening. It is also long-term, exhilarating and absolutely necessary. I would much rather scare people off who are not ready to make the commitment for a change of this scale than pretend they will be able to fix things by changing their electricity supplier, upgrading their cars and enlisting their friends in an orgy of 'greensumption'.[1]

Transparency is the by-word, then. By reading this chapter you will under-stand why I have proposed what I have later on in the book. If you don't like my train of thought, then you could try reading Chapters Seven, Ten and Eleven again and see if they clarify things; if that fails, then put this book down and come back to it in a few months' time. Before you do anything, I want you to feel comfortable in your own mind with what lies ahead.

Your Part in All This

In Chapter Thirteen I went some way towards describing how Industrial Civi-lization operates; in particular the methods used to make sure people are no threat to the dominant culture, and an explanation of where the power really lies. If you were expecting a conspiracy theory, which placed the elite members of society in some unassailable position, guiding our every move, then you proba-bly ended up disappointed. Yes, the rich and powerful do get a lot more material benefit from this unequal set-up, but they are also teetering on the brink of psy-chosis whenever the power rush gets too much. There are an increasing number of people who subscribe to 'New World Order' theories and the like; ideas that seem very appealing when you are stuck in a dark place, trying to get out. The internet is awash with conspiracy sites describing in minute detail every cartel, every meeting and every deal that takes place to ensure power is kept with the people who already have it.[2] The complex structures that actually exist to ensure economic growth continues are benefiting greatly from this paranoid activity.

Here's one example: suppose there is a large trawler that comes into port, day after day, its hold brimming with fish. Time passes, and the size of the other crews' hauls begin to diminish as the fish stocks are gradually depleted. The local population starts to become concerned about their future. One of the locals pro-poses a theory that the successful skipper is getting information about fresh shoals of fish from some mysterious source which has knowledge far beyond their understanding: a supernatural force, perhaps. This idea becomes accepted fact. Whispered discussions about this 'higher power' fill the inns for many nights, but nothing is ever done because there is nothing that *can* be done to defeat such powerful entities. Meanwhile, the successful skipper continues to bring home heavy catches, and the fishing stocks keep getting smaller.

It turns out that the successful boat is actually equipped with a better form of sonar than all the other boats, imported from another country where it is already widely used. This being a small isolated fishing port, nobody else is aware of this new technology. Had the other crews taken time to look closer to home and cleared their heads of thoughts about higher powers, they would have realized that one boat simply had better equipment than all the others. In order to protect the fishing stocks, their simple task then would have been to damage the sonar on the successful boat. Every time that sonar was repaired, they would damage it once again.

Ignoring the fact that the law may have eventually caught up with the protagonists – after all, *the law exists to maintain economic success above anything else* – their efforts in attacking the immediate cause of the heavy catches would have prevented the fish stocks falling for a while; but then other boats in other ports may have started to use this sonar, hitting the stocks even harder. If the fishermen wanted to deal with this further problem, they could have become even more ambitious, they might wish to block the supply lines for the import of sonar equipment; they might go to the country of origin, or enlist local help, to prevent the manufacture of the sonar. Eventually though, as this is the Culture of Maximum Harm, jealousy and greed would take over, and the other crews would realize it was in their immediate economic interests to install their own sonar systems, catch everything they could, and to hell with the terminal decline of the fishing stocks!

There are two lessons here. First, the answer to a problem usually lies in a far more mundane place than people realize; it is only the way that we have been manipulated that causes us to look in the wrong places for solutions: to the law, to business, to politics, to hope. We rarely look closer to home for answers. We rarely look in the mirror and question our own motives. Richard Heinberg, author of *Peak Everything*, has this to say about our addled state:

> As civilization has provided more and more for us, it's made us more and more infantile, so that we are less and less able to think for ourselves, less and less able to provide for ourselves, and this makes us more like a herd – we develop more of a herd mentality – where we take our cues from the people around us, the authority figures around us.[3]

Second, good intentions rarely last long in this culture. In a way, there was some higher power in play here: the power that makes people give up good intentions and follow the path chosen for them by Industrial Civilization. The fishermen stopped trying to prevent the problem getting worse and instead decided to put their own snouts into the trough. That's just the way it is: it's what we have been brought up to do.

When you think about it, humans in this culture seem to *want* conspiracy theories about strange things we don't understand; we seem to want unassailable forces running our lives from ivory towers; we seem to want this because we cannot accept that perhaps we are all in this together and the truth will hurt a bit too much. Driving a giant SUV, flying half-way across the world for pleasure, or buying the results of rainforest devastation because our culture makes these acts acceptable does not absolve the user – we must take some responsibility, for without accepting our role in this system then we have no chance of being freed from it.

You are part of the system.

*   *   *

The act of giving someone bad news is often easier than the thought of doing so: the period leading up to giving this news can get inside your head, invade your dreams and start to gnaw away at you; the act of passing on the news might be uncomfortable, but the moment is quickly gone, however difficult that moment is. The longer you leave things, the worse it feels. Receiving bad news works in much the same way; except that usually people don't realize they are going to get it. The thought that something bad might happen to you in the future; now, that really can play tricks with your mind – you try to avoid the situation, put it off for as long as you can but, as long as the outcome isn't truly terrible, the execution is rarely as bad as you imagine it might be.

In the movie *The Matrix*, the thought that something was wrong gnawed at Neo, the eventual perpetrator of change, for years; but when he found the truth, it was as much a liberation for him as it was a shock. Neo found that he could do something about his situation because he had knowledge, and because he fully understood his position. Once you accept things as they are – that you are part of the problem, and therefore you have a part to play in the solution – you actually start to feel better, as though the weight of ages has been lifted from your shoulders.

You are part of the system; you have to take responsibility for your part of the problem: how does that feel?

Your place in the system is as a component in a massive food web. Like all food webs, it is driven by energy; physical energy sources like oil, gas, coal and radioactive materials drive the machines that ensure money keeps floating to the top of the vat where the Elites skim it off to add to their wealth. If you are resourceful or in a role that holds some status, you can have some of this wealth too, and the material trappings that come with it. Without the energy that drives the web, though, there is no money, and there is no web. It is not just the oil, gas, coal and various sources of radiation that keep the web operating though – people are equally vital, more so, in fact. Unless people run the machines, staff the shops, build the products, drive the lorries, create the advertisements, read the news and enforce the law, the web will collapse upon itself, bringing the entire hierarchy down with it.

Think back to the chapter about cod. The cod are positioned high up in the food web in terms of the amount of food energy they require to remain alive: they operate at a high trophic level, but without the organisms at the lower levels – the sand eels, the tiny copepods and the minute plankton – they cannot exist. Without the cod, the scavenging hagfish might start to suffer (although the windfall of bodies would provide rich pickings for a long time) but the sand eels one level down would be delighted: they would flourish. Think of your place in civilization; think of your job, or your role in society, and how it relates to the people sitting right at the top, or even those somewhere in the middle, aspiring to move upwards. What do you want to be, a wheel or a cog?[4]

Yes, you are part of the system; but you are far more important than the people higher up in the web: you are the engine, the energy source, the reason for its continuation. You *are* the system. Without your co-operation, without your faith, the system would have no energy and then it would cease to exist.

Building Solutions

Industrial Civilization has to end; this was made clear in Part Three. There is no doubt that sooner or later it will collapse, taking much of its subjected population with it: oil crisis, credit crunch, environmental disaster, pandemic – whatever the reason, it will eventually fail in a catastrophic manner. This may not happen for 50 or 100 years, by which time global environmental collapse will be inevitable. That is one option; the other is for it to die, starting now, in such a way that those who have the nerve and the nous to leave it behind can save themselves and the natural environment that we are totally dependent upon.

Be assured, no one is going to go into the heart of the 'machine' and rip it limb from limb, because the machine has no heart, it has no brain. This civilization is what we have ended up with after a series of deliberate (and sometimes accidental) events intended primarily to give power and wealth to a privileged few. What we have now got is an entire culture that values economic growth above everything else, a toolkit of malicious methods for keeping that cultural belief in place, and an elite, ever-changing group of people who have become pathological megalomaniacs, unable to cope with the sheer amount of wealth and power this culture allows them to have.

Given that we all appear to be in this together, how on Earth is it possible to bring down something so monumental? The answer lies in the nature of Industrial Civilization itself – its key features are also its greatest weaknesses.

Take the simple article of faith that is Economic Growth. We have, I guess, agreed that there is nothing sustainable about it – however you cut the pie, the natural environment is bound to lose out all the time the economy is growing. In order to sustain a 'healthy' level of economic growth, the consuming public has to know that when they spend some money they will still have some left. The definition of 'having money to spare' has been stretched out of all proportion in recent years as creditors have extended people's ability to spend beyond their means, while still thinking they are solvent. Whether that spare money is in the form of savings, cash, investments or credit, though, the important factor is that potential consumers will stop being potential consumers as soon as they realize there is no more money left to spend. Having a paid job is one way of ensuring (at least for a while) that you can pay for things; in fact, this is the major factor affecting consumer confidence.

Across the world, governments and the corporations that control them are in a constant cycle of measuring consumer confidence. The USA Conference Board[5] provides the model for most of the indices used by the analysts. The importance of confidence to economies is critical:

> In the most simplistic terms, when . . . confidence is trending up, consumers spend money, indicating a healthy economy. When confidence is trending down, consumers are saving more than they are spending, indicating the economy is in trouble. The idea is that the more confident people feel about the stability of their incomes, the more likely they are to make purchases.[6]

This creates an interesting situation: it is possible, indeed probable, that to initiate collapse within an economy, and thus bring down a major pillar of Industrial Civilization, the public merely have to lose *confidence* in the system. This is reflected in other, related parts of civilization: following the attacks on the World Trade Center in 2001, the global air transport industry underwent a mini-collapse; the BSE outbreak in the UK in the early 1990s caused not only a temporary halt in the sale of UK beef but also a significant drop in global beef sales. Anything that can severely undermine confidence in a major part of the global economy can undermine civilization.

The need for confidence is a *psychological* feature of Industrial Civilization; there are also two *physical* features that work together to create critical weaknesses. The first of these is the complexity that so many systems now exhibit. I mentioned the 'farm to fork' concept in Chapter Eleven, indicating that the distance travelled by food items is becoming increasingly unsustainable. Overall, the methods used to produce food on a large scale, in particular the high energy cost involved in cultivating land, feeding livestock, transforming raw materials into processed foods, chilling and freezing food, retailing it and finally bringing it home to cook, not only demonstrate huge inefficiencies but also expose the number of different stages involved in such a complex system. The same applies to electricity: in most cases electricity is generated by the burning or decay of a non-renewable material, which has to be removed from the ground in the form of an ore, processed and then transported in bulk to the generation facility. Once the electricity is generated, in a facility with a capacity of anything up to five gigawatts,[7] it has to be distributed, initially over a series of very high voltage lines, and then through a number of different power transformation stages (all the time losing energy) until it reaches the place where the power is needed. Both of these examples – and there are many more, including global money markets and television broadcast systems – consist of a great many stages; most of which, if they individually fail, can cause the entire system to collapse.

The second of this potentially debilitating pair of features is the overdependence on hubs. Systems are usually described as containing links and nodes, a node being the thing that joins one or more links together; a road is a link, and the junctions that connect the different roads together are the nodes. Systems that have many links and nodes are called 'networks'; food webs are networks, with the energy users being the nodes, and the energy flows being the links. Networks made up of links that develop over time, based on need, are referred to as 'random' networks: the US interstate highway system is one such random network, as is the set of tunnels created by a family of rabbits. Networks created intentionally to fulfil a planned purpose, usually with the potential to expand, are called 'scale-free' networks, good examples being the routes of major airlines,electricity transmission grids and the food distribution networks of major supermarket chains.

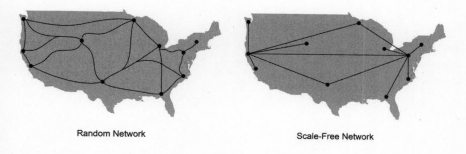

Random Network   Scale-Free Network

Figure 20: The two major types of infrastructure network

A node within a network that joins together a great many links is known as a hub; Industrial Civilization uses hubs a lot. Thomas Homer-Dixon describes the situation like this:

Although researchers long assumed that most networks were like the interstate highway system, recent study shows that a surprising number of the world's networks – both natural and human-made – are more like the air traffic system. These scale-free networks include most ecosystems, the World Wide Web, large electrical grids, petroleum distribution systems, and modern food processing and supply networks. If a scale-free network loses a hub, it can be disastrous, because many other nodes depend on that hub.

Scale-free networks are particularly vulnerable to intentional attack: if someone wants to wreck the whole network, he simply needs to identify and destroy some of its hubs.[8]

In July 2001, a railway tunnel fire in Baltimore, USA caused the shutdown of a large part of the downtown area due to the heat generated within the tunnel and the health risk posed by an acid spill. Over the next few days the surrounding rail networks were affected by the extra freight traffic diverted onto other lines, causing a number of bottlenecks in the greater Baltimore area.[9] There was also one unexpected impact: internet access across much of the USA slowed down dramatically. "The Howard Street Tunnel houses an internet pipe serving seven of the biggest US Internet Information Service Providers (ISPs), which were identified as those ISPs experiencing backbone slowdowns. The fire burned through the pipe and severed fibre optic cable used for voice and data transmission, causing backbone slowdowns for ISPs such as Metromedia Fiber Network, Inc., WorldCom, Inc., and PSINet, Inc."[10] The Howard Street tunnel was a major artery for internet traffic; its severance caused the same impact that the destruction of a major network hub would cause.

When you combine a set of key complex systems consisting of a large number of interdependent components, with networks that are increasingly becoming dependent on a small number of hubs, you create a structure that is extremely sensitive; irrespective of any safeguards that may have been built into it. Civilization is built upon these complex, interdependent systems, and these systems rely on networks to keep the flows of energy, data, money and materials moving. Civilization also depends upon its human constituents (you and I) having complete confidence in the way it operates: it needs faith. In both physical and psychological terms, Industrial Civilization is extremely fragile: one big push and it will go.

*   *   *

These are just thoughts, ideas, imperfect sketches for something that could work if it's done properly. I can't predict how things are going to turn out, even if what I am going to propose does succeed; nobody can predict something that hasn't started yet. My train of thought won't stop with the end of this book, but here's where I am at the moment:

- The world is changing rapidly and dangerously, and humans are the main reason for this change. If we fail to allow the Earth's physical systems to return to their natural state, then these systems will break down, taking humanity with them.

- Humans are part of nature; we have developed in such a way that we think we are more than just another organism; but in ecological terms we are irrelevant.

- Regardless of our place in the tree of life, humans always have been and always will be the most important things to humanity. We are survival machines.

- Our failure to connect the state of the planet with our own inarguable need to survive will ensure our fate is sealed. This must not happen.

- In order to bring us to a state of awareness, we must learn how to connect with the real world; the world we depend upon for our survival. We are all capable of connecting.

- Our lack of connection with the real world is a condition that has been created by the culture we live in. The various tools used to keep us disconnected from the real world are what make Industrial Civilization the destructive thing that it is.

- To understand how to remove Industrial Civilization we must realize that we, along with everyone else in Industrial Civilization, are the system.

- Industrial Civilization is complex, faith-driven and extremely sensitive to change and disruption. It will collapse on its own, but not in time to save humanity.

I have read a lot of books and a lot more articles and essays related to the problems that we face. I have heard people talking on the radio and on television proposing how everything can be sorted out. I have seen some wonderful movies that describe where we are going, how we got here and where we might be going. Some of these works reach an ecstatic crescendo before petering out in a gentle rain of hope. Some of them tell me what we should be doing; when it is obvious that the things suggested will not help, and could even make things worse. Some of them tell me I should not be looking for 'solutions' to the problem at all – that there are no solutions, no cures, probably no chance at all. I haven't read, heard or watched anything that could actually make things better.

Have I missed something?

I don't think so. For one thing, I don't subscribe to the idea that there are no solutions, although there is no way of knowing if I have left something out – I probably have – and no way of completely tidying up the fallout that will inevitably result from the massive shift in society that is required. But that doesn't mean you can't have solutions, providing you know what the problem is. I know what the problem is, and so do you: at its heart, it is not environmental change and it is not humanity itself – it is that we are disconnected from what it means to be human. The solution is the answer to this simple question:

How can we reconnect with the real world?

I'm not asking people to help build a new set of systems, construct a new world order, design a new future – that kind of ambition is the stuff of civilization; the stuff of control, hierarchy and power. Connection is the most liberating and most powerful step you can take. If you know what is happening, if you know why it matters, if you know how to connect, and if you have the strength to reject the way this culture disconnects us, then you can change your own world, at the very least. That is the start of everything.

There are two dimensions to the solution, both of which I want to briefly explain before I move on to the solution itself. The reason I am using dimensions is because the solution is not simple; it is much easier to understand something complex if you can break it down a bit.

The First Dimension: Cutting Across

In this dimension lie the different actions that can be carried out to deal with the problem itself: our lack of connection. There are a few different aspects to this, some of which are more useful than others; but the nature of them makes it difficult to just make lists – they do tend to cut across each other, depending on how you approach the problem. For instance, if we assume (correctly) that to bring civilization to its knees, economic growth has to stop, then it would seem logical to directly attack the instruments of the global economy: the investment banks, clearing houses, treasuries and the various things that link these nodes together. The problem is that, however exciting an idea this is, it doesn't deal with the deeper problem – that civilization actually wants economic growth to take place: unless this mindset is removed, then the systems will just be rebuilt in order to re-establish a growing economy.

Even more fundamentally, unless the reasons why people feel that economic growth is necessary (i.e. the Tools of Disconnection) are removed, then very few people are likely to spontaneously reconnect with the real world and reject economic growth. You can see straight away why a number of different dimensions are necessary. To put it simply, though, the 'cutting across' dimension consists of those actions that (a) remove the forces that stop us connecting, (b) help people to reconnect and (c) ensure that the Tools of Disconnection cannot be re-established.

The Second Dimension: Drilling Down

Almost every 'solution' I have come across only deals with the problem at one or, at most, two levels. I feel like a razor-blade salesman now, by saying I have a three-level solution ("Not one, not two, but three levels of problem-solving!"), but it's no accident there are three levels. I started thinking about the nature of the problem at a fairly superficial level – the kind of level most of the 'one million ways to green your world' lists pitch at – and immediately realized that, while suggesting what can be done to make things better is necessary, it assumes that there is a huge mass of people who actually *want* to do these things. You know already that very few people are connected enough to go ahead and do the, quite frankly, very radical things that need to be done: two more levels are necessary.

The second level, therefore, looks at the way individuals and groups of people change over time, and how the necessary changes in attitude can be transmitted throughout the population in a structured way, then accelerated beyond what conventional theory tells us is possible. I am only going to touch on the theory of this as it is pretty dry stuff, but the practical side of it makes for very interesting reading. The beautiful thing about using this multi-level approach is that activities can be taking place at the first level, amongst the people who are already connected and ready to act, which then makes the process of motivating the more stubborn sectors of the population progressively easier.

The final level is the most fundamental of all, without which none of this can happen. It's all very well me saying what people should do and how different sectors of the population can be progressively mobilized, but unless the individuals involved are ready to be engaged, nothing will happen. This level has to deal with the process of engagement and preparing people so that when asked, they actually want to act. The reason this is almost never addressed is a combination of (a) writers who make the assumption that things will turn out OK (the 'hope' trap), and (b) that this is a very difficult thing to do. I am going to attempt to resolve this.

Chapter Fifteen

Making the Change

Where do we need to end up? I suppose the best answer I can give at this stage is: humanity in a state of connection with the world around it, living with a dramatically reduced impact such that the Earth's natural systems can once again function normally – any further, and things start to get much more difficult to predict. In many ways that simple, non-prescriptive statement is exactly how it should be. My decision not to offer you a fully mapped-out, single new way of living, beyond the wonderful state of being connected was inspired by Daniel Quinn:

> There is a clear sense in which ours is just a special case of a much wider story, written in the living community itself from the beginning, some five billion years ago: There is no one right way for ANYTHING to live.
>
> This is how we humans got from there to here, by enacting this story, and it worked sensationally well until about ten thousand years ago, when one very odd culture sprang into being obsessed with the notion that there must be a single right way for people to live – and indeed a single right way to do almost everything.[1]

You realize now that our disconnected state is the outcome of this sprawling homogenous system that has one aim: to have more of everything. The way the vast majority of us are living has been decided for us by the culture that we live in, of which we are an intrinsic part. Because they are only present in civilizations, *neither governments nor corporations have any part to play in the solution.* Despite the protestations of the mainstream environmental movement, it is obvious now that the best thing corporations and governments can do is to shut up shop and leave humans to go back to the emphatically less destructive beings they were before Industrial Civilization took control. My job in all of this is to get us to a point where we can make the decision to change for ourselves – with a clear, open, connected mind, unfettered by blind ambition, uncontaminated by civilization.

Level One: Ways to Live

Given that this book's aim is to regain our lost connections with the real world, and given what I have said about the superficial nature of 'green' lists, it might seem odd that I am now going to describe some key 'greening' actions: actions that will dramatically reduce our impact on the natural environment. The reason for this is that I believe the best actions are those with multiple impacts – the direct impact of the actions I am going to propose is, indeed, to reduce the amount of greenhouse gases being emitted by human activity, reduce the amount of ecological degradation taking place, and to allow the Earth's natural biological and chemical processes to begin to return to a stable state. The very welcome side-effect of these actions is they trigger the rapid reversal of the industrial or capital-based economy.[2] Just as the success of Industrial Civilization is defined in terms of economic growth, a lack of economic growth will cause Industrial Civilization to break down:[3]

> Modern capitalism's stability – and increasingly the global economy's stability – requires the cultivation of material discontent, endlessly rising personal consumption, and the steady economic growth this consumption generates.[4]

The author of this statement goes on to insist that a failure to grow will result in rapid and fierce societal breakdown: a 'zero-sum conflict' (i.e. a battle to gain the most of a finite resource). To a person rooted in the Culture of Maximum Harm, that sounds like a good reason to maintain economic growth forever; to ensure there is always enough to go round to satisfy an insatiable desire for more of everything. To me this sounds like a system that is fatally flawed and needs to be removed from the face of the Earth, before the inevitable ecological collapse brings it down in far more horrible circumstances. Whether you agree with this thesis depends on whether you place any value on having a liberated, connected and survivable future.

There is a third role that these actions fulfil, and that is of engaging individuals with their actions; in other words, allowing people to think about the impact – both positive and negative – of the things they do. As an example, simply by localizing your food supply, you have to understand the processes by which your food gets to you, and thus you become engaged. Even deciding not to do something (by which I mean, making a conscious decision to reject a suggestion), you still have to engage your thought processes in the issues. Not surprisingly, this works at many levels, particularly Level Three: Influencing, which we will come to later on.

The following list is not exhaustive, but based on my own work, and that of countless other writers, scientists and thinkers; they are the things which I believe to be potentially most effective in fulfilling the joint purpose set out above. The quicker and more thoroughly the suggestions are followed, the more rapid the impact will be. I have intentionally left out the act of Connecting from this list as it is implicit in everything that humans do in their lives – if you need a reminder on the reasons for connecting and how to do it, please re-read Chapters Eleven and Twelve. Finally, there is one more item near the end of the list which may not seem to fit in with the rest – the act of Undermining – but in leaving it out I would be ignoring an essential tool in the armoury of anyone truly serious about reclaiming their liberty: it can be as much a constructive action as all of the rest I have listed.

Consuming

There are commonly thought to be three R's in environmental parlance: reduce, reuse and recycle. However, very few people in this culture bother doing the first two because we have been led to believe that doing the last one is enough – which would be funny if it weren't so serious. It's time to add a couple more R's to the list, and get rid of one: here are my four:

Reduce: Do I need to buy this thing at all?

Repair: Can I repair or refurbish this thing, or have somebody do it for me?

Reuse: Can I buy or obtain this thing, or something similar, pre-owned?

Respect: Can I look after this thing better?

To take the simple act of reducing: if every person in Industrial Civilization were to reduce their consumption of all goods and services by 25%, this would cause a contraction in the size of the economy (in fact, even if everyone just bought the same amount of stuff each year the economy would start to sputter!) sufficient to cause serious problems for speculators and governments alike. If you focus that overall reduction on non-essentials – such as consumer electronics, leisure goods and services, and cosmetic home improvements – then those parts of the economy will fall apart rapidly. It is those parts of the industrial economy that maintain overall economic growth, because they take up the slack left by the 'essential' economy (staple food, healthcare, utilities, education etc.)[5] which, because of its non-consumer nature, grows very little or not at all. Giving up a new TV or a cinema trip won't do anything to save the world, but it will curtail overall economic growth and also hit advertising and promotional (i.e. Tools of Disconnection) budgets. That said, reducing your consumption of 'essential' items, such as energy, also has an obvious environmental benefit, and again helps to move the economy in the right direction. It is vital to remember that *we are not consumers*; we are individuals who may or may not choose to buy things – individuals who cannot be pigeonholed into convenient categories for the benefit of the economy.

Repairing, which includes refurbishing and renewing parts of the things that you already have, makes the act of reducing the purchase of new things far easier. Of course, Industrial Civilization will try to convince you that you need to upgrade that thing because having the latest thing is part of living the consumer dream: but there is more to repairing than just keeping the same thing functional – it also brings a sense of pride and ownership. A chair with a broken leg is, in the eyes of the consumer culture, crying out to be replaced with a new chair – hell! Go and by a whole set of them! But if you insert a small piece of dowel, and then glue or screw the leg back in place, you now have a chair that *you repaired*. How could you just throw it away now? Repairing and building from scratch – things we have clearly forgotten how to do, by virtue of the off-the-shelf economy – are ways of connecting with the belongings you have: they allow you to Respect what you have. Once you start to respect the things you have, then you don't want to throw them away – and you treat them with care. Manufacturers may give goods 'planned obsolescence', so that they stop working after a short time, but you can extend the lifetime of something indefinitely if you look after it.

Then there is the important act of Reusing. Logging onto eBay, or going to the charity shop is certainly one way of reusing pre-owned goods – again, this results in the reduction of goods that are bought new, causing the economy to contract – but these activities can be brought closer to home by selling things directly that you no longer need, or just giving them away. Two simple activities are almost absent from the money-based lives we now lead: donation and bartering. Donation is just giving something away. Don't want that table that has been cluttering up the shed? Just give it to someone. Want a bicycle but don't even have a broken one to repair? Go and see what other people have thrown out in their skip or dumpster. Donation can work both ways. Barter, on the other hand, always works in two (or more) ways: if you have a service you can offer, or something you have made or grown, then exchange it for something someone else has. I may have a glut of tomatoes this summer from my garden, and someone up the road has some seasoned firewood I could use in my burner.

Donation and barter are invisible activities as far as Industrial Civilization is concerned, because they are of no value to the market economy; but they are perfect as tools for beginning a new way of life that doesn't require the exchange of cash or the needless production of goods. One measure of how threatened a civilization is, is the laws it makes: George Bush Jr. and his economic advisers may have found it prudent in 2008 to bribe middle- and high-income earners to spend more money on consumer goods,[6] but the moment certain activities start to threaten the industrial economy you can be sure they will be made illegal.

In all cases where an activity has a negative impact on the natural environment, and hence human survival, *the act of reducing must always be the first option in the decision-making process.*

Eating

There are three facets to eating that should all be taken into account: how much you eat, what you eat, and how it is produced. It would be easy to fill an entire book with analysis on this very emotive subject – emotive because what you put in your body, in a very real sense, defines what you are – but a few words on each should be sufficient to make things clear. First, how much you eat goes back to the last section on consuming. Obviously the less you eat, the less energy, soil, chemicals and labour is required to produce it; but there is clearly a minimum amount of food that can be healthily consumed depending on what kind of life you lead – it's about 2,500 calories daily for a man, and 2,000 for a woman. If you are eating more food than you need, then reducing it will go some way to reducing your impact, but not very far.

Obesity is a major health issue for societies – not just in highly Westernized areas, but also in those areas just beginning to be touched by the aggressive hand of commercialism: why eat a sandwich when you can have a Big Mac; why have a glass of water when you can have a Coke? Overweight and obese people, surprisingly, aren't eating more calories than those people of a healthy weight – they may even be eating fewer, as those with very physical lives have to consume more to stay healthy – but they are eating more calories contained in fats and processed sugars.[7] Obesity is a symptom of the lifestyle that most benefits the consumer culture: sedentary, digital and mechanized living; a diet dominated by processed, high-profit foods. What you eat, the second facet, is very important here.

As I showed earlier, unless you are self-sufficient, a diet containing a high volume of meat is environmentally unsustainable; so the first, and simplest way of reducing the environmental impact of a diet is to reduce the amount of meat contained in it. As I also alluded to in Chapter Fourteen, a diet dominated by meat or processed foods requires far more stages of production than a diet which is based around things that come straight out of the ground and into your mouth. Obviously some element of processing is required for many foods, but the fewer stages that are required, the lower the environmental impact of that food, and the less the user of that food depends upon the industrial food-processing system.

This takes us neatly into the third facet: how your food is produced. As I see it, there are three skills that every person will have to have in order to survive the future (whether it changes by accident or design): the ability to make simple things, including building basic structures, from scratch; the ability to cook good, nutritious meals from basic ingredients; and the ability to grow, and rear if necessary, your own food. Step back only a few decades and it would have been extremely unusual for someone not to be able to do these things, yet it seems that part of the disconnection that civilization has forced upon us is to make us lose these critical life skills. *We have become dependent upon the various systems of this culture to provide us with what we, until recently, could provide for ourselves*: right down to the insipid, packaged ready-meals that masquerade as food.

Since giving up paid work as part of the industrial economy a year ago – making myself no longer 'economically viable' – I have learnt to repair and make lots of things from scratch; cook a huge variety of meals with whatever food is local, in season and from my store cupboard; and, starting with herbs and leafy vegetables, have gradually learnt how to grow my own food. Taken together, these three things have made me feel extraordinarily liberated and given me the confidence to do more. Not surprisingly, I have also become connected with the things I have made, the food I use, and the small patch of earth that will be providing my family with more and more good stuff as time goes on.

I wonder how long it will be before growing food in back yards is made illegal.

Travelling

There are two major types of transport: motorized and non-motorized. They are easy to distinguish, especially in the eyes of a child who hasn't yet been indoctrinated in the ways of the machine: cars, trucks, trains, aeroplanes, mechanized boats, motorcycles and coaches are all motorized; legs, bicycles, sailboats and animal-drawn vehicles are not motorized. Deciding between a mode of transport that is very energy-efficient (non-motorized) and one that is not (motorized) is simple, really; although you would be forgiven for thinking it is not. You see, manufacturers, and all of the other vested interests involved in a particular mode of transport – especially the money-rich car and air industries – will do anything to ensure you stick to that mode of transport. Aircraft manufacturers make a big deal of the energy-saving potential of the new Airbus-A380 or Boeing 787, whilst conveniently glossing over the need to burn tonnes of fuel to keep an enormous lump of metal in the air. Car manufacturers (along with their good friends in the oil industry) bring out all sorts of new 'green' vehicles, whilst at the same time fighting to ensure that fuel economy regulations are kept strictly voluntary.[8] Changing the way we travel is about far more than changing the model of vehicle or the airline we use – these are blatant distractions from the real issue – it is about the method of transportation we use, and the distance and rate by which we travel in the first place.

In essence, the method we use to get around is far more important than distinguishing between different versions of the same method. Some recent work concluded that the humble bicycle was the most efficient (land-based) form of transport by a long way,[9] which makes perfect sense when you consider the combination of gear system, efficient traction wheels and most importantly, being powered by a human being, rather than a combustion or electrical engine. Human beings produce only 100g of CO_2 in their breath cycling or walking twenty kilometres, compared with a car producing between three and six kilograms of carbon dioxide.[10] However, this kind of exertion would require about 500 calories, which if taken in the form of beef would emit around seven kilograms of carbon dioxide.[11] This latter information has, not surprisingly, been used as a reason to drive rather than walk[12] – assuming people eat nothing but beef. If you have an average global diet, though, with only 15% of your calories from meat, then the total carbon dioxide emissions of human and bicycle (or on foot) are well under a kilogram.

The point of this analysis is not only to debunk some of the more fatuous arguments put forward by transport industry lobbyists, but also to show how obvious it is – by using a little bit of common sense – that motorized transport is not the way forwards, regardless how 'green' a manufacturer may claim their vehicle is. Bear in mind, also, that a vegan (based on discussions in Part One) would emit less than half a kilogram of carbon dioxide all-in over that twenty kilometres: far better even than a fully laden bus or coach. Self-propelled, non-motorized transport is a threat to civilization; which is the perfect reason to switch the engine off for good:

> The cyclist creates everything from almost nothing, becoming the most energy-efficient of all moving animals and machines and, as such, has a disingenuous ability to challenge the entire value system of a society. Cyclists don't consume enough. The bicycle may be too cheap, too available, too healthy, too independent and too equitable for its own good. In an age of excess it is minimal and has the subversive potential to make people happy in an economy fuelled by consumer discontent.[13]

More important even than method, though, is distance and speed. Culturally, the world is getting faster, not only in terms of transportation but also the accelerating flow of information intended to keep us consuming, and keep us disconnected from the real world. The automobile made door-to-door rapid transportation possible, as well as being responsible for a large proportion of the anthropogenic greenhouse effect. In every industrial nation, the car is king, with the aeroplane coming up a close second – able to take people further and more quickly than any other form of mass transport. The 'need for speed' is a symptom of our perceived lack of time: no longer is the journey part of the experience; it is merely an adjunct to the destination we must reach. The relationship between speed and distance is two-way, with great distances being achievable due to the great speeds we can attain, and great speeds being 'necessary' due to the great distances we wish to travel. The desire for extreme speed and the desire to travel great distances are not natural human instincts – Industrial Civilization, wishing to squeeze more and more profit out of synthetic desires, has placed them in our minds. The reason speed creates a frisson is because humans are, rightly, afraid of its potential to injure or kill – yet travelling faster than our legs can carry us is made out to be a positive thing, largely because there is money to be made out of it. The reason we desire to travel long distances is because the travel industry encourages us to.

About fifteen or sixteen years ago I made the decision to travel only within my own country: not for any jingoistic reason, but simply because I realized that there was so much to discover and enjoy close to home – I didn't need anywhere else. Around the same time as making this decision (and perhaps they were related), I completed a transport study of the road network on the small island of Guernsey. What I discovered was that, before 1800 (around the time when roads were built to protect against Napoleonic invasion) the vast majority of travel took place within individual parishes, little more than a couple of miles across: a holiday was a week in a neighbouring parish. Travel took place from home to the market, to friends and family, to places of worship and to places of work – all of which were within easy walking distance.

The logical response to the immense pressure on us to travel further, faster and by more technically complex forms of transport is to draw back; to only travel where and in a way that you consider absolutely essential, not that which has been decided by civilization on your behalf. This is the way humanity was until very recently: *having what we needed close to us* (like food, family and friends), learning what the local environment had to offer and making the best of it. It may not be possible where you are to live in such a way, but then perhaps that is the best reason of all to step outside of the system and make your own decisions.

Living

Everyone needs a place to call home, but not every place people call home is a place desirable to live in. Without clean water, clean air and an appropriate level of shelter and warmth, no one can reasonably be expected to live for long: yet across the world, the civilized world of cities, industry and democratic governments; people live in conditions that an Inuit, an Apache, a !Kung or a Taíno would never call 'home'. Those at the bottom live in conditions of grinding poverty, kept afloat by the crumbs of the industrial economy and the daily promises of material fulfilment. Those at the bottom of civilization are far worse off as regards the real needs of humans than most of those who lived (and still live) 'uncivilized' lives.

Those above the breadline, living in Industrial Civilization, have the basic necessities of a fulfilled life: then they are exhorted to pack these lives out with excess as soon as a bit more money becomes available. The excess – the entertainment system, the air conditioning, the conservatory, the fully-fitted kitchen – provides some superficial pleasure, while at the same time driving a wedge between individuals, their families, their communities and nature. The plastic bubble of modern living provides the perfect cultural prophylactic: a barrier between you and the real world.

Is there no middle ground?

In this culture, I don't believe there is, unless somehow you are able to distance yourself from every attempt to disconnect you. There reaches a point, though, when you can go no further: you cannot go beyond civilization if you exist within civilization.[14] When I suggest a raft of different means for reversing the damage and disconnection caused by our consuming, our eating and our travelling, I know that at some point we are all going to have to say, "I would love to, but I can't, because the system doesn't allow it." That is the point at which you need to step outside of the system, and go beyond civilization.

If you consider the home – the typical brick, wood or concrete-built home of a typical Westerner, with space and water heating, running water and sewerage, lighting and various electrical appliances – certainly there are huge steps that can be made in order to reduce its environmental impact. There are huge steps that can be taken to reduce the dependency of that home, and that of the people living in it, on the infrastructure laid down by the various profit-making utilities – some of which are even recommended by authorities and suppliers. Most of these run off the tongue of the average 'consumer': turn your heating and your air conditioning down; switch off lights and appliances; buy energy-efficient devices; have showers instead of baths; install double-glazing and loft insulation. There are options for going a bit further, too: you can install solar heating and electricity; you can install a wood-burner for space-heating, and also use it to heat water; you can install ground or air-sourced heat pumps, wind turbines, combined heat and power; you can plant cooling greenery, fix louvers and shutters, add passive solar capture systems. Use some common sense, and you can make quite a big difference.

But there is a catch: governments and utility companies assume that most people won't do these things, so the overall impact of these actions is minimal; as soon as the majority of people start doing these things, the energy companies start to cry foul – the grants dry up and the exhortations mysteriously stop. This suggests that, as with consuming, eating and travelling, a large number of people changing the impact of their daily lives will start to hurt the economy; and that is why governments, utilities and the environmental organizations that usually follow their lead, stop short of asking for major societal change in the way that people live within Industrial Civilization. It is not in their interests for things to change too much – in fact it would be commercial suicide.

Just how easy is it to really take yourself 'off grid'? At what point do you decide that you don't need mains water or sewerage? When exactly do you ask the local authorities to stop collecting your trash? Just about the point at which your use of energy and water, and your production of waste, have dropped to less than the level of a 'civilized' person. That's the point at which you probably start experiencing freedom.

Working

At what age do you think your working future is planned out for you? I think by now you wouldn't be surprised that the answer is: 'from birth'. There is a separate section in this chapter called Educating, but it's nothing to do with the education system and it is nothing to do with on-the-job learning or career paths; after all, working is what people have been brought up to do in Industrial Civilization, and not just any old work. If you cast your mind back to Chapter Eight, where we thought about population, you will remember that it was the Industrial Revolution that was largely responsible for the beginning of the population explosion: a mass of willing slaves brought up in the cities to be components of the industrial machine. To create wealth you need product; to create product you need people.

There were a few who saw what was going on and realized that some of the most brutal aspects of physical work needed changing: the reputations of the Great Philanthropists of the West – Titus Salt, Lord Leverhulme, Joseph Rowntree – have stood the test of time, mellowed into a whimsical tale of pure goodness; ignoring the fact that the philanthropists were largely ensuring that their workforces remained loyal and hard-working. To be blunt, working during the Industrial Revolution in the West was hell; working in the new Industrial Revolution in the sweatshops, mines and factories of China, India, Indonesia, Vietnam . . . different sets of eyes, but the same vision of hell. Time may have passed, but all that has really changed is the location.

Yet, incredibly, the participants see such conditions as a necessary evil. Unionization, a living wage and the promise that the company will do its best not to shorten your life is the best that can be hoped for. Such 'victories' make life tolerable for those people working to make the shoes you wear, the food you eat and the televisions you watch, but they do not change the fact that we are all part of the machine. The education system is where it starts.

For centuries governments and dictators have twisted a population's knowledge base to their own ends. We may look back in history, and gape at the ritual burning or enforced suppression of the works of authors whose printed ideas did not match those of the accepted orthodoxy, but the flames are closer than we like to admit. The Nazi elite stirred up hatred of anti-Nazi materials in a co-ordinated "synchronization of culture",[15] while only a decade later the US government elite stirred up hatred of left-leaning beliefs in a co-ordinated exhumation of so-called Communist sympathizers; the Chinese government installed the Great Chinese Firewall to suppress 'immoral' internet access, while at the same time the US government continue to control information coming out of wartime Iraq and Afghanistan through the use of 'embedded journalists'. In the last few decades, stories of censored schoolbooks in far-off lands have made those in supposedly more enlightened nations cringe,[16] yet in a culture that apparently promotes freedom of thought and expression, teachers are forced to become mouthpieces for the Culture of Maximum Harm:

> The Government has worked with partners from the statutory and voluntary and community sectors to define what the five outcomes mean. We have identified 25 specific aims for children and young people and the support needed from parents, carers and families in order to achieve those aims. . . .[17]

This is from the UK Government's Every Child Matters programme, which "sets out the national framework for local change programmes to build services around the needs of children and young people so that we maximize opportunity and minimize risk."[18] Twenty-five aims, supposedly to promote the well-being of children, yet containing the following items:

- Ready for school

- Attend and enjoy school

- Achieve stretching national educational standards at primary school

- Achieve stretching national educational standards at secondary school

- Develop enterprising behaviour

- Engage in further education, employment or training on leaving school

- Ready for employment

- Access to transport and material goods

- Parents, carers and families are supported to be economically active

National educational standards; enterprising behaviour; ready for employment; access to material goods; economically active – the progression is there for everyone to see. Even when veiled as being in order to 'improve the lives of children', the educational system is little more than an instruction manual for creating little wheels and cogs. I urge you to look at your own national curriculum, searching for words like Citizenship, Enterprise and Skills – it won't take long to find the real motivation behind the education system where you live. "A child in the work culture is asked, 'What do you want to be?', rather than 'What do you want to do?' or 'Where do you want to go?' The brainwashing to become some kind of worker starts young and never stops." [19]

This is a wake-up call: look at the work you do and how it neatly fits into the industrial machine, ensuring economic growth and continued global degradation; think about your job and what part it plays in ensuring we remain disconnected from the real world; read your children's books, talk to their teachers – find out how your own flesh and blood is being shaped into a machine part. As we are encouraged to work more and more in order to feed our inherited desire for material wealth and artificial realities, we lose touch with the real world; we pack our children off to day centres and child-minders in order that we can remain economic units, and stop being parents; most of us work to produce things that nobody needs, and we are unable to perceive the things that we do need – food, shelter, clean air, clean water, love, friendship, connection.

The vast majority of us don't need to do the job we do. The lucky few, who through chance or design have found work that is a fulfilling part of their lives rather than their lives being a slave to work, provide examples for the rest of us. Once you decide to break out of this cycle for all the right reasons and reduce your expenses to the bare minimum by refusing to follow the instructions of civilization, leaving your job and taking on something that provides you with a real living becomes easy.

Reproducing

Some truths are far harder to give than others; one of them is that people will die in huge numbers when civilization collapses. Step outside civilization and you stand a pretty good chance of surviving the inevitable; stay inside and when the crash happens there may be nothing at all you can do to save yourself. The speed and intensity of the crash will depend an awful lot on the number of people who are caught up in it: greater numbers of people have more structural needs – such as food production, power generation and healthcare – which need to be provided by the collapsing civilization; greater numbers of people create more social tension and more opportunity for extremism and violence; greater numbers of people create more sewage, more waste, more bodies – all of which cause further illness and death.

Civilization is defined, more than anything else, by the cities in which it primarily operates: as the cities get larger, they must import more and more energy, food, materials and finished goods from a larger area outside of the city; and they must also become more complex. You cannot simply make systems bigger to support larger numbers of people; above a certain threshold a 'step change' is required, and a layer of complexity has to be added – such as requiring a distribution system to feed a million people, compared with a single farmer who can directly feed a few dozen people. This leads to considerable stresses. As Joseph Tainter writes:

> More complex societies are more costly to maintain than simpler ones, requiring greater support levels per capita. As societies increase in complexity, more networks are created among individuals, more hierarchical controls are created to regulate these networks, more information is processed, there is more centralization of information flow, there is increasing need to support specialists not directly involved in resource production, and the like. All this complexity is dependent upon energy flow at a scale vastly greater than that characterizing small groups of self-sufficient foragers or agriculturalists.[20]

The city progressively becomes a helpless foetus feeding through the city's umbilical linkages with itself and the outside world – particularly the energy gleaned from it. If those links are severed, or the multi-level systems that civilization depends upon start to break down, then the city becomes helpless: it starves to death. The more complex and interdependent the systems required to support the larger number of people are, the more rapid and more intense the crash is likely to be. More fundamentally; the larger the city, the larger the mass of people in one dependent location, and thus the more people will be killed at once by any catastrophic systemic failure. As Industrial Civilization becomes more urbanized, passing 50% of the global population and 90% of the population of many highly industrialized nations,[21] the risk of catastrophic collapse continues to intensify.

In short, the greatest immediate risk to the population living in the conditions created by Industrial Civilization is the population itself. Civilization has created the perfect conditions for a terrible tragedy on a scale never seen before in the history of humanity. That is one reason for there to be fewer people, providing you are planning on staying within civilization – I really wouldn't recommend it, though.

The second reason is slightly more obvious, and has been covered earlier in this book: the more people there are, the more resources they will use up, the more greenhouse gases they will release and the more damage they will do, as more people become consumers within the Culture of Maximum Harm. The plan, after all, is for every human on planet Earth to become a good consumer. Reducing the population in an increasingly resource-hungry society is essential to prevent a net increase in environmental degradation. Even if you are planning to leave civilization, it's not the kind of thing you can rush into, and the vast majority of people walking the road from hell are going to spend a few years on that road. You will remain a *de facto* civilian until you leave and, within the system, are bound to create more waste, emissions and degradation than outside it: Industrial Civilization makes a virtue of excess. Morally, having fewer offspring is something you need to seriously consider, until you are no longer dependent upon civilization.

A third, and rather more proactive reason to have fewer children, is to hasten the shut down of the industrial machine. This seems a little contradictory, considering that fewer children will reduce the intensity of societal collapse, but there is a big difference between wanting to bring down civilization in a measured way (well, as measured as we can manage, given its complexity), and wanting to ensure that millions of people die in a catastrophic implosion. The key point here is that civilization needs people to keep it going: as I said in the last section, humans are the feedstock of the industrial machine. The fewer people there are, the fewer empty, consumer-driven 'opportunities' can be filled. Of course, commerce being what it is, the desire for production will move from an area bereft of willing slaves to one where the population has been suitably primed to leap on the new positions being created – apparently for their benefit. But that is ignoring the fact that Western economies in particular, at least on a national scale, really do suffer when there is a drop in the availability of suitable local workers.[22] Not having children could be a very useful strategy, both for destabilizing an economy, and removing the worries of bringing up children in a collapsing society.

There is a fourth reason, but it is nothing to do with living within civilization. Later on I'll discuss why balancing the number of children you have with the need to keep humanity going will be critical in ensuring you can thrive in a world outside of civilization.

Restoring

The Earth's natural systems will, over time, do a wonderful job of restoring the planet to a stable condition – providing Industrial Civilization has gone. In the presence of Industrial Civilization, these systems are struggling to overturn the changes that our culture is heaping upon the planet. The increase in atmospheric greenhouse gases exceeds any previous increase in terms of speed and intensity; the removal of forests and other critical ecosystems is – in any normal sense of the word – irreversible through natural processes; rivers, seas and groundwater are being toxified not only by excessive quantities of basic elements and natural molecules, but also by large amounts of synthetic chemicals for which there are no natural restorative processes. Civilization has placed a burden on the Earth that – if we are to survive beyond the next 100 years – will have to be peeled back by humans.

There are two ways to do this: the first is a combination of Unloading and Setting Aside; the second is Active Restoration. Within the Culture of Maximum Harm the first option is impossible to achieve.

Unloading essentially means the removal of an existing burden: for instance, removing grazing domesticated animals, razing cities to the ground, blowing up dams and switching off the greenhouse gas emissions machine. The process of ecological unloading is an accumulation of many of the things I have already explained in this chapter, along with an (almost certainly necessary) element of major structural change. If carried out willingly and on a sufficiently large scale, this process would require dismantling many of the key components of civiliza-tion; but no person would be foolish enough to cut off their own limbs unless they were suffering from some kind of psychotic delusion, and no civilization would be willing to remove any of the pillars of its own existence. Looking from the outside, though, a civilization hacking off its own extremities would seem like exactly the right thing to do. It's not going to happen, of course.

Setting Aside is similarly suicidal for civilization. In order to continue the upward spiral of economic development, acquiring all of the symbols and cultural attitudes that entails, an increasing amount of resources have to be used by civi-lization. For example, in order to support an increasing desire for a civilized diet containing fish, the oceans have to be stripped of life – yet, in order for the ocean's natural balance to return to a semblance of its previous condition at least 40% of its area would need to be set aside in perpetuity.[23] Such a step is totally incompat-ible with the current ambitions of this culture: it will not happen. Similarly, if a third (to be conservative) of all of the major land habitats on Earth were to be set aside, not only would many of civilization's processes have to halt, or at least con-tract significantly, but those countries with larger proportions of those key habi-tats within their borders would not accept having to take on the 'burden' of setting aside potential economic resources. The extreme difficulty experienced by such groups as The Wilderness Society (in the USA and Australia), Greenpeace (in Brazil) and the International Conservation Union to increase the amount of land set aside from agriculture and other development, and strengthen the level of protection in the face of determined government and corporate opposition, makes this all too clear.[24] Once again, though, Setting Aside is an inevitable con-sequence of following the suggestions set out in this chapter.

Active Restoration is all that is left; and you would be forgiven for thinking that there is hope for this methodology, given the types of suggestion coming from corporations, authorities, scientific institutions and other groups of people. Ideas include seeding the ocean with iron to restore levels of carbon-absorbing plankton;[25] replanting rainforest areas with native species; sucking carbon out of the atmosphere and into the ocean basin;[26] and instigating a process of 'managed retreat' in salt marshes. Predictably, all of this is insufficient at best, and cynical profit-mongering at worst. The insufficiency is simply because the scale of environmental degradation being carried out in the name of economic growth dwarfs even the most ambitious plans of the proponents of active restoration. Much of the 'restoration' work is in the form of the heralded 'techno-fix': the idea that the tools of Industrial Civilization can be used to build solutions to the problems of civilization.[27] The two fundamental flaws with techno-fixes, though, are that (a) they are almost all profit-motivated, backed by corporations who have no intention of changing the way they operate and (b) they assume that technology is an adequate replacement for natural restorative processes, further widening the disconnection between humanity and the real world.

Now, I'm not suggesting for a moment that restoration is unnecessary, nor that it is the wrong thing to do, but it must be carried out in such a way that it complements natural processes. I have a small meadow at the bottom of my heavily-wooded garden, which I have planted with native grasses and flowers, and which I allow to grow in whatever way it likes – a tiny memento of the wide meadows that once crossed southern England, but something positive nonetheless. Managed retreat to restore salt marshes is a good thing, and I can think of few things more satisfying than breaching the sea walls that once allowed farmland to reign over the coastal ecosystem. Even some of the more unusual ideas, such as burying biomass in the form of whole trees[28] or far more stable biochar (charcoal), have their merits but, as with the processes of unloading and setting aside, they are only going to achieve anything substantial in the context of Industrial Civilization becoming a thing of the past. Do what you think is right and encourage others to do the same; but never forget that restoration is just a stepping-stone to our real future.

Undermining

I think we can confidently say that civilization is not going to go down without a fight, and the forces unleashed in its defence could be truly terrible if the past and current behaviour of governments, their corporate owners and their military marionettes, is anything to go by. In Chapter Thirteen I wrote: "The laws in each country are tailored to suit the appetite of the population for change." This statement is especially relevant to any attempt to undermine Industrial Civilization: if the ruling Elites feel that their beloved system is under threat, they will do their best to suppress this threat. This suppression may be carried out legally and visibly, or illegally and invisibly. Public activities that were once permitted will be criminalized, and anyone who directly challenges the stability of the machine will be taken out of harm's way and, if deemed necessary, made an example of.

It would be wrong of me not to tell you this.

The system has legitimized all its efforts to prevent change and suppress opposition because the vast majority of people who are subjected to its activities are fully paid-up members of Industrial Civilization. It is 'right' that civilization maintains its stability because without stability, civilization collapses and can no longer impose its will upon the population. Does that sound like a coherent argument to you? In all truth, that really is the best argument civilization has for its continued existence: it has to be maintained because it has to be maintained. Even a heroin addict, shooting up to get the fix that he agonizingly craves, knows that his habit will eventually kill him. Even a lifelong nicotine addict will admit that smoking is bad for her and she should stop. Hands up if you think Industrial Civilization should be stopped.

* * *

I take no great pride in knowing that for a large part of my working life, over the last five or so years, I could have caused a breakdown in the global economy; yet I chose not to make this happen. My position placed me in charge of key data centres, front-line IT security and technical disaster recovery mechanisms, the failure of which would have caused major disruptions in the global financial trading engine. I could have been a hero of the anti-civilization movement; but I didn't do anything. My lack of motivation to make the change – to undermine the global economy in some way – was largely down to living, for many years, the life of the industrial worker; a slave to my mortgage and to the system that told me that this was what life was all about. I wasn't connected enough; I wasn't motivated enough; I thought this was just the way it had to be. I guess there are lots of people in the same situation that I was, to a greater or lesser extent: perfectly poised to undermine the system in some way, but not sure how or what to do; not even sure whether it is right to do anything at all.

How on Earth do you decide?

Only you can really decide whether Undermining is something you want to take part in, but I can help you to a certain extent. What follows is a set of **simple rules** that underpin this process – once you have read and understood the rules then you will be in a far better position to decide whether Undermining is for you.

* * *

First, I want to make one thing clear: I am not talking about mindlessly sabotaging the first thing you lay your hands on, nor am I condoning anything that will cause harm to innocent people – when I talk about 'Undermining' I am specifically referring to the act of giving people back their liberty, their freedom to choose. Nothing more.

So what kinds of actions are we talking about? No doubt it's a major achievement to bring down a corrupt government, but in the Culture of Maximum Harm it will only be replaced by one that operates along the same lines as its predecessor – to promote the 'need' for economic growth and to spread the influence of Industrial Civilization around the world on behalf of its corporate masters. Bringing down an oil company or even a single refinery will, indeed, cause a halt in the production and sale of a large amount of climate-changing hydrocarbons and, if the company or refinery is large enough, could trigger economic unrest; but there are other oil companies and many more refineries, and there are always powerful institutions, and huge numbers of deluded people, who will ensure that the oil keeps flowing – at least until it runs out. As I said, the primary targets, if enough people are to carry out the other tasks necessary to reclaim the Earth for those who actually want to survive, are the things that are stopping people from connecting with the real world: the Tools of Disconnection.

Rule One: *Concentrate your efforts on the Tools of Disconnection.*

The first reason for this is that disconnection is the biggest problem humanity is facing, and we are trying to deal with the root of the problem here. It may be satisfying to burn down a garage full of SUVs if you have a virulent hatred of gas-guzzling road transport; but these places are insured and there are plenty more SUVs where they came from. In the context of reconnecting humanity, it turns out that such actions are only symbolic – they don't actually achieve anything useful. Far better to undermine and halt the activities of the advertisers and marketing media that encourage people to buy SUVs in the first place; far better to hijack the work of the government agencies and trade bodies that ensure that vehicle sales and production remain a high priority; far better to expose the efforts of the oil and motor companies in convincing people that climate change is nothing to do with them, and even if it is, the disappearing icecaps are not really that much of a problem. All of these activities are within the means of any intelligent, motivated and connected person.

The second reason to concentrate on the Tools of Disconnection is that the laws that protect the global economy, and the forces that ensure the global economy remains the primary concern of humanity, are currently focussed on protecting the symbolic elements of Industrial Civilization. I don't believe for a moment that these forces won't move to protect the Tools of Disconnection if, and when, a concerted Undermining effort takes place; I don't believe for a second that laws will not be made to ensure those of us who want to opt out of the system are 'encouraged' to stay: but for the moment, it is the traditional targets of the symbolic protester – the buildings and vehicles and individual 'elite' members of society, for example – that are best protected. If you attack a corporate headquarters or chief executive then you will be stopped and probably imprisoned; if you divert or copy all confidential documents coming out of a corporate lobby group to a publisher of 'subversive' materials or a local friendly radio station, then who is going to come off worse?

As I said at the beginning of this section, there are risks involved in at least some aspects of this Undermining process, and like any of the Level One activities, I don't expect more than a small number of people, at least initially, are going to be keen to take part. In fact, many of the ways in which this can be done are actually far less risky, and far more fulfilling than you might imagine. It could be that you are in a position to do something that might be of great value to safeguarding the future of humanity but have never realized it.

Even if you are in a position to act, you may have concerns about the morality of what you are about to do. To make a judgement, you need to weigh up Risks and Rewards: the Risks being the various negative outcomes of your actions, the Rewards, the positive ones. When it comes to Risk, you must go into things with a clear mind – Risk is not just a measure of the risk to you; it is a measure of the risk to everyone who might be affected by what you do. You may have a rabid loathing for some part of the system, but you still *have to take responsibility for your actions*. If you take Rule One into account, you are very unlikely to encounter any serious moral dilemmas; the vast majority of Undermining activities that are likely to be effective are relatively small acts that are part of a larger, beneficial, whole – small acts that, in themselves do not cause harm to people. If you do encounter difficult choices, though, then Reward can play a part.

Reward is a measure of the net improvement in the long-term survival of humanity; based ultimately upon the improvement in the condition of our natural life-support system. It is most certainly not about fame and glory – if that is your intention then I suggest you reconsider your actions. Few, if any, people are qualified to judge whether an action has sufficient reward to justify a high degree of collateral damage: the best advice I can give is that for all undermining activities – large or small, morally complex or not – always abide by Rule Two.

Rule Two: *Only act if the rewards far outweigh the risks.*

Though the battle-worn troops of World War II resolutely denied that Europe ever had a 'soft underbelly', Winston Churchill nevertheless piled the combined forces of the Western Allied armies into north Africa, across the

Mediterranean and into southern Europe in 1943. The Russian forces, along with the Russian people, died in their millions to hold off a rampant Axis army on the Eastern Front; while all the time the Allies were working their way north-wards, peeling off division after division of German soldiers, weakening the Nazi defences as they went. Only after Hitler's fighting machine had been diminished through a combination of eastern attrition and southern guile was it possible for the D-Day landings to take place on the northern coast of France. Beating the unbeatable was a slow, but highly calculated process: at no point after the disas-trous attempt to land at Dieppe, did the Allied forces ever attempt a direct assault upon a full-strength enemy. The Allied troops were successful because they knew what to expect, and how to make the most of their advantages.

An effective computer hacker will spend a large amount of time not only planning his or her attack methodology (this is known as 'scoping') but also ensuring that once the attack has been completed, no trace of it remains. This is not too difficult if the attack is a quick 'smash and grab' to extract information, change data or bring down all or part of an IT system; where it gets difficult is in the more destructive and less reversible hacks – those that install some kind of mechanism that allows the hacked system to be remotely controlled or re-entered easily though a 'back door', or those that are designed to keep on attack-ing the system automatically. Such attacks require a tremendously detailed level of planning and are rarely carried out alone; in most cases an 'insider' is required to gather information and also create the necessary distraction while the real work is taking place. Because IT systems have become among the most critical components within all the major corporate and political institutions, Industrial Civilization is increasingly at the mercy of hackers and, by extension, those who would seek to undermine the Tools of Disconnection.

But computer hacking is only one of many different undermining actions, and a high risk one at that. As we have already seen, there are many other effec-tive types of Undermining, most of which carry a far lower risk, and can be just as effective in their outcome, or even more so. Whatever you do, though, make sure you plan ahead.

Rule Three: *Don't go blundering in – plan your approach.*

I was in a perfect position to, at least partly, halt the economic machine, had I wished to, but I would have been a prime suspect due to my multiple positions of authority and my well-known environmental leanings: if caught my first action may well have been my last. It won't surprise you then, that the best per-petrators of Undermining are not just those who have the skills and the position to make their actions effective, but are also the people whom no one will ever suspect – who have no obvious motive and are seen as unlikely to ever exploit their position. Dmitry Orlov, an authority on the collapse of the Soviet Union, says the following about sabotage in general, although it applies to many forms of Undermining just as well:

> To do it right, you have to get paid to do it. Good industrial sabotage is indistinguishable from black magic: nobody should know that it was sabotage, or how it worked, especially not the person actually doing it. The absolutely worst thing that a half-competent saboteur can be accused of is negligence, but it really should be more of a 'mistakes were made' sort of thing.[29]

It is no accident that some of the most effective Undermining actions are carried out from inside – as Bruce Schneier writes: "Insiders can be impossible to stop because they're the exact same people you're forced to trust."[30] Exploiting the trust of someone may feel morally reprehensible, but remember that you are being trusted by someone who is a willing (and possibly eager) participant in the most destructive culture ever seen on the face of the Earth.

The most recent UK Labour Government was almost brought down through leaks made by individuals within its own departments: the leaks concerned something that had forced countless people to reflect on their inner feelings about the morality of a single activity – the Iraq War. Dr David Kelly, the only named source in the revelation that a dossier specifically produced for the Blair Government as a case for going to war was hopelessly inaccurate, paid for his 'going public' with his life. Whether he died at his own hands, or those of other agencies will never be known for sure, but Kelly was not the only source of leaks concerning the 'Dodgy Dossier', and was certainly not the only source of the many off-the-record conversations, anonymous memos and uncensored government files related to the Iraq War. When something like a questionable war, a genocide or a global ecological catastrophe invokes a moral reaction in people who are in positions of trust, they can – and will – use whatever tools they have at their disposal to undermine whatever is the cause of the problem. If the protagonist is able to remain in that position of trust, much as Cold War spies were able to pass on secrets for years undetected, then they are all the more effective.

Rule Four: *Don't get caught.*

No one should make you feel guilty for not taking part in Undermining, just as no one should make you feel guilty for having meat in your diet or using a car – your participation in any of these Level One activities is voluntary and personal; it can hardly be anything else, for by saying you don't have a choice, I would be no better than those who seek to deny you the right to make things better. It is important to add, though, that Undermining is not some arcane dark art to be practised by a few gifted individuals; it is something that we can all do to a certain extent. Granted, there are complex and high-risk activities that only a few people are ever going to have the means or motivation to carry out – those people (of which you may be one) are almost certainly far better equipped than me, and also know how to do it far more effectively and secretively than I could outline in a book of this nature – but whatever you do, be sure you follow the rules I have laid out:

1. Make the Tools of Disconnection your priority; anything else is a waste of time and effort.

2. Carefully weigh up all the pros and cons, and then ask yourself, "Do the benefits far outweigh the costs?" Only act if the answer is "Yes".

3. Plan ahead, and plan well, accounting for every possible eventuality.

4. Even if you value the worth of your actions, don't get caught.

* * *

One question still remains unanswered, but has been well covered by Derrick Jensen in his Endgame books: "How can just a few determined people make it easier for the rest of humanity to reconnect with the real world?" The simple answer is that far fewer people have to make the first move than you might suppose. As Jensen revealed during a conversation with a former military officer:

> They don't have to break everything in sight. All they have to do is give the first in each line of dominoes a hearty enough heave. Once the reaction has achieved a critical threshold a fire will feed itself and grow uncontrollably. Part of the key is winning the minds of the people who would otherwise plug all the machinery right back in again.[31] Once they realize they can actually walk away, without repercussions, they'll be able to exercise their human freedoms in prodigious ways.[32]

If you hark back to the discussions about the fragility of civilization, then it becomes less of a pipe dream and more of a reality to think that a few people can start the dominoes tipping. And anyway, who is to say that thousands of people are not already partaking in a healthy slice of Undermining? Even if you simply post a suspicious internal corporate memo to your local newspaper in an unmarked envelope in a postbox far from your home; or you alter a billboard near a busy road junction in the dead of night; or if you switch off the television sets in public areas broadcasting their endless consumer messages and propaganda, you are already joining the swelling ranks of those attempting to undermine the very things which prevent us from changing.

Educating

Knowledge is power, and the greatest threat to Industrial Civilization is a knowledgeable population. As we saw in Part Three, the huge effort undertaken by countless authorities over many centuries to ensure that information is controlled, bears testament to the danger they see of information falling into the wrong (or rather, the right) hands. Remember, we are not talking about conspiracies and dark secrets here, but basic information about the way companies and governments operate on a day-to-day basis; objective information about the damage we are doing to the very environment we need to remain healthy in order for us to survive; the way in which we are being systematically disconnected from the real world; and the simple but devastatingly effective measures everyone can take to change all of this. But it doesn't stop there.

Just as Undermining is vital in cutting the arteries of civilization's disconnection machine, education in its purest form is vital in healing the deep divisions that have been created by that machine. Real education is a form of passive sabotage: it undermines the education system that turns children into potential employees, potential voters and potential consumers. Children, and adults for that matter, need to become world-wise, connected and able individuals; they also need to become people who want to work together, not as economic units, but as communities of people striving to achieve something far more real than anything Industrial Civilization could ever offer them. Not only is such an education far more relevant to the real world; it is imperative that people are equipped with the skills to survive whatever will happen in the next few decades. David Orr starkly laid out one of the future decisions we will have to make following the inevitable collapse of cities, in a 1994 lecture:

> The choice is whether those returning to rural areas in the century ahead will do so, in the main, willingly and expectantly with the appropriate knowledge, attitudes, and skills . . . or arrive as ecological refugees driven by necessity, perhaps desperation. For all of the fashionable talk about cultural diversity, schools, colleges, and universities have been agents of fossil-energy-powered urban homogenization.[33]

As a people, we are losing basic and vital skills with frightening ease; partly out of ignorance, but mainly because we have been made to believe that civilization will look after us, provide for our every need and make such skills as growing, building, cooking and caring obsolete. We have become incapable of looking after and thinking for ourselves. One of your tasks as an intelligent, knowledgeable and connected person is to ensure that useful information stays out there – in the minds of as many people as possible.

The classrooms in the education systems of Industrial Civilization only provide sufficient knowledge to turn humans into good workers; that is not where the educating should take place. It should take place in the homes of families and friends; in pubs and restaurants; in sports venues; at pop concerts and music festivals; in parks, woods, fields, beaches and on the street; in trains and buses; in offices, shops and factories; even in playgrounds. Person to person, unfiltered and uncensored – just information that can be discussed, debated, added to, written down, remembered and passed on again and again. You need to keep this information alive and accurate; you need to keep it interesting and relevant; you need to be a teacher because, like it or not, the system is not going to educate anyone on how to live in a world where the system is not in charge.

Level Two: Ways to Accelerate Change

This is the point when most environmental guidebooks tail off into a happy conclusion, generally along the lines of, "If we all follow these suggestions, the world will be a better place." That is, of course, complete garbage. For a start, the recommendations in these guidebooks are generally no more radical than installing a wind turbine on your roof, or lobbying your government representative / friend of the global economy for change. Also, as I said in the last chapter, the assumption that everyone reading the book (let alone a large enough number of people to really make a difference) will follow the recommendations is foolish at best. A conclusion at this point would make no sense at all – you can't change a society if only a tiny minority of people are prepared to change themselves. I know that the things I have suggested, as well as those I have warned against, will only initially be taken up by a very few people: what is needed is a way of propagating that change to a far larger group in the shortest time possible.

Innovators, Early Adopters, and the Rest

If you have read up to this point of your own accord, and are prepared to take on the challenge of using various methods to gradually crumble Industrial Civilization, then that makes you an Innovator. The first way of accelerating the change process is based upon the Diffusion of Innovations theory, which the American sociologist Everett Rogers developed into something far-reaching and rather brilliant.[34] An Innovation can be anything that has not been done before; whether that be adopting a new technology, watching a new television programme or changing a society. Rogers proposed five different groups of people through which the innovation has to pass before an entire population can be said to have adopted it: Innovators (sometimes called Pioneers), which account for around 2.5% of the population; Early Adopters, 12.5% of the population; Early Majority, 35%; Late Majority, 35% and, finally, Laggards who are the last 15% of people to take on an innovation. The percentage figures can change depending on the type of innovation and also the nature of the population; but what is more important is that the five groups each describe a time-lag: the Early Majority will not adopt an innovation until the Early Adopters have, and so on.

On its own, that seems simple enough, but what makes things more complicated is that each individual within each group usually has to go through a number of different phases in order for their personal adoption to be achieved, as follows:[35]

1. Knowledge – person becomes aware of an innovation and has some idea of how it functions,

2. Persuasion – person forms a favourable or unfavourable attitude toward the innovation,

3. Decision – person engages in activities that lead to a choice to adopt or reject the innovation,

4. Implementation – person puts an innovation into use,

5. Confirmation – person evaluates the results of an innovation-decision already made.

People in one group are unlikely to start their adoption process until those in the previous group have, at least, started their Implementation phase, and probably not until the Confirmation phase: 'Leaps of Faith' are as uncommon as they are risky. The Confirmation phase is when the adopter decides whether he or she is happy with the outcome of the adoption, and is in the best position to encourage others – friends, family, colleagues, neighbours and so on – to start the adoption process themselves. If the members of one group never reach the Confirmation phase, there is very little chance of the innovation passing to the next group.

With all that said, it sounds as though any major change in society towards a survivable future is going to take an age, especially when you consider the enormous pressure constantly placed on individuals to ensure that they don't change at all. This is where you come in.

*   *   *

I said in the last chapter that some of this theory was a bit dry so, rather than plough on and risk losing you through sheer boredom, I'm going to explain how this needs to work in practice. I'm going to describe the most important innovation of all: the one that comprises the raft of different radical measures described in the last section; the one that people need to adopt in order for them to become part of the solution.

The difference between a population deciding to watch a new television programme and their taking on a completely new way of living is profound: for a start, switching over a TV channel, even arranging things so you are near to your television at the time the programme starts takes very little time – changing your life can take years, especially if you are a deeply ingrained 'consumer'. More obviously, persuading someone to change their life as opposed to changing their TV channel requires a lot more effort (something I will deal with in the Level Three section). Figure 21 shows the process graphically, with the thin bands indicating the smaller population groups, and the increasing adoption time for each group indicating the additional effort required for a more ingrained person to change their life. The 'Innovators / Pioneers' group is highlighted because nothing can happen until this group begins adopting the change. There is no absolute time scale; you will see shortly that it is almost impossible to predict how quickly the population will change because there are so many factors to consider.

Consider lighting a fire: you can't send a spark to a large, dense piece of timber and expect it to ignite – you have to start with the smaller, more reactive materials. First the newspaper or tinder catches; then the small sticks – the kindling – begin to burn; then the larger pieces of wood and, when the flames have reached a high enough temperature, the logs will start to burn. You end up with a powerful, intense fire, hot enough to set light to almost anything that is placed near to it. Now, what if you are lighting the fire under different conditions: in some cases your materials may be dry, you have a good air flow but not so much that the flames are blown out; compare this with a fire made from slightly damp materials – it's raining, the wind is blowing hard.

In Level One I suggested lots of different changes, some of which are harder to achieve than others. Change isn't going to happen in one big bang, even among the Innovators; it will require different levels of effort and different time scales, so it's important to keep plugging on, even when you have made what you consider to be big changes in your life. When you have made a significant change – say you have stopped being a conspicuous consumer or you have stopped flying and driving entirely – that is a good point to start influencing the people in the next phase, while still continuing with your personal efforts. I know it sounds a bit convoluted, but it's actually a very natural way of doing things; after all, your friends who may be quite keen to change are more likely to be put off from changing when they see what a massive gulf there is between you and them. Instead, if you are in a position to guide your friends through the same change you have just completed, they are far more likely to go along with you; and also pass on their more comfortable (albeit quite radical) experience to others.

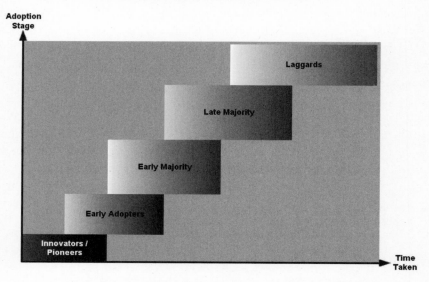

Figure 21: Simplified Diffusion of Innovations graph for fundamental life changes

It is important to also understand that you are very unlikely to persuade someone to change if they are two or more phases behind you: I long ago gave up trying to discuss environmental and social changes with many of the people I knew – the conversation might have been interesting, but there was no chance of them agreeing to actually do anything about it. Miracles do happen and people do have moments of revelation, but the best strategy – as shown by the abject failure of groups like Greenpeace and Friends of the Earth to change a defiant public *en masse* – is to *concentrate your efforts on those most likely to be persuaded.* Any other approach flies in the face of social theory and, to be honest, common sense.

Finally, I just want to mention something that was pointed out by a close relation just a few days ago: how do you deal with the situation where someone is trying to persuade you *not* to change? This is all about peer pressure, and peer pressure can be extremely toxic at its worst. A person who decides to go vegetarian, for instance, will come up against not only the system itself, using its Tools of Disconnection, but lots of people who might persuade him or her to 'just have a bit of meat' or to not change on the grounds of health, convenience and the multitude of other reasons people give for avoiding a change in their diet. I'm not suggesting for a second that you should avoid your friends or relations (although it might be a good time to consider who your real friends are), but I would say that times like this require a great deal of self-confidence, and not a little tact. It is possible that the people asking you not to change are actually closer to changing themselves than they will ever admit – as Carol Adams writes, with reference to people that try to sabotage vegetarian behaviour: "Saboteurs may be the group most truly threatened by vegetarianism. That's the last thing they can admit to themselves or you." [36]

I suggested earlier on that if you were not ready to take the plunge, then you should take time out to reflect and re-read certain sections of this book. One reason is to ensure that you are in a position to disregard any potential distractions and plough your own furrow – there is little point going into this half-heartedly and being right back where you started a few days later because a relative told you that you were being foolish. Don't get mad at someone because they don't know any better: explain why you are doing what you are doing; describe what civilization is doing to humanity in the simplest terms; show them how your life has improved immeasurably because of the changes you have already made and, if that doesn't stop them, just ignore them. I find that works very well!

Mavens, Connectors and Salespeople

It wouldn't be fair of me to take the credit for this section, but I bet when he was writing about Sesame Street and Hush Puppies, Malcolm Gladwell never thought the ideas he proposed in *The Tipping Point* [37] would be used to try to bring down Industrial Civilization. If you create something compelling, effective and yet infinitely flexible, though, then it is bound to be used for things other than for which it was intended.

There are three key elements to *The Tipping Point*, each of which has its own relevance to triggering major change: the first is known as The Law of the Few. This presupposes that for each successful idea or innovation, to use the previous terminology, you have three different types of people involved. Mavens are people who identify trends and have an instinct for knowing when something is right. Connectors are those people who, usually through their job or social standing, are able to link together the kinds of people who can broadcast and propagate an idea to other similar people. Salesmen (or women) are those people who are experts in persuading large numbers of people that the idea should be adopted.

Who can we use to bring down civilization?

Well, it's clear that, given what we are trying to get rid of, we are not talking

about the usual network of fashionistas, marketing executives or used car salesmen – although such people might themselves be persuaded to join the other
side. In fact we don't actually need Mavens here, because the idea has already
been identified at Level One in this chapter: whether it is the kind of idea that is
likely to succeed is a moot point – it has to succeed, which is why Connectors
and Salespeople are so important.

The Connectors are pretty well established and, again, this is where you play
your part if you are in a position to do so: bloggers with a readership consisting
of other bloggers, along with a range of influential people; journalists and broadcasters not shackled by a particular editorial regime; people who are regular
commentators on popular websites; regularly published letter writers to newspapers and people who can get spots on radio and television shows; finally, people
who have large social networks consisting of those people who are most likely to
change themselves. If you are this kind of person, or can persuade any that you
know to be a Connector, then so much the better.

The Salespeople are such a diverse bunch that I'm not going to list them here,
but they are essentially the kinds of people who are ready to make the change
themselves, and are persuasive enough to get ideas across that would normally
be anathema to this culture. We all know people who can sell things; they just
need to be convinced that they have a far more important job to do than selling
cars, vacations, houses or hi-fi equipment. More likely, the best people for the job
are those who are already used to selling ideas rather than things – musicians,
actors, teachers and lecturers for example[38] – but you never know who might be
willing to help. If you are, or are good friends with a Salesperson who is also a
Connector then you have a real star on your hands!

The second Tipping Point element is the Stickiness Factor. The message in
this book is pretty simple, but takes quite a lot of digesting: what if the message
could be presented in such a way that everyone gets it? At least it would give the
largest number of people a chance of changing. The problem is that the message
'Industrial Civilization must end' is not very sticky at all: the statement makes no
sense to most people. It will appeal to the converted, the people who are already
on their way down the path out of civilization, but those people exist in such
small numbers that they have little chance of triggering any kind of movement –
the message needs to stick with enough people to create genuine momentum.

Paul Revere started a word-of-mouth epidemic with the phrase "The British are
coming." If he had instead gone on that midnight ride to tell people he was having a sale on the pewter mugs at his silversmith shop, even he, with all his enormous personal gifts, could not have galvanized the Massachusetts countryside.

The specific quality that a message needs to be successful is the quality of 'stickiness.' Is the message memorable? Is it so memorable, in fact, that it can create change that can spur someone to action?[39]

This is not a small book, and I would be fooling myself if I thought millions of people were going to read it; and even if they did, most of those people would be recreational readers who are not yet ready to make the change. The point is that, somehow, the key messages in this book need to be condensed down and conveyed in such a way that those messages stick with a large enough number of people. I had a go at this near the end of Chapter 14, breaking what had been said into eight key points; but even that may be too much for some people to convey in a short time, and none of the summarized information is qualified in any way – you need to read the book for that. It's a dilemma. At some point you're going to have to decide which bits of the message are likely to stick with the people who are going to be the main recipients: the Connectors and the Salespeople, and key people in the next phase of Innovation. Already the need for a third level is emerging; and it is in that section that the nature of the message itself will be covered.

The third and last Tipping Point element is The Power of Context: whether the idea is relevant to the environment in which it is presented. We can bang on all we like about how the planet is being degraded by Industrial Civilization; about how we have been forcibly disconnected from wild nature; about how there are many ways to deal with this, most of which don't follow the cosy ideology of the mainstream environmentalist – but unless the context is right then the message just won't sink in. Here's a quick example: last year I wrote a comment on an influential blog about Al Gore's Live Earth concerts in which I said that they had almost no chance of influencing people due to their superficial nature. This comment was picked up by MTV, who called me for an interview, which duly appeared on the front page of the mtv.com website for over a week.[40] Subsequently, I was interviewed by CBC, the Canadian broadcaster and appeared on their bulletins for the whole day that the Live Earth concerts were taking place.

This is not to say that my efforts and the criticisms of others had any impact on the public, although Al Gore was forced to develop a '7 Point Pledge' and defend the concerts publicly; the point is that I was asked to speak because the context was just right. Live Earth was happening, and my comments hit a nerve. The wider context of this book is that environmentalism is everywhere and we are being implored to 'do something',[41] but sadly that context is so broad as to be irrelevant: the general environmental context is not going to help push the necessary changes through society. Nevertheless, as the Live Earth example showed, it is possible to take advantage of particular events, especially those that are media-friendly, and put an anti-civilization slant on them – this is where the Salespeople can really come to the fore. You can even force the context by associating or juxtaposing the ideas you want to get across with something of more interest to your audience: recycling is important to lots of people, so saying to a friend or colleague that recycling is largely a way of distracting people from actually doing something effective, after they tell you that they religiously recycle all their cans and bottles, will certainly be memorable.

The context of an idea and its stickiness are, regardless of the power of the idea, culture-specific. If an idea is only relevant to a small sector of society then it will never make the leap to a wider audience without some form of cultural translation. Some of the examples of how companies have made cultural changes to their marketing to sell products are cringe-inducing, to say the least, and not a little cynical – well, all commercial marketing is cynical by its nature: the 'World's local bank' campaign by HSBC springs to mind,[42] but there are many others. Regardless of cynicism, though, subtle cultural adjustments do work; largely because, as we saw in Chapter Ten, there is already a dominant culture that most people on Earth are affected by. This book was originally written in English, and I have lived in the UK all my life, so many of the references and examples are close to home for me. That said, I have taken a global and culture-neutral viewpoint as far as my experiences allow, which is designed to appeal to a far wider audience. Ironically, the more people on Earth that experience the Culture of Maximum Harm, the more people the ideas in this book will be relevant to: but I would like to think that there are Connectors out there who can cross over the cultural boundaries that still exist (particularly in large, recently industrialized societies like India, China and Indonesia), and who can short-circuit this cultural dependency before the whole world loses its identity.

Gumming Up the Works

All the while phases are being considered and tipping points are being targeted there remains one big stumbling block: the one all the 'how to save the world' purveyors manage (or more likely choose) to ignore. This is the elephant in the room that was discussed at length in Chapter Thirteen: the Tools of Disconnection. At Level One we cut across, showing the huge range of different things that need changing in our lives if we are to stand any chance of making progress with surviving the next century or more, while acknowledging the huge power that Industrial Civilization has over our activities. Educating outside of the educational system was shown to be a key way of undermining this control, and this educating effort – as you have seen in the last few pages – is a key part of the Diffusion of Innovations and Tipping Point concepts. By educating people about the power of the system and how it seeks to prevent change, people can understand better how to reach each subsequent sector of the population. It's still extremely difficult – the elephant is still there, glowering at all attempts to move it.

I prefer to let the poor elephant run free – it may be big and grey, but it has been done a grave disservice in metaphor-land. Elephants live as sustainably as all other non-civilized living creatures: they control their populations and the areas they use through natural processes – any attempt to be unsustainable would be suicide for an elephant herd. No, I prefer to use a different metaphor: a gigantic machine chewing up the Earth's natural resources, belching out polluting liquids and gases, run by a workforce made up of billions of willing slaves. One of the machine's jobs is to make sure everyone ignores what the machine is doing and just carries on working for it, through thick and thin. *Unless the machine is slowed down it will carry on until there is nothing left to feed it*, and no one left to operate it. Some of us may wish to stop shopping, stop travelling, change our eating habits, leave our jobs and live sustainable lives; some of us may wish to reverse population growth and help restore the degraded land; some of us may wish to educate people and undermine the Tools of Disconnection but – and here is the paradox – unless the undermining is taking place, none of this will get any easier. Undermining helps create the conditions for change and allows that change to accelerate, rather than be dragged backwards by the influence of civilization.

This is why Undermining is probably both the single most important Level One *and* Level Two activity. We know there are people ready to do the work, and you may well be among them. Those people, you included, are the key to getting this process moving at the speed it needs to go. I'm sorry if this sounds like needless repetition, but I wouldn't repeat it if it wasn't important: *in order to motivate entire groups of people to change, the things holding them back must be removed.*

* * *

It might feel as though we are leaving the suggestions provided in Level One behind, but that couldn't be further from the truth: the list of 'Ways To Live' is still completely relevant and lies at the heart of preventing catastrophic environmental damage. Read it, print it out, stick it on your wall. You may also think that I have gone into more than enough detail about the mechanisms of change in Level Two; and, indeed, I have spent quite a bit of time on them – suggesting how we should live is all very well, but without many people adopting these changes, there is no chance of these catastrophes being prevented. Level Two is also vitally important.

There is one more level that is missing, though: the one that lies far deeper than anything I have yet seen in an environmental book – the level that shows how to actually lift people out of their civilization-induced slumber in the first place. Without something that actually picks people up and, at least metaphorically, gives them a good shake, even the very best Salesperson has nothing to work with. That is what we need to discuss now.

Level Three: Ways to Influence People

My younger daughter told me recently that if we were to show all the people driving 4x4s the last few minutes of *The Day After Tomorrow* then they would stop driving. I think this level of confidence is wonderful in a nine-year old, but I had to be honest and tell her that most people driving 4x4s weren't ready to change (I didn't explain Diffusion of Innovations to her – I'm not that mean!) It got me thinking, though, that there must be something that can wake at least the Early Adopters up to smell the green grass, newly watered soil and fresh air. As I said earlier, there is a big problem with creating a message that is sufficiently 'sticky' and also contains the information necessary to steer people in the right direction. We can concoct a decent message from the huge amount of information I have included in this book – perhaps something that fills a poster, or a short burst of conversation – but what would make that message good enough to cut through the consumer noise and light-green platitudes that are currently occupying people's minds?

The idea of the Meme is a good starting point. Richard Dawkins first coined the term 'meme' (pronounced 'meem') in his book *The Selfish Gene*; describing it as a replicator, which acts, not on genes, but on cultural ideas like songs, religions, sports, fashions, art, methods of construction, or ideas like evolution, gravity and faith.[43] Unlike genes, which have been literally pulled apart by scientists, we have a pretty poor understanding of how memes work: the best that can be said is that they share some of the characteristics of genetic behaviour but, unless you include their physical representations – books, paintings, recorded music etc. – they only exist in the minds of the carriers. Dawkins suggests there are two ways in which a meme might successfully replicate to the next generation or group of humans: either they have 'merit' (in other words they have some intrinsic ability to remain, regardless of anything that surrounds them), or they are highly compatible with the cultural environment.[44] The idea that it is good to survive, rather than die, has merit and has thus replicated throughout all of humanity. The idea that the daily habits of a particular movie or music star are worthy of discussion has little merit in itself but, as long as that star is shining brightly, then that meme will be replicated: when the star is no longer a star, then the meme fails.

One characteristic that memes do share with genes is that if they mutate more rapidly, or to a greater extent, than is beneficial to their continued success, then they quickly lose their advantage over other memes. Rapid mutation can be a good thing if we are prepared to accept huge collateral damage for the sake of one highly adapted super-meme; but if that final meme bears little resemblance to the thing you wanted to be replicated, then it is little better than no meme at all. In fact, in the world of environmental information, the super-meme may be extremely damaging!

What we are seeing in a so-called age of Environmental Enlightenment is actually a set of basic ideas about the way we need to act and the reasons for acting, being mutated out of existence in the cacophony of competing ideas, which no one can seem to agree upon. This is in part due to the presence of the powerful commercially-funded body of sceptics; but made worse by a huge range of environmental groups that are each trying to compete for a slice of the 'we helped save the world' pie.[45] The ideas and messages are changing so often that there is currently little chance of a genuinely effective idea dealing with the competition.

Or is there?

I believe it is possible to create something that will motivate people to act in the right way, regardless of everything else that is taking place. Such an Eco-Meme must have the following three characteristics:

1. *It is sufficiently 'sticky' to get an individual's attention.*
The uniqueness of the message is an important factor here – we are not talking about '10 Ways To Save The World' but something far more interesting and far more striking: the need to bring down something that we have been brainwashed into thinking we cannot do without. To make the message very sticky, though, it needs to be short, easy to understand and memorable. A message that is too complicated will fail to stick.

2. *It is powerful enough to appeal to an individual's basest instincts to act.*
The message needs to harness the things that go to the heart of what it means to be human: survival is one of them; another is the unique experience of being connected – something that is impossible to achieve without 'tuning out' of civilization; the final one is the natural anger that comes from realizing you are being forcibly disconnected by the system you have trusted, possibly for all of your life.

3. It is robust enough to avoid losing its meaning when passed on.

Again, simplicity is a key here – if everyone can understand the message then there is a greater chance of it remaining intact when it is passed on: the shorter the message, the greater the chance of it being passed on in its entirety. This book is not the message, but because it has been written to be easily understood by a large number of people then the message can be reinforced by the supporting material.

To create a message that is suitable as an Eco-Meme, we need to first boil down all the relevant material into a short burst of information. The first part needs to contain the 'why?' information, i.e. 'Why do I need to do something?' It looks something like this:

Human activity is destroying the natural systems that we depend upon for our survival. Our most basic instinct as humans is to survive; yet we continue to destroy our life-support machine. Connected humans understand this terrible contradiction; disconnected humans are not able to.

Not all humans are responsible: just those who are part of Industrial Civilization. Industrial Civilization depends on economic growth and the unsustainable use of natural resources, so it has developed a complex set of tools for keeping people disconnected from the real world and living a life that keeps civilization running. Humans have been manipulated in order to be part of a destructive system.

The only way to prevent global ecological collapse and thus ensure the survival of humanity is to rid the world of Industrial Civilization.

The second part needs to contain the 'how?' information, i.e. 'How can I make this happen?' Again, it needs to be in such a form that it is suitable as an Eco-Meme:

Civilization is complex and delicate: it depends on everything running smoothly and also depends upon people having faith in its goodness. Global ecological systems are changing in unpredictable and major ways; natural resources are running out rapidly; the population is growing, particularly the population of urban areas; there is considerable political and civil unrest developing throughout the world: any combination of these factors is likely to lead to a sudden and cata-strophic collapse of civilization during the 21st century.

It is possible to create a situation where civilization is left to crumble gradually, reducing the impact on humanity, and the sooner this is done, the less the global environment will be harmed. The key things we need to do are:

1) Reconnect with the real world, so that we can understand our close relationships with it in everything we do. The more you connect, the more you will realize how unreal civilization is.

2) Live in such a way that we do not contribute to the expansion of the global economy, reducing our impact on the natural environment in the process. Be aware that authority figures within the system, such as political leaders and corporations, will attempt to provide you with 'green' advice: this advice is designed to ensure that civilization continues, and should be ignored.

3) Create the conditions so that others may also change through education and, even more importantly, undermining the tools that civilization uses to keep us part of the machine. Don't waste time protesting: this changes nothing – that is why it is legal.

A future outside civilization is a better life; one in which we can actually decide for ourselves how we are going to live.

I'm sure a better writer than me could go through this and construct something more eloquent, but that is the essence of the message; and that is what I think needs to go out to humanity – at first to a receptive minority and then, as conditions become more conducive to change, to a progressively larger audience.

* * *

Now we have the basis of a simple, but comprehensive message, we need to ensure it stands the best chance of being successful in the big, bad world that is the Culture of Maximum Harm. There are a few things we can do to help.

First, we need to be careful about the *words we use*. Some words, which we unwittingly use in neutral terms, are deeply grounded in civilization; as though that is the only way of being. 'Consumer' has become a general term for a person going about their daily life, when it actually means someone who is taking part in a consuming activity, like shopping or tourism. 'Advanced' and 'Developed' are terms used to describe cultures that are at the peak of human endeavour, when they are actually very specific terms to describe a high level of technological or economic activity; likewise, 'Backward' and 'Undeveloped' are used to put non-industrial, low-resource-use societies in a poor light, as opposed to 'good' civilization. 'Developing' is purely aspirational: it implies that a society or country that is not 'developed' is aspiring to become so. 'Civilized' and 'Uncivilized' are similarly used to imply positive and negative aspects of a culture or society when these words actually describe to what level it is based around living in cities. Words like 'Savage', 'Wild' and 'Animal' have been framed in almost completely negative terms, when they simply imply that something is natural.

Redefining such words will, in the short term, just be confusing: instead, where a word is always going to be seen as negative, like 'Savage', it should be avoided; and where a word specifically relates to Industrial Civilization in positive terms, we should try to use it negatively. It is surprising how quickly this type of meme (the definition of a word) can spread throughout a population.

On a related point, we need to start talking as though not having stuff, not consuming, not travelling etc. is a positive thing: how can being genuinely environmentally friendly be anything but positive? Typically, a person in the Culture of Maximum Harm, if asked about something relatively non-destructive they own or have done, tries to play it down in order to seem 'normal'. For instance, they might say: "I just went camping / holidayed locally" or "I'm going to get one next week" or "Sorry, I can't afford it at the moment." We have become extraordinarily coy about not being rabid consumers, when we should be proud of it. Again, this is a kind of language change that can be extremely effective.

In order for a message to get out in its strongest possible form and remain untainted, civilization must not be allowed to mess around with it. It is not possible for a corporation to be 'green', therefore at no point must the message be allowed to include business as an ally; politicians are not enablers of change, for they exist to maintain the status quo, so are not going to play a part in the solution (at least not in their role as politicians); connection can only be made with an artefact of the real world, it cannot be reproduced in a technological 'experience'. In all of these cases, the process of Undermining may need to be employed once again, *focused on exposing the damaging and ineffective alternatives to real change* as greenwash, time-wasting or just plain lies. Exposing such duplicity is something everyone can take an active part in.

Finally, we must never forget *the way in which the message is delivered*: trust is by far the most important factor here. The best person to persuade someone why and how they need to change is a person that they trust, however humble and unassuming. The best salesperson isn't always the person who has been in the game the longest or has the best track record; he or she may just be someone who has the ear of someone else. You are delivering a message that is critically important and undeniably positive in its outcome: it will not be a breach of trust to deliver this message, however hard it may be to digest. We may not all be heroes, but we can all be part of the change.

* * *

What we have experienced over the last thousand or more years is a progressive addiction to a way of life that cannot, under any circumstances be maintained. There is no cure to addiction and almost all of us will feel a certain amount of withdrawal as we move away from a life of toxic abuse to one that provides little or none of the paraphernalia we have become so dependent upon. The next generation, though, will not be addicted: they can grow up in a culture that doesn't try to cut them off from reality. The current generation may become a generation of ex-civilians; the next generation will simply be free.

Getting rid of civilization is not going to be easy, but the alternative is far, far worse. In the next chapter I am going to show you how to make the process of withdrawing from this culture easier for yourself, and help insulate you from the worst of the after-effects of Industrial Civilization: when something that big comes down, however it comes down, it is bound to make a bit of a mess. It doesn't hurt to be prepared.

Chapter Sixteen

Being Ourselves

Find a patch of sunshine or a place where it is warm and still; sit or stand, whichever is most comfortable. You'll need to put the book down in a moment because I want you to shut your eyes and imagine what it will be like after civilization has gone. If you have ever been somewhere truly wild, even just for a camping trip or a long walk, then that will help your imagination. If you already live somewhere truly wild, then this will be an easy exercise; if you are dependent upon Industrial Civilization to provide you with everything, then it will be hard, maybe impossible. Imagine no cities, no paved roads, no pylons, no offices or factories – imagine having to grow everything, make everything, do everything for yourself.

Now close your eyes and go there for a while . . .

* * *

Mixed feelings. Loss, emptiness, a sense of solitary isolation. Tough work, endless toil, dirt, disease and death. Rubble, dust, twisted metal and poisoned water; constant battles, tribal rivalries and extreme hostility between people. Distance; a depraved past and a promising future. Cleanliness, fresh air, fresh water, open to the elements and a feeling of raw, real living. Richness, fulfilment, connection, freedom.

Most of us are not mentally or physically ready to cope with the loss of something we have been made to believe is so important to us. Take away civilization tomorrow and we could fall too far to save ourselves. We have to start thinking like survivors again because, one way or another – suddenly, through this culture's self-destructive behaviour, or more gradually, by our own caring hands – that is the world we will be seeing in two or three generations, possibly only one.

If you are prepared for it, then the journey and the eventual destination can show you what it is really like to be human. Prepare, and your existence outside civilization can be something that you can *only* find outside civilization: something real and truly good.

Preparing

Civilization has taught us that there is only one way to go, and that's forwards in a straight line – always increasing, always renewing, always disposing of the past and reaching for something 'more'. We rush headlong into the future with over-wound enthusiasm, trusting our survival to the blind faith that keeps us moving forwards with the current, getting faster and faster, pulling us towards a place that has not been made, yet one that we are told is the only place to go. We are stuck in a rip current of our own making; sucking us into the open sea, out of control.

It's surprisingly easy to get out of a rip current: just swim sideways.

We rightly look to the past as a way of understanding how we got here, and also so we can learn lessons about the right and the wrong way to do things; but remember what we talked about in Part Two, about the way we are bound to our temporal life – we have to live for the future, rather than the past: it's just that *there is more than one future*. As a good friend of mine wrote: "What we do in the future is what counts. And I think we need to become something new, not return to some earlier state. Now we have to use our brains and our knowledge to change ourselves in deliberate ways."[1] Step out of the rip current and step into something else: a more docile, less urgent flow of time, one that understands how we relate to the natural processes of the world, that allows us to grab hold of a branch or a piece of weed as it drifts into our path and see what it has to offer.

> Obviously, we cannot turn back the clock. But we are at a point in history where we not only can, but must pick and choose among all the present and past elements of human culture to find those that are most humane and sustainable. While the new culture we will create by doing so will not likely represent simply an immediate return to wild food gathering, it could restore much of the freedom, naturalness, and spontaneity that we have traded for civilization's artifices...We need not slavishly imitate the past; we might, rather, be inspired by the best examples of human adaptation, past and present. Instead of 'going back,' we should think of this process as 'getting back on track.'[2]

"Getting back on track." I like that. Industrial Civilization is a blink in human history; a rapid, artificial cataract on our many and varied courses downstream. Grab hold of something if you can, or step sideways and join a flow that you can control. Here's how to build your own boat, with its own sail.[3]

* * *

Quite a few pages back there was a section called 'Ways To Live'. I intentionally avoided suggesting technological 'solutions' and ways of living that depend upon the system rather than your own free will. Every way of living written there runs counter to the needs of civilization; every change that I laid down is a change that pulls you out of the uncontrollable flowing water. Take Consuming, for example: I talked about reducing, repairing, bartering and donating – all anathema to the Culture of Maximum Harm. What about Travelling: there was no energy-efficient technology, or government-sponsored travel plans; we need to remove our dependence on motorized transport, and reduce the speed and distance we travel. The same with Working: no 'switching off computers in the office', no telecommuting, no corporate carbon offsetting – just the simple message to stop living as part of the growth economy.

By following 'Ways To Live' you are preparing yourself for a life without civilization; you are distancing yourself, drawing yourself away from the culture that you feel so attached to. The Level One solutions are about far more than reducing our impact on the natural environment – they are ways of stopping the system in its tracks and helping you prepare for when the inevitable happens. When civilization collapses, starting with the inner cities, but rapidly progressing to the infrastructure-dependent suburbs and the smaller towns that have stopped being self-sufficient, then the survivors (I mean those who are *really* living, not those scrabbling around in a post-apocalyptic swill) will be those who have loosened enough ties with civilization to be able to get on without it. Dmitry Orlov writes:

> If the economy, and your place within it, is really important to you, you will be really hurt when it goes away. You can cultivate an attitude of studied indifference, but it has to be more than just a conceit. You have to develop the lifestyle and the habits and the physical stamina to back it up.[4]

Now we're starting to discover a few more needs. Physical stamina and strength are necessary: you can't saw and cut logs, dig half an acre of land or even cycle a few miles to do some errands if you spend your life slumped in front of a computer screen; although it's surprising how quickly the fat drops off and the muscle builds up once you decide the best use for your hands is something other than pressing the remote control or hitting the indicator lever. Mental strength is equally important – probably more so. Firstly, because unless you have the willingness to keep at it, you can quickly find yourself slipping back towards the 'easy' consumer life; secondly, because, however good and complete the living is, adjusting to a life that is fundamentally different from what you have become used to is never easy. Attitude is vital: primarily a positive attitude that, if you are doing something for the right reason, is not really that hard to start off with. To maintain it, though, is something you have to work at. Brent Ladd went headlong into a subsistence way of life that he wasn't adequately prepared for, so had a tough time dealing with things as they happened. His attitude helped him tremendously:[5]

> It is important to know skills like fire-making inside and out, but if you're caught in a rainstorm or blizzard or whatever, and you let the weather get to you psychologically – it could mean hypothermia. I am learning that I need a sense of confidence and courage to live the way I have in the past two years. Many doubts have entered my mind about what I am doing. I have had to suck it up and get past the fears and let myself know I can do it. If I fail, I try again.
>
> A sense of humour is a big part of the right attitude. Being able to laugh at myself (I do it often) helps a great deal. When things don't go just the way I've planned, I can either get down on myself, blame someone else, or laugh at myself or the situation. Having been through what I have, I can say that laughter is indeed the best medicine. When I began to live a free lifestyle, my personality also became more free.[5]

Learning to live outside of civilization is possible on your own, if you are uniquely able to deal with everything wild nature can throw at you – but let's be honest, most of us have no idea what nature is really like close up. In reality, you are not going to be going about this on your own, even as just a family group: you will need others on the boat with you.

> You may feel like you want to do it alone, but you have never done it alone. To survive the breakdown of this world and build a better one, you will have to trade your sterile, insulated links of money and law for raw, messy links of friendship and conflict. The big lie of post-apocalypse movies like Omegaman and Mad Max is that the survivors will be loners. In the real apocalypse, the survivors will be members of multi-skilled well-balanced co-operative groups.[6]

Apocalypse, fallen by the wayside or managed, intentional defection; whatever the reason for living without civilization, community is where you will have to end up living. Looking at the two-metre panel fences and brick walls surrounding the homes of the civilized, I can see there is a huge difference between the way we are now, the way we were and the way we need to be. I have some photographs of gardens from the 1930s and 1940s in Britain: there are no solid fences, no impenetrable barriers – just a bit of chicken mesh, often to stop rabbits and chickens from getting into the next garden. This was not some halcyon age of evergreen landscapes; the skies were often full of coal smoke, although the amount of carbon dioxide in the air was some 20% less than it is now (low enough to keep the Arctic ice frozen) – but people talked to each other. The endless tittle-tattle across the flimsy dividers often crossed many gardens; people would chat in the street, walk along together rather than jump in their cars and drive anonymously from one place to another; people really did leave their doors unlocked because they knew someone would always be watching out for them. What happened? We became so enmeshed in our drive to become economically successful that we segregated ourselves from those that mattered: families have become subdivided by a perceived lack of time and shattered by financial pressures; the age of the three generation household is gone[7] – the elderly are packed away to 'care' homes to live out their remaining years in virtual isolation; children and parents have forgotten how to talk to each other. The segregated society may benefit the economic dream where people compete to materially outdo each other, but as a place for survivors, the segregated society is a hopeless case.

We need people to discuss plans and ideas with, to help us get things off our chests, to laugh and enjoy things together, to just be there when we are feeling low; we need people because humans are social animals. It's not just a psychological need, though: however multi-skilled we may be, there will always be someone else who knows more than us about something and can teach us; who can lend a hand when a job gets too tough, or we are not feeling well enough to complete it; who is part of a team that has a variety of different roles, all essential, all as valuable as one another. Barn-raising, once so common in rural America but now limited to Amish and other more traditional communities, was – until the advent of building contractors – impossible without the help of a sizeable number of willing workers, all focused on a single task for the longer-term benefit of the community. A substantial barn could be raised in less than a week using the combined labour of all those who had the necessary strength and stamina[8] – which, in a self-sufficient community, was almost everyone. But the work wasn't just about getting something done as quickly as possible: it was a chance to eat, talk, sing, and (except for the Amish) drink together; it was a demonstration of people's confidence in each other. A community or tribe[9] – for that is where we need to be headed – that cannot rely on its own people is bound to fail: a tribe that draws together, recognizes the importance of the individuals within it, and whose individuals recognize the importance of the tribe as a functional whole, can thrive indefinitely.[10]

We all have our own specialities as individuals: many, but by no means all of them, are required in the community and, over time, the tribe. Many of the skills we have learnt in civilization may be transferable, particularly for those who work closely with the land, with people and with materials – artistic skills can also be important for morale. Equally, many of the skills we have picked up in civilization are irrelevant to sustainable living outside civilization and could be dangerous, for they may be intrinsically linked to the continuation of civilization: make no mistake, there is a trade-off to be made.

The following list is gathered from a number of different sources,[11] as well as from the personal experiences of people I have the privilege to know. It doesn't contain every skill you may need, but it does provide a starting point over a number of timescales. If the list were any more specific, it would imply that each tribe and group of people working to become self-sufficient is going to be the same: of course it will not. Remember that there is no one right way to live.

Key Skills for Going Beyond Civilization

Short-Term / Emergency (surviving for a few days or weeks)
- Water discovery / capture, purification and storage

- Fire-making

- Shelter-building

- Wild food identification and discovery; food preparation and cooking

- Friendship and community spirit

- Basic first aid

Medium-Term (surviving for a few months or years)
- People skills:[12] conflict resolution; entertaining; consensus decision-making; objective setting and planning; counselling and psychology

- Sustainable food gathering and trapping

- Food production (Permaculture):[13] land and soil management; food growing; preparation, storage and preservation; cooking

- Sanitation and waste management

- Baby and child care: birthing, feeding, caring, educating

- Medical skills: first aid, herbology and anatomy

- Local knowledge: plant and animal lore; meteorology; physical geography

- Home economics (domestic management of resources – not finance)

- Building construction and maintenance

- Mechanics, electricals, chemistry and other useful scientific skills (largely to assist the transition process).

Long-Term (surviving forever)

This is not so much a list of needs as an idea of some of the key skills you should develop or retain for improving your chances. Notice that none of them are practical – by this stage you are likely to have identified most of the practical skills you will ever need.

- Sociology and political analysis: to map out options for the society / community / tribe you are evolving

- Teaching, learning skills and adaptation: to pass on skills and knowledge, and encourage their acquisition

- History and folklore: to learn from the past and protect the future

- The willingness to learn

Over the time I have been writing, blogging and making a general nuisance of myself, people have sent me notes explaining how they are preparing themselves for the future in all sorts of ways – going 'off-grid'; becoming self-sufficient in food; building their own homes away from the dangers of civilization (as far as that is possible); learning about everything they possibly can. Some people who have seen these notes have suggested they are simply dropping out of life and making a move that is the preserve of the affluent few: if you can afford to do it, then that's OK, but what about the rest of us? To me that's missing the point entirely: we simply cannot afford *not* to make the change. I applaud the brave few who have taken the plunge. Where they lead, others have to follow.

*   *   *

In the section called Reproducing, I mentioned there was a fourth reason to have fewer children. Civilization needs a continuous supply of workers in order to feed the growing economy, and this feedstock has to be produced for generation after generation. Sometimes 'problems' occur, such as with unexpected immigration, which can cause a shortage in the supply of houses, school places, workplaces, prison places and so on – but these are temporary aberrations: civilization is very good at consuming more resources in order to produce more of what it needs as required. As we know, the resources Industrial Civilization depends upon are finite – both the ones that it removes from the Earth, and the ones into which it throws all the crap we don't need any more – and Industrial Civilization is hitting all sorts of resource limitations which will, in combination, lead to its downfall.

We have to take these lessons very seriously: like all species on Earth, humans have to observe the natural limits we are provided with. When we live a connected life that doesn't let us ignore these limits, we have to adjust as conditions change, and – if we aren't able to glean out more from less – one of the fundamental adjustments we have to make is to the number of people living in a particular geographical area. That is why ensuring that populations are kept below the level that can be comfortably supported is critical. Balance is the key: between the number of people you need to maintain a successful community; the number of people that can be comfortably supported; and also the wider world in which you live, so you have no need to intrude on other communities, however much the grass may seem greener on their side.

I need to finish this section on a contentious note. A factor that keeps rearing its head in discussions about leaving civilization behind is healthcare: the fear that the moment we step outside of the comfortable arms of modern living we will be subjected to all sorts of medical horrors that will strike us down, and which we will have no defence against. To this there are four things that need to be said: first, the kind of healthcare that has made eternal preservation a distinct possibility is restricted to a very privileged few in Industrial Civilization. Even a nation like the USA which spends more on healthcare per person than any other civilized nation on Earth has dramatic health inequalities[14] – if you don't have health insurance, you only get treated as a last resort. Second, Industrial Civilization may have produced new and innovative ways of fighting human disease, but at the expense of tens of millions of other animals each year,[15] and the release of unknown quantities of synthetic antibiotics and other substances into the natural environment. Third, probably the single biggest killer of newly exposed tribal peoples is the introduction of foreign pathogens to which they have no immunity.[16] Building immunity from scratch takes time, but in the absence of a glut of antibiotics, most humans are able to increase their levels of immunity to common pathogens quickly; after only a single exposure, in the case of viruses. This is not to say that people will not die from disease – that happens regardless of healthcare provision – but medicine doesn't need to be synthetic, we just need to learn how to find the metaphorical dock-leaf; a skill we have lost in the cosseted world of hospitals and over-the-counter remedies.

Finally, civilization itself is the worst disease of all; not only because of the raft of cancers, diet- and habit-related diseases and mental conditions unique to the Culture of Maximum Harm; not only because it has turned largely benign, isolated organisms into global killing machines;[17] not only because of the complete failure of civilization to equip us with the basic tools to look after ourselves; but also, and primarily, because of the catastrophe that is edging towards us in the form of irreversible climatic and environmental change – all civilization's doing. Losing your cabinet of synthetic pharmaceuticals and your ambulance service may be one kind of loss; but in the big scheme of things, it's a loss that has many gains attached to it.

Giving the Earth a Future

Early in 2006, I started to write on a small and insignificant website called The Earth Blog. From the beginning it was subtitled, 'Giving the Earth a Future', and people had often said to me things like: "But, the Earth has got a future, it's just that we might not be a part of it." That's what got me thinking about many things that culminated in the writing of this book: it forced me to get a grip on the complexity of the change that was taking place, which seemed to have no beginning and no end, and which no one seemed to have made any sense of, and it made me realize how far we had lost contact with the real world, and to understand how this could have happened beneath our very noses. Most unexpectedly – I think it was while taking a shower of all things – it brought me to the conclusion that, despite the harm that many humans have inflicted on the Earth, and despite our insignificance as just one of millions of species; to us, we really are the most important things on the entire planet. If we snuff ourselves out, then nothing that happens afterwards can possibly matter.

I also have one slightly more pragmatic response to those who doubt that we have a duty to give the Earth a future: if, through the activities of Industrial Civilization, humanity ceases to exist, it will undoubtedly leave a legacy of turmoil. Climatic systems that will take eons to readjust; rivers, soil, oceans and animals full of the toxic by-products of our industrial past; and probably worst of all, at least 70% of all species on Earth wiped off the face of the planet in a synthetic replay of the great Permian extinction event that occurred around 250 million years ago – one that was accompanied by the kinds of climatic conditions that we are bringing the Earth towards at an ever-increasing rate.

We can look at the results of the experiment called civilization and feel helpless, or we can look at what we have in ourselves, and what remains undamaged on the Earth, and think, "We can do better." The future is still ours if we have the determination to survive it and, whether you like it or not, the future will be determined by the decisions you make. 'Giving the Earth a Future' seems about right in these circumstances, and we have just the solution at our fingertips: all we have to do is wave goodbye to civilization, and learn once again to be ourselves.

Afterword

That would have been a good place to finish, but some people are never satisfied. I can't predict where we are going to end up, but I can predict what some people are going to think upon finishing this book: "What about the long-term future? What about the next 100,000 years, when we might be wiped out by an asteroid; or what about the next five billion years, when the Earth will cease to exist – why are you so concerned about the short term? Why do you want to stop civilization in its tracks and prevent any hope of us stopping the asteroid or hopping from planet to planet in search of other habitable worlds?"

My simple answer is this: if we don't deal with the next 100 years, then what happens 100,000 years or five billion years in the future doesn't matter at all. We can plan ahead a few decades, maybe a bit longer – enough for two or three more generations, but at least a starting point for what comes after. When we have managed to survive the next few decades in one piece, then maybe our grandchildren can talk about the distant future; sitting by the sparkling, clean river; breathing in the fresh air; surrounded by an abundance of life.

Does that sound like a plan?

References and Notes

You can find hyperlinks to the web references below at www.amatterofscale.com.

Chapter 1

1. UNAIDS, '2006 Report on the Global AIDS Epidemic', 2006, http://data.unaids.org/pub/GlobalReport/2006/2006_GR_CH02_en.pdf (accessed 28 November, 2007).

2. Not everyone infected with HIV will develop full-blown AIDS; the main reason being that many will die of other causes before the incubation period has passed. If the recipient of the infection does survive the incubation period (up to ten years, but far less without drug therapy) then it is almost certain that they will contract AIDS.

3. www.who.int/mediacentre/factsheets/fs117/en/ (accessed 28 November, 2007).

4. Stephen King, *The Stand*, 1978, New English Library.

5. Alfred W. Crosby, *America's Forgotten Pandemic: The Influenza of 1918*, Cambridge University Press, 2003.

6. www.who.int/vaccine_research/diseases/ari/en/index.html (accessed 28 November, 2007).

7. Information from Symantec Corp. www.symantec.com/norton/security_response/definitions.jsp (accessed 28 November, 2007). An 'in the wild' virus is one that has been detected on a computer other than the one on which it was developed, i.e. it has multiplied.

8. George Rice, 'Are Viruses Alive?', http://serc.carleton.edu/microbelife/yellowstone/viruslive.html (accessed 28 November, 2007).

9. British Antarctic Survey, 'Climate Change – Our View', www.antarctica.ac.uk/bas_research/our_views/climate_change.php (accessed 30 November, 2007).

10. *The Independent*, 'Second case of bluetongue found in Suffolk', http://news.independent.co.uk/uk/this_britain/article2996099.ece (accessed 30 November, 2007).

11. Jirí Olejnícek and Ivan Gelbic, 'Differences in response to temperature and density between two strains of the mosquito, Culex pipiens molestus Forskal', *J. Vector Ecology* (25), 2000.

12. *Washington Post*, 'Climate Change Drives Disease To New Territory', 2006.

13. Indian Railways Yearbook 2005-6, www.indianrailways.gov.in/deptts/stat-eco/YB-05-06/passenger-business.pdf (accessed 4 December, 2007).

14. 'The Great Mumbai Rail Experience', http://cosmic-confusion.blogspot.com/2006/08/great-mumbai-rail-experience.html (accessed 3 January, 2008).

15. *Demographia*, 'Selected Current and Historic City, Ward & Neighborhood Densities', www.demographia.com/db-citydenshist.htm (accessed 4 December, 2007).

16. Karl Taro Greenfeld, *China Syndrome*, 2006, Penguin Books.

17. USDA Foreign Agricultural Service, 'China, People's Republic of, Poultry and Products Semi-Annual Report 2006', 2006, www.fas.usda.gov/gainfiles/200602/146176724.pdf (accessed 4 December, 2007).

18. World Health Organization, 'Avian influenza – Fact Sheet', 2006, www.who.int/mediacentre/factsheets/avian_influenza/en/ (accessed 6 December, 2007).

19. See Greenfeld, reference 16 above.

20. Ontario Genomics Institute, 'Is it possible that avian flu can combine with Spanish Flu?', www.ontariogenomics.ca/education/episode13.asp (accessed 6 December, 2007).

21. *New Scientist*, 'European airlines to trade emissions allowances', http://technology.newscientist.com/channel/tech/aviation/dn10829-european-airlines-to-trade-emissions-allowances.html (accessed 6 December, 2007).

22. As described in the (former) Chicago Convention, 1944: "Fuel, lubricating oils, spare parts, regular equipment and aircraft stores on board an aircraft of a contracting State, on arrival in the territory of another contracting State and retained on board on leaving the territory of that State shall be exempt from

customs duty, inspection fees or similar national or local duties and charges." International Civil Aviation Organization, 'Convention on International Civil Aviation: Ninth Edition, 2006', www.icao.int/icaonet/dcs/7300_cons.pdf (accessed 13 June, 2008).

23. *Nature*, 'Planes play big role in spreading flu', http://network.nature.com/boston/news/articles/2006/09/12/planes-play-big-role-in-spreading-flu (accessed 6 December, 2007).

24. Richard Preston, *The Hot Zone*, Doubleday, 1994.

25. World Health Organization, 'Ebola haemorrhagic fever', www.who.int/mediacentre/factsheets/fs103/en/ (accessed 6 December, 2007).

26. Martin Wiselka, personal communication, 7 November, 2007.

27. 'State of the World's Forests 2007', UN FAO, www.fao.org/docrep/009/a0773e/a0773e00.htm (accessed 6 December, 2007).

28. A carbon sink is anything that locks away carbon rather than it being released into the atmosphere.

29. See UN FAO, reference 27 above.

30. Nadine T. Laporte, Jared A. Stabach, Robert Grosch, Tiffany S. Lin, Scott J. Goetz, 'Expansion of Industrial Logging in Central Africa', Science (8), 2007, (quoted in http://news.mongabay.com/2007/0607-congo.html, accessed 6 December, 2007).

31. Ibid.

Chapter 2

1. L. Kappen, 'Field measurements of carbon dioxide exchange of the Antarctic lichen Usnea sphacekta in the frozen state', *Antarctic Science* (1), 1989.

2. Toni Gabaldon and Martijn A. Huynen, 'Reconstruction of the Proto-Mitochondrial Metabolism', *Science* 301 (2003).

3. Jeremy K. Nicholson, Elaine Holmes, John C. Lindon & Ian D. Wilson, 'The challenges of modeling mammalian biocomplexity', *Nature Biotechnology* (22), 2004, (quoted in www.wired.com/medtech/health/news/2004/10/65252 (accessed 10 December, 2007)).

4. Ibid.

5. When dealing with many smaller life forms, pluralization can be confusing. Bacteria is the plural of bacterium, and virii is sometimes used mistakenly as the plural of virus, particularly in reference to computer viruses.

6. R.G. Eagon, 'Pseudomonas natriegens, a marine bacterium with a generation time of less than 10 minutes', *J. Bacteriology* (83), 1962.

7. National Institute of Standards and Technology, 'Cornell Discusses His Recovery from Necrotizing Fasciitis with Reporters', www.nist.gov/public_affairs/newsfromnist_Cornell_mediaevent.htm (accessed 13 December, 2007).

8. www.ni.unimelb.edu.au/docs/forum/5-Carapetis.pdf (accessed 13 December, 2007) which takes its figures from Jonathan R. Carapetis, Andrew C. Steer, E. Kim Mulholland and Martin Weber, 'The global burden of group A streptococcal diseases', Lancet Infect Dis (5), 2005.

9. WHO Statistical Information System, www.who.int/research/en/ (accessed 14 December, 2007).

10. 'Trialling a new vaccine for tuberculosis', Wellcome Trust, www.wellcome.ac.uk/News/News-archive/Browse-by-date/2001/Features/WTX024018.htm (accessed 14 December, 2007).

11. A.R. Zink, C. Sola, U. Reischl, W. Grabner, N. Rastogi, H. Wolf, A.G. Nerlich, 'Characterization of Mycobacterium tuberculosis complex DNAs from Egyptian mummies by spoligotyping', *J Clin Microbiol.* (41), 2003.

12. Richard Fortey, *Life: An Unauthorized Biography*, HarperCollins, 1997.

13. Martin Wiselka, personal communication, 7 November, 2007.

14. D. A. Ratkowsky, Jone Olley, T. A. McMeekin and A. Ball, 'Relationship Between Temperature and Growth Rate of Bacterial Cultures', *J. Bacteriology* (149), 1982.

15. Paul S. Mead et al., 'Food-Related Illness and Death in the United States', Centers for Disease Control, www.cdc.gov/ncidod/eid/vol5no5/mead.htm (accessed 18 December, 2007).

16. World Health Organization, 'Diarrhoeal Diseases: Typhoid Fever', www.who.int/vaccine_research/diseases/diarrhoeal/en/index7.html (accessed 18 December, 2007).

17. Philippe Roumagnac et al., 'Evolutionary History of Salmonella Typhi', *Science* (24), 2006.

18. Buddha Basnyat, Ashish P. Maskey, Mark D. Zimmerman and David R. Murdoch, 'Enteric (Typhoid) Fever in Travelers', CID (41), 2005.

19. Spike Milligan (edited by Jack Hobbs), *Mussolini: His Part In My Downfall*, Penguin Books, 1978.

20. From the Simpsons archive. To see the full quotation, go to www.snpp.com/episodes/7F19.html

21. Centers for Disease Control, 'Lyme Disease – United States, 2001-2002', www.cdc.gov/mmwr/preview/mmwrhtml/mm5317a4.htm and 'Lyme Disease – United States, 2003-2005', www.cdc.gov/mmwr/preview/mmwrhtml/mm5623a1.htm (accessed 20 December, 2007).

22. Kathleen LoGiudice et al., 'The ecology of infectious disease: Effects of host diversity and community composition on Lyme disease risk', *PNAS* (100), 2003.

23. World Health Organization, Weekly Epidemiological Record (79), 2004, www.who.int/wer/2004/en/wer7933.pdf (accessed 20 December, 2007).

24. Keith Farnish, 'What If . . . We All Became Vegan?', The Earth Blog, http://earth-blog.bravejournal.com/entry/17001 (accessed 20 December, 2007).

25. T.E. Amerault and T.O. Roby, 'Card test an accurate and simple procedure for detecting anaplasmosis', *World Animal Review*, 1981, www.fao.org/DOCREP/004/X6538E/X6538E04.htm (accessed 13 June, 2008).

26. Secretariat of the Pacific Community, 'Cattle Tick', www.spc.int/rahs/Manual/BOVINE/CATTLE%20TICKE.HTM (accessed 20 December, 2007).

27. For example, all leopards are of the same genus as each other, as are all honey-bees.

28. Chris J. D. Zarafonetis, 'The Typhus Fevers' in 'Internal Medicine In World War II', http://history.amedd.army.mil/booksdocs/wwii/infectiousdisvolii/chapter7.htm (accessed 20 December, 2007).

29. David W. Tschanz, 'Typhus Fever On The Eastern Front In World War I', http://entomology.montana.edu/historybug/WWI/TEF.htm (accessed 20 December, 2007).

30. Michael W. Gray, 'Rickettsia, typhus and the mitochondrial connection', *Nature* (396), 1998.

Chapter 3

1. In the world of commercial 'pest' control almost everything that moves is a potential pest. A few commentators have observed that maybe the only true pests are humans, e.g. http://query.nytimes.com/gst/fullpage.html?res=9801E2DB123FF931A25757C0A9619C8B63 (accessed 13 June, 2008).

2. 'Plant Parasitic Nematodes', USDA ARS, www.ars.usda.gov/Services/docs.htm?docid=9628 (accessed 3 January, 2008).

3. N. A. Cobb, 'Nematodes and their relationships', Dept. Agric. Yearbook, 1914 (quoted in R. N. Huettel and A. M. Golden, 'Nathan Augustus Cobb', *Ann. Rev. Phytopathology* (29), 1991).

4. Ibid.

5. Victor H. Dropkin, *Introduction to Plant Nematology*, John Wiley and Sons, 1980.

6. Meat & Wool New Zealand, 'Wool Exports', www.meatandwoolnz.com/main.cfm?id=259#331 (accessed 3 January, 2008).

7. R. Danovaro et al., 'Exponential Decline of Deep-Sea Ecosystem Functioning Linked to Benthic Biodiversity Loss', *Curr. Biology* (17), 2007.

8. The Scottish Government, 'Potato cyst nematodes - a technical overview for Scotland', www.scotland.gov.uk/consultations/agriculture/PCN_Technical_Paper_Scotland_SEERAD.pdf (accessed 30 December, 2007).

9. SeedQuest, 'BASF expects European Union approval of Amflora potato within weeks', www.seedquest.com/News/releases/2007/december/21250.htm (accessed 30 December, 2007).

10. M. Toparlak et al., 'Contamination of Children's Playground Sandpits with Toxocara eggs in Istanbul, Turkey', *Turk J Vet Anim Sci* (26), 2002.

11. 'A History of Crop Protection and Pest Control in our Society', *Croplife Canada*, www.croplife.ca/english/pdf/Analyzing2003/T1History.pdf (accessed 7 January, 2007).

12. CAMEO Chemicals, 'Chemical data sheet for: Copper Acetoarsenite', http://cameochemicals.noaa.gov/chemical/2981 (accessed 7 January, 2007).

13. Sorry about the terminology – it just means 'insect killer'.

14. Randy Gaugler, 'Nematodes', Cornell University, www.nysaes.cornell.edu/ent/biocontrol/pathogens/nematodes.html (accessed 2 February, 2008).

15. William T. Crow, 'Using Nematodes to Control Insects: Overview and Frequently Asked Questions', http://edis.ifas.ufl.edu/IN468 (accessed 8 January, 2008).

16. Simon Gowan, University of Reading, personal communication.

17. G. C. Smart Jr. 'Entomopathogenic Nematodes for the Biological Control of Insects', *Supp. J. Nematology* (27), 1995.

18. A.H. Jay Burr and A. Forest Robinson, 'Locomotion Behavior' in Eds. Randy Gaugler, Anwar L. Bilgrami, *Nematode Behavior*, CABI Publishing, 2004.

19. Southern Illinois University Carbondale, 'Root-knot nematode moving into Illinois fields', 2001, http://news.siu.edu/news/June02/060402k2114.html (accessed 9 January, 2008).

20. Iowa State University, 'Researchers Bioengineer Plants Resistant to Devastating Pathogen', 2006, www.ag.iastate.edu/aginfo/news/2006releases/baum.html (accessed 10 January. 2008).

21. University of California IPM, 'Phenology Model Database: Columbia Root Knot Nematode', http://ucipm.ucdavis.edu/PHENOLOGY/mn-columbia_root_knot.html (accessed 10 January, 2008).

22. Fred Pearce, 'Bye Bye Bananas', Boston Globe, www.thedominican.net/articles/banana.htm (accessed 10 January 2008).

23. Dan Koeppel, 'Can This Fruit Be Saved?', *Popular Science*, www.popsci.com/popsci/science/5a4d4c3ee4d05010vgnvcm1000004eecbccdrcrd.html (accessed 10 January, 2008).

24. Alexandra Abrahams, 'Adopt A Veg', *The Ecologist*, www.theecologist.org/archive_detail.asp?content_id=231 (accessed 10 January, 2008).

25. 'Burrowing and Lesion Nematodes of Banana', Secretariat of the Pacific Community, www.spc.int/PPS/PDF%20PALs/PAL%2005%20Banana%20Burrowing%20Nematode.pdf (accessed 10 January, 2008).

Chapter 4

1. Alexie Barrioneuvo, 'Honeybees Vanish, Leaving Keepers in Peril', *New York Times*, www.nytimes.com/2007/02/27/business/27bees.html (accessed 15 January, 2008).

2. This is a particularly good (bad) example of the bizarre thought processes that lead to scare stories: www.i-sis.org.uk/MobilePhonesVanishingBees.php. Mobile phones don't even use the same microwave frequencies as DECT phones. A friend of mine dug out even more examples including: www.monstersandcritics.com/tech/news/article_1293113.php/Mobile_phones_massacring_honeybees_,ww w.newscientist.com/blog/environment/2007/04/are-cellphones-wiping-out-bees.html, http://conservativeculture.com/2007/04/your-talking-the-honey-bees-to-death and www.hese-project.org/hese-uk/en/issues/nature.php (all accessed 13 June, 2008).

3. Diana Cox-Foster, 'Prepared Testimony before the U.S. House of Representatives Committee on Agriculture Subcommittee on Horticulture and Organic Agriculture on Colony Collapse Disorder in Honey Bee Colonies in the United States', http://maarec.cas.psu.edu/CCDPpt/CoxFosterTestimonyFinal.pdf (accessed 18 January, 2008).

4. J.R. Minkel, 'Mysterious Honeybee Disappearance Linked to Rare Virus', *Scientific American*, www.sciam.com/article.cfm?id=E0E0362F-E7F2-99DF-3F4F781839D6C879&page=1 (accessed 18 January, 2007).

5. S. Testi et al., 'Severe anaphylaxis to royal jelly attributed to cefonicid', *J Investig Allergol Clin Immunology* (17), 2007.

6. Alan Campion, *Bees at the bottom of the garden*, Northern Bee Books, 2001.

7. Quoted in many places, including 'Bee decline threatens our dinner and the countryside', *Daily Telegraph*, www.telegraph.co.uk/earth/main.jhtml?xml=/earth/2007/08/03/eabees103.xml (accessed 29 June, 2008).

8. www.pbs.org/aboutpbs/ (accessed 18 January, 2008).

9. You can watch the whole, hilarious trailer at: www.pbs.org/wnet/nature/bees/ (accessed 18 January, 2008).

10. L. McClure, 'Is a Paleolithic Age Diet an Optimal Diet for Modern Human Beings?', http://escholarship.umassmed.edu/ssp/27/.

11. World Health Organization, 'Diet, Nutrition and the Prevention of Chronic Diseases', www.fao.org/docrep/005/ac911e/ac911e00.HTM (accessed 18 January, 2008).

12. Mildred M. Haley, 'Changing Consumer Demand for Meat: The U.S. Example, 1970 – 2000', USDA, www.ers.usda.gov/publications/wrs011/wrs011g.pdf (accessed 18 January, 2008).

13. Alexadra-Maria Klein et al., 'Importance of Pollinators in Changing Landscapes for World Crops', *Proc. R. Soc. B.* (272), 2007.

14. Ibid.

15. Ibid.

16. 'Current world fertilizer trends and outlook to 2009/10', UN FAO, ftp://ftp.fao.org/agl/agll/docs/cwfto09.pdf (accessed 18 January, 2007).

17. 'Climate Change 2007, The Physical Science Basis', IPCC Working Group 1, http://ipcc-wg1.ucar.edu/wg1/wg1-report.html (accessed 21 January, 2008).

18. Quoted in George Raine, 'Many causes blamed for honeybee die-off', San Francisco Chronicle, www.sfgate.com/cgi-bin/article.cgi?f=/c/a/2007/06/01/BUGQ2Q5AAI22.DTL (accessed 21 January, 2008).

19. At this stage I need to define the word, which repeats throughout the text in ever more accusative terms: Civilization. Definitions of Civilization vary but in essence the word means, 'city dwelling', and is defined by its dependence for resources on a larger geographical area than the civilization actually occupies. The best general summary for 'civilization' I can find (from http://anthropik.com/2005/03/what-is-civilization/, accessed 29 April, 2008):

> Primary Criteria:

1. Settlement of cities of 5,000 or more people. 2. Full-time labor specialization.

3. Concentration of surplus. 4. Class structure. 5. State-level political organization.

> Secondary Criteria:

1. Monumental architecture. 2. Long-distance trade. 3. Sophisticated art.

4. Writing. 5. Predictive sciences (math, astronomy, etc.)

> The secondary criteria have a general correspondence with civilization, but are not definitive. There are plenty of civilizations that lack one or more of them, two out of five (predictive sciences and sophisticated art) are human universals, and two of the remaining items (monumental architecture and long-distance trade) are known among non-civilized societies.

> The primary criteria, though, help us to begin to understand the true nature of civilization. It is my supposition that these criteria form a reflexive set; that no one of these criteria can be met without also fulfilling the other four. That these five primary criteria form a single cultural 'package', best defined by the word 'civilization'.

> I have used the extended term 'Industrial Civilization' to distinguish the current, most destructive form of civilization from the various civilizations that have existed in the past. It is Industrial Civilization that needs to be dealt with. Inevitably, other civilizations will follow – that problem will have to be dealt with when it happens.

20. T.O. Lloyd, *Empire: The History of the British Empire*, Continuum, 2001.

Chapter 5

1. '"Nemo" mania poses threat to clownfish', *The Independent*, www.independent.co.uk/environment/nemo-mania-poses-threat-to-clownfish-581465.html (accessed 28 January, 2008).

2. 'From Ocean To Aquarium: The global trade in marine ornamental species', UNEP / WCMC, 2003.

3. Vaclav Smil, 'Worldwide transformation of diets, burdens of meat production and opportunities for novel food proteins', Enzyme and Microbial Technology (30), 2002.

4. Fisheries Research Services, www.frs-scotland.gov.uk/FRS.Web/Delivery/display_standalone.aspx?contentid=472 (accessed 29 January, 2008).

5. Personal communications (January, 2008). The name has been changed; there is a great deal of sensitivity amongst fisherman over these issues – they are often loath to talk to anyone who may give the fishing industry a bad name.

6. 'The State of World Fisheries and Aquaculture – 2006', FAO, www.fao.org/docrep/009/a0699e/a0699e00.htm (accessed 2 February, 2008).

7. Garrett Hardin, 'The Tragedy of the Commons', Science (162), 1968. The original wording is: 'The individual benefits as an individual from his ability to deny the truth even though society as a whole, of which he is a part, suffers.' I'm sure he would appreciate the sentiment.

8. Mark Kurlansky, *Cod*, 1997, Vintage.

9. UN FAO, 'World aquaculture production of fish, crustaceans, molluscs, etc., by principal producers in 2005', ftp://ftp.fao.org/fi/STAT/summary/a-4.pdf (accessed 22 February, 2007).

10. Rosamond L. Naylor et al., 'Effects of Aquaculture on World Fish Supplies', US EPA, www.epa.gov/watertrain/pdf/issue8.pdf (accessed 22 February, 2008).

11. The IPCC report says: "The observed widespread warming of the atmosphere and ocean, together with ice mass loss, support the conclusion that it is extremely unlikely that global climate change of the past 50 years can be explained without external forcing, and very likely that it is not due to known natural causes alone." IPCC 4th Assessment Report, Working Group 1, 'Summary for Policymakers', IPCC, 2007.

12. John Gordon, 'Deep Sea Demersal Fisheries', Joint Nature Conservation Committee, www.jncc.gov.uk/page-2525.

13. More properly known as Kalaallit Nunaat, in Greenlandic, but for convenience I will refer to it as Greenland.

14. 'Ice melts opening up Northwest Passage', *Daily Telegraph*, www.telegraph.co.uk/earth/main.jhtml?xml=/earth/2007/09/15/eaNW115.xml (accessed 1 February, 2008).

15. A simple but striking presentation of this can be found at http://maps.grida.no/go/graphic/climate-feedbacks-the-connectivity-of-the-positive-ice-snow-albedo-feedback-terrestrial-snow-and-vegetation-feedbacks-and-the-negative-cloud-radiation-feedback (accessed 1 February, 2008), which shows both feedback loops and a web of connections between the different components.

16. Government of British Columbia, Ministry of Environment, 'Ambient Water Quality Criteria for Dissolved Oxygen', www.env.gov.bc.ca/wat/wq/BCguidelines/do/do-01.htm (accessed 4 February, 2008).

17. Laurence Challier et al., 'Environmental and stock effects on recruitment variability in the English Channel squid Loligo forbesi', *Aquat. Living Resour.* (18), 2005.

18. NASA GISS, 'GISS Surface Temperature Analysis: August 2007 Update and Effects', http://data.giss.nasa.gov/gistemp/updates/200708.html (accessed 23 February, 2008).

19. Michael Fumento, 'James Hansen's Hacks', www.fumento.com/environment/globalwarming.html (accessed 5 February, 2008).

20. '2007 Annual Climate Review U.S. Summary', US NCDC, www.ncdc.noaa.gov/oa/climate/research/2007/ann/us-summary.html (accessed 5 February, 2008).

21. E. Otterlei et al., 'Temperature dependent otolith growth of larval and early juvenile Atlantic cod (Gadus morhua)', *ICES Journal of Marine Science* (59), 2002.

22. David O. Conover, 'Effects of Climate Change on Fisheries', www.stonybrook.edu/sb/testimony.pdf (accessed 5 February, 2008).

23. NASA GISS, 'GISS Surface Temperature Analysis: Global Temperature Trends: 2007 Summation', http://data.giss.nasa.gov/gistemp/2007/ (accessed 4 February, 2008). The average is officially between 1951 and 1980, but this works out to be very close to the average for the entire century.

24. Michael J. Behrenfeld et al., 'Climate-driven trends in contemporary ocean productivity', *Nature* (444), 2006.

Chapter 6

1. *Encyclopaedia Britannica*, XXIII, 1888: 'They [the Altai] are chiefly hunters, passionately loving their taiga, or wild forest.'

2. WWF, 'Eastern Siberian Taiga - A Global Ecoregion', www.panda.org/about_wwf/where_we_work/ecoregions/eastern_siberian_taiga.cfm (accessed 7 February, 2008).

3. Eyewitness testimony from N. V. Vasiliev et al., 'Eyewitness accounts of Tunguska (Crash)', 1981, http://tunguska.tsc.ru/ru/science/1/0 (accessed 8 February, 2008).

4. Simon Welware and John Fairley, *Arthur C. Clarke's Mysterious World*, Fontana, 1980.

5. More correctly known as Cyanobacteria, these are a range of functionally evolved bacteria, the green varieties which are able to extract energy from the sun and produce oxygen, and are an immediate precursor to plant cells which they form part of (Richard Dawkins, *The Ancestor's Tale*, Weidenfeld and Nicolson, 2006).

6. The slow battle is explained beautifully by Richard Fortey in *Life*, HarperCollins, 1997.

7. The Carboniferous period stretched from 360 to 290 million years before present, and takes its name from the carbon-based fossil fuels laid down during this time of extreme foliage production.

8. Janet Marinelli, 'Power Plants—The Origin of Fossil Fuels', www.bbg.org/gar2/pgn/2003su_fossilfuels.html (accessed 8 February, 2008).

9. CDLI Canada, 'Boreal Forest Fact Sheets', www.stemnet.nf.ca/CITE/artsmarts/boreal_factsheets.PDF and Canadian Wildlife Services: Niterland Who's Who, 'Canada's Boreal Forest', www.hww.ca/hww2.asp?id=354 (accessed 8 February, 2008).

10. 'Revised 1996 IPCC Guidelines for National Greenhouse Gas Inventories', IPCC, www.ipcc-nggip.iges.or.jp/public/gl/invs6d.htm (accessed 11 February, 2008).

11. S. H. Lamlom and R. A. Savidge, 'A reassessment of carbon content in wood: variation within and between 41 North American species', *Biomass and Bioenergy* (25), 2003.

12. Natural Resources Canada, 'Boreal Forest', http://atlas.nrcan.gc.ca/site/english/learningresources/theme_modules/borealforest/index.html (accessed 11 February, 2008).

13. Energy Information Administration, 'International Energy Annual 2005', www.eia.doe.gov/pub/international/iealf/tableh1co2.xls (accessed 11 February, 2008).

14. The Kyoto Protocol, ratified by Canada in 2002, committed the government to reduce emissions to 6% below 1990 levels during 2008-2012. This would mean a 30% reduction in carbon dioxide alone, from 2005, and certainly more from 2008-2012. There is almost no chance of this being achieved.

15. 'Envoys take overnight break as Bali conference extended', CBC News, www.cbc.ca/world/story/2007/12/14/bali-conference.html (accessed 11 February, 2008).

16. You can try to find them yourself – the best I could do was the 'Intensity' figures at www3.gov.ab.ca/env/soe/climate_indicators/15_ghg.html. British Columbia are happy to post theirs at www.env.gov.bc.ca/soerpt/996greenhouse/emissionsglance.html (both accessed 11 February, 2008).

17. Gross Domestic Product is an indicator of the financial earnings of a country or region. As it is based on earnings only it is no indicator of the overall economic strength of a country, nor does it say anything about the overall quality of life of the people in that country. It would be better renamed Grossly Damaging Production.

18. 'Alberta's Economic Performance 1994-2004', Alberta Office of Budget and Management, www.finance.alberta.ca/aboutalberta/spotlights/2006_0323_alberta_economic_performance.pdf (accessed 11 February, 2008).

19. 'State Of The World's Forests 2007', UN FAO, ftp://ftp.fao.org/docrep/fao/009/a0773e/a0773e07.pdf (accessed 16 February, 2008).

20. Forest Products Association of Canada, 'Forest Products Industry Calls for Greater Scrutiny of Forest Management Practices in the World's Forests', 2007, www.fpac.ca/en/media_centre/press_releases/2007/2007-08-20_greenpeaceAnnouncement.php (accessed 16 February, 2008).

21. See UN FAO, reference 19 above.

22. Aesop's fable, 'The Tortoise and the Hare', tells the story of an overconfident hare that challenges a

humble tortoise to a race. The hare, so enamoured by its lead, halfway through the race, decided to take a nap, during which time the tortoise plods past and wins the race.

23. 'Trends, Friends and Enemies', Taiga Rescue Network, 2003, www.taigarescue.org/_v3/files/pdf/39.pdf (accessed 16 February, 2008).

24. UN FAO, ForesSTAT, http://faostat.fao.org/site/381/default.aspx

25. Forestry Commission, 'Management of great spruce bark beetle', www.forestresearch.gov.uk/fr/INFD-6XPC8D (accessed 16 February, 2008).

26. *Forest Health Conditions In Alaska 2006*, USDA, 2007.

27. Dan Glaister, 'Plague of beetles raises climate change fears for American beauty', *The Guardian*, www.guardian.co.uk/environment/2007/mar/19/usnews.conservationandendangeredspecies (accessed 18 February, 2008).

28. F. Lieutier, 'Host Resistance to Bark Beetles and its Variations', in *Bark and Wood Boring Insects in Living Trees in Europe, a Synthesis*, Kluwer Academic Publishers, 2003.

29. A.M. Johnson et al., 'Increased Bark Beetle Damage due to Changing Climate Extremes?', *Geophys. R. Abstracts* (6), 2004.

30. 'Climate Change Impacts, Adaptation and Vulnerability', IPCC Working Group II, www.ipcc-wg2.org/ (accessed 18 February, 2008).

31. F.S. Chapin et al., 'Arctic and boreal ecosystems of western North America as components of the climate system', *Global Change Biology* (6), 2000.

32. According to Amber J. Soja, et al., 'Climate-induced boreal forest change: Predictions versus current observations', *Global and Planetary Change* (56), 2007, "In Siberia, 7 of the last 9 years have resulted in extreme fire seasons, and extreme fire years have also been more frequent in both Alaska and Canada."

33. M. Wang and J. Overland, 'Detecting Arctic Climate Change Using Köppen Climate Classification', *Climatic Change* (67), 2004.

34. Fred Pearce, 'Climate Warning as Siberia Melts', *New Scientist*, 2005.

35. Keith Farnish, 'Defusing The Methane Timebomb', The Earth Blog, http://earth-blog.bravejournal.com/entry/22611 (accessed 18 February, 2008).

36. Trausti Valsson, *How The World Will Change With Global Warming*, University of Iceland Press, 2006.

Chapter 7

1. GM Freeze, 'Independent assessment of the implications of patents on genetic resources', www.gmfreeze.org/page.asp?id=233&iType=1081 (accessed 22 February, 2008).

2. Money Morning, 'Monsanto Reaps Huge Rewards From Its Blossoming Seed Business', www.moneymorning.com/2008/01/07/monsanto-reaps-huge-rewards-from-its-blossoming-seed-business/ (accessed 22 February, 2008).

3. Definition from http://syntheticbiology.org/ (accessed 22 February, 2008).

4. OpenWetWare, http://openwetware.org/wiki/Materials (accessed 23 February, 2008).

5. Terrorism is in the eye of the target. The word has been ridiculously misused in recent years, such that you can be branded a terrorist in both the USA and the UK simply for suggesting that suicide bombers may sometimes have just motivation for acting as they do. 'Terrorism' has become a classic propaganda word, in the same sense that 'Communism' was a propaganda word during the McCarthy era (USA from the mid-1950s until the late 1960s): it instils fear, thus allowing for greater control over those who are persuaded to be afraid.

6. John Stuart Mill, *Utilitarianism*, Hackett, 2001 (second edition).

7. 'Synthetic Life', *The Economist*, 2006, http://web.rollins.edu/~tlairson/tech/synlife5.html (accessed 23 February, 2008).

8. J.W. von Goethe, 'Epirrhema', from *Goethe: Selected Verse*, translated by David Luke, Penguin, 1964.

9. Deep Impact post-encounter factsheet, NASA, http://solarsystem.nasa.gov/deepimpact/mission/factsheet-postencounter.pdf (accessed 23 February, 2008).

10. Carl Sagan, *Cosmos*, Macdonald, 1981.

Chapter 8

1. I like the term 'Survival Machine'. You can read more about this term at www.edge.org/documents/ThirdCulture/j-Ch.3.html (accessed 10 October, 2007).

2. These opinions are taken from friends, common beliefs and my own thoughts. You might like to add some of your own.

3. Or 'COmmon aNCESTORS': Richard Dawkins, *The Ancestor's Tale*, Houghton Mifflin, 2004.

4. Richard Fortey, *Life: An Unauthorized Biography*, HarperCollins, 1997.

5. ITIS (the Interagency Taxonomic Information System) is a US Government resource, but is available to all Internet users. See www.itis.gov/itis_phy.html (accessed 11 October, 2007).

6. I am trying to remain consistent with my spelling of words that are different, depending upon the 'type' of English being used. Many Americanized spellings – like 'Americanized' – are actually derived from the original British spellings. Mid-Atlantic is the best way of describing my approach.

7. William F. Bynum, 'The Great Chain Of Being After Forty Years: An Appraisal', *History Of Science* (13), 1975.

8. Edward O. Wilson, *Success And Dominance In Ecosystems: The Case of Social Insects*, 1990, Ecology Institute.

9. May R. Berenbaum, *Buzzwords*, Joseph Henry, 2000.

10. It is true that the archaea bacteria that sit at the very roots of life are anaerobes, i.e. they can live without oxygen, and oxygen is lethal to many of these bacteria (Richard Fortey, *Life*, Flamingo, 1998), but it is also true that the majority of autotrophs do not require such harsh conditions.

11. UN Department of Economic and Social Affairs: http://esa.un.org/unpp/ (accessed 15 October, 2007).

12. Sources: http://esa.un.org/unpp/ (UN Department of Economic and Social Affairs) and www.census.gov/ipc/www/worldhis.html (US Census Bureau) (accessed 15 October, 2007).

13. BCE: Before Common Era. This is a standard convention for historical dating. Equivalent to BC in Christian cultures.

14. CE: Common Era. CE is another standard convention. This is equivalent to AD (*Anno Domini*).

15. Optimum Population Trust, 'Ecological footprinting and the Living Planet Report', www.optimumpopulation.org/opt.sustainable.numbers.html (accessed 15 October, 2007). Their figures are based on the WWF report mentioned in the reference, along with widely available demographic data.

16. Jeff Hecht, 'Donkey Domestication Began in Africa', www.newscientist.com/article.ns?id=dn6032 (accessed 15 October 2007).

17. Charles More, *Understanding The Industrial Revolution*, Routledge, 2000.

18. UN Population Division, 'The World at Six Billion', www.un.org/esa/population/publications/sixbillion/sixbilpart1.pdf (accessed 15 October, 2007).

19. Ed. Geoffrey Parker, *The Times Atlas Of World History*, Times Books, 1993.

20. UN Population Division, 'World Population Prospects: The 2005 Revision', www.un.org/esa/population/publications/WUP2005/2005WUPHighlights_Exec_Sum.pdf (accessed 18 October, 2007).

21. Subsistence is another way of saying 'living off the land'. You catch, pick, dig up and fell anything that you need to survive.

22. Andy Collier, 'Self Sufficiency', http://thesietch.org/mysietch/greenspree/2007/07/17/self-sufficiency/ (accessed 18 October, 2007) and personal communication.

23. Derrick Jensen, *Endgame. Volume 1: The Problem Of Civilization*, Seven Stories Press, 2006.

Chapter 9

1. R. Engelman and E. Leahy, 'How Many Children Does It Take to Replace Their Parents? Variation in Replacement Fertility as an Indicator of Child Survival and Gender Status', http://paa2006.princeton.edu/download.aspx?submissionId=60125 (accessed 15 October, 2007). It's 2.07 in the UK, but a great deal higher in most other countries.

2. M. Potts and M. Campbell, 'History Of Contraception', *Gynaecology and Obstetrics* (6), 2002.

3. Advert for The Guardian, 'The Whole Picture'. This can be viewed at www.youtube.com/watch?v=E3h-T3KQNxU (accessed 28 February, 2008).

4. Mirja Iivonen, Diane H. Sonnenwald, Maria Parma and Evelyn Poole-Kober, 'Analyzing and Understanding Cultural Differences: Experiences from Education in Library and Information Studies', 1998, www.ifla.org/IV/ifla64/077-155e.htm (accessed 24 October, 2007).

5. J. Rawls, *A Theory Of Justice*, Oxford University Press, 1999.

6. 'New Directions in the Study of Happiness: United States and International Perspectives', 2006 (www.nd.edu/~adutt/activities/documents/McMahonNotreDameTalk.pdf).

7. *Concise Oxford English Dictionary*, OUP, 2004.

8. Searches carried out on www.google.com, 22 October, 2007.

9. Ranch Rider, 'Self Drive Tours', www.ranchrider.com/drivetours.html (accessed 22 October, 2007).

10. Tourism New South Wales, 'National Visitor Survey and International Visitor Survey research findings', http://corporate.tourism.nsw.gov.au/Sites/SiteID6/objLib13/ 4_nature_tourism_research_findings.pdf (accessed 22 October 2007).

11. Keith Farnish, 'Did You Have A Good Life?', http://earth-blog.bravejournal.com/entry/19828 (accessed 28 October, 2007).

12. Thom Hartmann, 'The Lessons Ancient People Have For Us', www.thomhartmann.com/index.php?option=com_content&task=view&id=203&Itemid=80 (accessed 28 February, 2008).

13. Erna Gunther, *A Further Analysis Of The First Salmon Ceremony*, University of Washington Publications in Anthropology, 1928.

14. Save Our Wild Salmon, 'Lewis and Clark', www.wildsalmon.org/library/lewis-clark.cfm (accessed 1 November, 2007)

15. Douglas H. Ubelaker, 'North American Indian population size, A.D. 1500 to 1985', *Amer. J. Physical Anthropology* (77), 1988.

16. Many of the salmon runs are now dead – industrial humans have taken it upon themselves to dam the rivers for electricity generation.

17. Native American Documents Project, 'Annual Report of the Commissioner of Indian Affairs to the Secretary for the Year 1872' from www.csusm.edu/nadp/r872001d.htm (accessed 11 December, 2007).

18. Marshall Sahlins, 'The Original Affluent Society' from www.eco-action.org/dt/affluent.html (accessed 1 November 2007).

19. American Indian and Native American are used interchangeably throughout the literature. I prefer the term 'Native American' simply because it implies prior habitation of the North American continent.

20. Rodney Frey, 'Original Affluent Society', www.webpages.uidaho.edu/~rfrey/220original.html (accessed 1 November, 2007).

21. The increasing figures for food reflect the way that food is grown, transported and processed. The figures for domesticated animals reflect this in terms of the way their feed is produced, as well as the amount of animal products we consume.

22. Nigel Warburton, *Philosophy: The Classics*, Routledge, 2001 (2nd Edition).

Chapter 10

1. English Heritage, 'Normanton Down Barrows - Burial Preparations in the Neolithic period', www.english-heritage.org.uk/stonehengeinteractivemap/sites/normanton/02.html (accessed 6 November, 2007).

2. Religion Facts, 'The Big Religion Chart', www.religionfacts.com/big_religion_chart.htm (accessed 6 November, 2007).

3. Shannon Burkes, 'God, Self, and Death. The shape of religious transformation in the second Temple Period', J. Study of Judaism Supplements (79), 2003.

4. William Wordsworth, *Guide through the District of the Lakes* (quoted in W.G. Hoskins, *The Making of the English Landscape*, Penguin, 1985).

5. Ana Salote, *Tree Talk*, Speaking Tree, 2007.

6. Bob Holmes, 'Imagine Earth Without People', www.newscientist.com/channel/life/mg19225731.100 (accessed 8 November, 2007). I purposely inserted the '[sic]' in relation to the discussion of our place on Earth. Use of the word 'advanced' needs an awful lot of qualification – the word 'industrial' would have been far more suitable.

7. Derrick Jensen discusses this brilliantly in *Endgame*, Seven Stories Press, 2006.

8. That's not to say that democracy is a good thing in itself. Ethically it's almost certainly a better choice than totalitarianism in all its forms, but it still doesn't seem to work very well in solving the problems we find ourselves in.

9. Michio Kaku, *Parallel Worlds*, Penguin Books, 2006.

10. European Foundation for the Improvement of Living and Working Conditions, 'Fourth European Working Conditions Surveys', 2005, www.eurofound.europa.eu/ewco/surveys/EWCS2005/ewcs2005individualchapters.htm (accessed 13 November, 2007).

11. New Economics Foundation, 'A map of the world colour-coded by HPI', www.happyplanetindex.org/map.htm (accessed 13 November, 2007).

12. Both Thomas Nagel and Derek Parfit have influenced my thinking here.

13. Judith A. Lothian, 'Why Natural Childbirth?', *J. Perinatal Education* (4), 2000.

14. The Internet Encyclopedia of Philosophy, 'Time', www.iep.utm.edu/t/time.htm (accessed 14 November, 2007).

15. World Health Organization, 'Suicide prevention (SUPRE)', www.who.int/mental_health/prevention/suicide/suicideprevent/en/ (accessed 19 November, 2007).

16. Margaret Thatcher Foundation, 'Interview for Woman's Own ('no such thing as society')', 1987, www.margaretthatcher.org/speeches/displaydocument.asp?docid=106689 (accessed 11 December, 2007). Margaret Thatcher actually said "and so they are casting their problems on society and who is society? There is no such thing! There are individual men and women and there are families and no government can do anything except through people and people look to themselves first." Effectively she was washing her hands of social responsibility.

17. This is a large subject and there is no space to explore it here. The subject is covered extensively in Robert E. Lane, *The Loss of Happiness in Market Democracies*, Yale University Press, 2001.

18. Tim Kasser, *The High Price Of Materialism*, MIT Press, 2002.

19. Matthew Gage, 'Evolution: Sex and Cannibalism in Redback Spiders', *Current Biology* (15), 2005.

Chapter 11

1. NOAA: Trends in Atmospheric Carbon Dioxide, www.esrl.noaa.gov/gmd/ccgg/trends/ (accessed 4 March, 2008). Parts Per Million, or PPM, is the standard measure of the volume of carbon dioxide gas in the atmosphere. Methane and Nitrous Oxide are measured in Parts Per Billion because they are present in smaller quantities.

2. James Hansen, 'Global Warming: The Perfect Storm', Presentation made to the Royal College of Physicians, London, www.columbia.edu/~jeh1/RoyalCollPhyscns_Jan08.pdf (accessed 13 March, 2008).

3. Fred Pearce, 'Greenland ice cap "doomed to meltdown"', *New Scientist*, 2004, http://environment.newscientist.com/channel/earth/climate-change/dn4864 (accessed 13 June, 2008).

4. http://flood.firetree.net/ (accessed 13 March, 2008).

5. Until very recently, water vapour was not considered an anthropogenic greenhouse gas, but recent work by David Wasdell (www.meridian.org.uk) among others has found a number of feedback loops which could place the amount of water vapour very much in the our hands. Water vapour is responsible for a great deal of the natural Greenhouse Effect, which makes life on Earth possible.

6. With the increase in ruminant animal consumption, methane levels are almost inevitably going to start to increase again after the recent drop in levels caused by drying wetlands (www.noaanews.noaa.gov/stories2006/s2709.htm: accessed 31 March 2008). Nitrous oxide levels could also increase again as aircraft use rises exponentially, and more land is opened up for agriculture using nitrogen-based fertilizers (see www.epa.gov/nitrousoxide/sources.html: accessed 31 March 2008).

7. Figures are superficially derived from a nice chart at http://en.wikipedia.org/wiki/ List_of_countries_by_carbon_dioxide_emissions, but have been cross-checked through the Carbon Dioxide Information Analysis Center, http://cdiac.ornl.gov/trends/emis/tre_coun.htm (accessed 5 March, 2008).

8. Based on figures from the World Trade Organization, www.wto.org/english/res_e/statis_e/statis_e.htm (accessed 5 March, 2008).

9. Thomas Homer-Dixon, *The Upside Of Down*, Souvenir Press, 2007.

10. Domestic trade (within the same country) figures are unreliable for the whole world, but even so, some explanation is needed as to why I have used international trade as an indicator instead. Between 1975 and 2000, total manufacturing output in the United States went up by 180% (based on figures from the US Census Bureau, www.census.gov/indicator/www/m3/hist/m3bendoc.htm - accessed 10 March, 2008) to $1.9 trillion. In the same period, imports into the USA went up by 1100% (Based on figures from the World Trade Organization, www.wto.org/english/res_e/statis_e/ statis_e.htm - accessed 5 March, 2008) to $1.3 trillion – an increase more than five times that of domestic production. Given the powerhouse status that the USA still has in global economics, it is clear that international trade is a good indicator for the world economy after 1975.

11. Analysed in detail in: Keith Farnish, 'Whose Carbon Is It Anyway?' The Earth Blog, http://earth-blog.bravejournal.com/entry/20579 (accessed 11 March, 2008).

12. We have looked at a number of them in Parts One and Two, such as the link between genetic modification and profit, and that between happiness and the consumption of goods. There is also the connection between the urgency for war and the desire by businesses to increase their profits, and a number of others that will become clear in Chapter 13. Very few of these social, political and economic connections are coincidental.

13. Personal communication.

14. No records exist earlier than about 600CE (see www.garhwalhimalayas.com/feel_garhwal/earlyhistory.html: accessed 13 March, 2008), but the nature of many tribes is that they leave no evidence of their existence except through oral histories.

15. Brian Nelson, 'Chipko revisited – Chipko Andolan forest protection movement; India', Whole Earth Review, 1993: accessed via http://findarticles.com/p/articles/mi_m1510/is_n79/ ai_13805372/pg_1 (accessed 13 March, 2008).

16. Quoted in Al Gedicks, *Resource Rebels: Native Challenges to Mining and Oil Corporations*, South End Press, 2001.

17. Ibid.

18. United Nations General Assembly, 'Report of the Special Representative of the Secretary-General on the situation of human rights defenders, Ms. Hina Jilani. Addendum: Mission to Indonesia.' www.unhcr.org/cgi-bin/texis/vtx/refworld/rwmain?page=&docid=47baaeb62 (accessed 18 March, 2008)

19. See US State department reports for various years, e.g.: www.state.gov/g/drl/rls/hrrpt/2005/61609.htm ("In February the Human Rights Commission in South Sulawesi concluded that the police committed a gross human rights violation in 2003 when they fired on farmers and indigenous persons attempting to reoccupy lands leased by the government to the London Sumatra Company; four persons were killed and more than a dozen were injured") and www.state.gov/g/drl/rls/hrrpt/2006/78774.htm ("During the year indigenous people, most notably in Papua, remained subject to widespread discrimination, and there was little improvement in respect for their traditional land rights. Mining and logging activities, many of them illegal, posed significant social, economic, and logistical problems to indigenous communities. The government failed to prevent domestic and multinational companies, often in collusion with the local military and police, from encroaching on indigenous people's land.")

20. Quoted in Brian Halweil, *Home Grown: The Case For Local Food In A Home Grown Market*, Worldwatch Institute, 2001.

21. Curtis White, 'The Ecology Of Work', Orion Magazine, www.orionmagazine.org/index.php/articles/article/267 (accessed 21 April, 2008).

22. James Speth, transcript of speech made at The Brookings Institution, 16 April 2008, www.brookings.edu/~/media/Files/events/2008/0416_speth/20080416_speth.pdf (accessed 19 April, 2008).

Chapter 12

1. David Hughes, 'Being A Poet', from the album *Recognized*, The Folk Corporation, 2002.
2. James Reeves, ed. Preface to *Selected Poems of John Clare*, Heinemann, 1954.
3. Excerpt from John Clare, 'Insects', in James Reeves, ed., *Selected Poems of John Clare*, Heinemann, 1954.
4. Jonathan Heawood, 'Poor Clare - rhyme, but no reason', *The Observer*, http://books.guardian.co.uk/reviews/biography/0,,1091069,00.html (accessed 29 March, 2008). The title of this article reveals much about the way a simple love for nature is treated in the 21st century. There was every reason in the world for Clare to write as he did; more reason than most modern journalists have to write what they do!
5. Excerpt from John Clare, 'The Nightingale's Nest'; see reference 3 above.
6. Personal communications.

Chapter 13

1. 'Baile Gean', Highland Folk Museum, http://highlandfolk.museum/bailegean.php (accessed 15 April, 2008).
2. Ed. Douglas MacGowan, *The Stonemason: Donald Macleod's Chronicle of Scotland's Highland Clearances*, Greenwood Publishing Group, 2001.
3. Victor Lebow, 'Price Competition in 1955', *Journal Of Retailing* (31), 1955.
4. Lexus, 'Hybrid Living Is Easy. Just Follow These Tips.' www.lexus.com/hybriddrive/pdf/hybrid_living_tips.pdf (accessed 16 April, 2008).
5. George Carlin, taken from HBO special, 'Life is Worth Losing', available to hear at www.informationclearinghouse.info/article18690.htm (accessed 23 June, 2008).
6. George Monbiot, 'Hurray! We're Going Backwards!' www.monbiot.com/archives/2007/12/17/hurray-were-going-backwards/ (accessed 20 April, 2008).
7. Ward Churchill, *Pacifism As Pathology*, AK Press, 2007.
8. Benjamin J. Barber, *Jihad vs. McWorld*, Corgi Books, 2003.
9. Charles Loft, 'The Beeching Myth: Forty Years On', *History Today* (53), 2003.
10. Derrick Jensen, *Endgame Volume II: Resistance*, Seven Stories Press, 2006.
11. Patrick Burgoyne, 'São Paulo: The City That Said No To Advertising', *Business Week*, www.businessweek.com/innovate/content/jun2007/id20070618_505580.htm (accessed 17 April, 2008).
12. Naomi Klein, *No Logo*, Flamingo, 2001.
13. 'Taíno' was the name given by the native island people to Christopher Columbus on being asked who they were: it means 'good' or 'noble' and is prefixed by the name of the island on which each tribe lives.
14. Michael D. Lemonick. 'Before Columbus Destroyed almost overnight by Spanish invaders, the culture of the gentle Taino is finally coming to light', *Archeology* (152), 1998.
15. Quoted in Noam Chomsky, 'Year 501: The Conquest Continues', Verso, 1993. This book is available in full, online at www.zmag.org/Chomsky/year/year-contents.html (accessed 17 April, 2008).
16. Quoted in Hans Schmidt, *The United States Occupation of Haiti, 1915-1934*, Rutgers University Press, 1995.
17. Milgram's work is described in detail in Stanley Milgram, *Obedience To Authority: An Experimental View*, HarperCollins, 1974.
18. Bob Altemayer, *The Authoritarians*, University of Winnipeg, 2006. This important book can be downloaded or read online at http://home.cc.umanitoba.ca/~altemey/ (accessed 26 June, 2008).
19. Ibid.
20. I'm assuming the operator is male – there may be female feller-buncher operators and lumberjacks, but they are very few and far between. For the sake of readability, sometimes you have to make assumptions.
21. I accept that it is possible to use renewable resources such as wind, solar power, some forms of biomass or wave power, but these are in a tiny minority and do not constitute the majority of raw materials from which Industrial Civilization is constructed.

22. George Monbiot, *Heat: How To Stop The Planet Burning*, Penguin, 2006.

23. 'Greenwash' is a portmanteau, a combination of the words 'green' and 'whitewash', which describes a raft of methods that businesses and political leaders, in particular, employ to pretend what they are doing is environmentally sound, when it is nothing of the sort. Examples include the advertising of 'green' cars, and the use of 'sustainability' policies to cover up damaging activities.

24. Keith Farnish, 'BHP Billiton: Olympic Sponsors – Toxic Tyrants', The Unsuitablog, http://thesietch.org/mysietch/keith/2008/03/14/bhp-billiton-olympic-sponsors-toxic-tyrants/ (accessed 21 April, 2008).

25. Bill Bryson, *The Life and Times of the Thunderbolt Kid*, Doubleday, 2007.

26. Dan Glaister, 'Bush unveils record $3.1 trillion budget', *The Guardian*, www.guardian.co.uk/world/2008/feb/05/usa.international1 (accessed 22 April, 2008).

27. Conservatively extrapolated from Centers for Disease Control statistics: http://webappa.cdc.gov/sasweb/ncipc/leadcaus10.html (accessed 22 April, 2008).

28. 'Defend the Soviet Union: Manifesto of the Socialist Workers Party', 1941, reprinted in The Encyclopedia of Trotskyism, www.marxists.org/history/etol/document/fi/1938-1949/ww/1941-ww03.htm (accessed 22 April, 2008).

29. Jim Myers, 'Heat wave has senator sticking to beliefs', *Tulsa World*, www.tulsaworld.com/news/article.aspx?articleID=060722_Ne_A1_Heatw72040 (accessed 22 April, 2008).

30. Non-Governmental Organization: essentially an organization performing a public service without government involvement. There is nothing to stop an NGO having corporate involvement, and WWF are sadly all too wiling to allow corporations – regardless of reputation – to carry their logo for a fee, so long as they carry out some trivial environmental activity.

31. Larry Rohter, 'In the Amazon: Conservation or Colonialism?' *New York Times*, www.nytimes.com/2007/07/27/world/americas/27amazon.html?_r=1&oref=slogin (accessed 22 April, 2008).

32. Conor Foley, 'Sister Dorothy can rest in peace', *The Guardian*, http://commentisfree.guardian.co.uk/conor_foley/2007/05/sister_dorothy_can_rest_in_peace.html (accessed 23 April, 2008).

33. Adam Hochschild, *Bury The Chains: The British Struggle to Abolish Slavery*, Pan Books, 2005.

34. Ibid.

35. Human Rights Watch, 'Sudan: Events Of 2007', http://hrw.org/englishwr2k8/docs/2008/01/31/sudan17759.htm (accessed 23 April, 2008).

36. Figures from Iraq Body Count (www.iraqbodycount.org/) as of 23 April, 2008. These are relatively conservative figures: in 2004, the British Medical Journal produced a civilian death figure in excess of 100,000 after just eighteen months of conflict, based on anecdotal evidence: www.bmj.com/cgi/content/full/329/7474/1066 (accessed 23 April, 2008).

37. Riane Eisler, *The Real Wealth Of Nations*, Berrett Koehler, 2007.

38. This section is partly re-edited from Keith Farnish, 'The Problem With . . . Hope', The Earth Blog, http://earth-blog.bravejournal.com/entry/24287 (accessed 24 April, 2008).

39. B. A. Robertson, 'Effectiveness of 'distant healing' prayer used in addition to medical treatment', Ontario Consultants on Religious Tolerance, www.religioustolerance.org/medical6.htm (accessed 24 April, 2008).

40. Donal P. O'Mathuna, 'Prayer Research: What Are We Measuring?' *Jn of Christian Nursing* (16), 1999.

41. Herbert Benson et al., 'Study of the Therapeutic Effects of Intercessory Prayer (STEP) in cardiac bypass patients: A multicenter randomized trial of uncertainty and certainty of receiving intercessory prayer', *American Heart Journal* (151), 2006.

42. Derrick Jensen, *Endgame Volume I: The Problem Of Civilization*, Seven Stories Press, 2006.

43. Daniel Quinn, *Beyond Civilization*, Three Rivers Press, 1999.

44. Franz J. Broswimmer, *Ecocide*, Pluto Press, 2003.

45. Erich Fromm, *To Have Or To Be?*, Abacus, 1976.

46. Daniel Quinn, see reference 43 above.

Chapter 14

1. That's 'green' consumption. A marvellous misnomer that I would use far more if anyone understood what it meant.

2. For examples you can visit www.conspiracyarchive.com, www.conspiracyplanet.com, www.theforbiddenknowledge.com and www.abovetopsecret.com. There are lots more you can try. The sad thing is that there are a lot of clever people writing a lot of good stuff, but conspiracy theories keep sidetracking them. Remember, a conspiracy is simply groups or individuals working together out of the public eye: you only have to read Chapter Thirteen to realize that the really sinister operations of Industrial Civilization are widely known; but we ignore them because 'that's the way it has to be'.

3. Quoted in *What A Way To Go: Life At The End Of Empire*, 2007, Directed by Tim Bennett, www.whatawaytogomovie.com.

4. Dmitry Orlov, 'Civilization Sabotages Itself', www.culturechange.org/cms/index.php?option=com_content&task=view&id=111&Itemid=42 (accessed 7 May, 2008).

5. As of April 2008, the US Consumer Confidence Index was down, reflecting the dicey position of the global economy: a combination of the 'sub-prime' market collapse, and the huge rise in oil prices. www.conference-board.org/economics/ConsumerConfidence.cfm (accessed 7 May, 2008).

6. Jim McWhinney, 'Understanding the Consumer Confidence Index', Investopedia, www.investopedia.com/articles/05/010604.asp (accessed 7 May, 2008).

7. Derived from MWh figure for global generating stations at http://carma.org/plant (accessed 8 May, 2008).

8. Thomas Homer-Dixon, *The Upside Of Down*, Souvenir Press, 2007.

9. Mark R. Carter et al., 'Effects of Catastrophic events on Transportation System Management and Operations: Howard Street Tunnel Fire.' US Department of Transportation, 2001.

10. Ibid.

Chapter 15

1. Daniel Quinn, *Beyond Civilization*, Three Rivers Press, 1999.

2. The Capital Economy is the newest type of economy – that which relies on the transfer and acquisition of material (monetary and object) wealth. Economics is actually the management of the home, and all of the most basic things needed to ensure it can be run effectively. Riane Eisler (*The Real Wealth Of Nations*, Berrett Koehler, 2007) posits six sectors of the economy, the first three being most critical but largely ignored in Industrial Civilization: Household Economy, Unpaid Community Economy and Natural Economy. The other three sectors are Market Economy, Government Economy and Illegal Economy (essentially the non-legal Market Economy).

3. The economic system is headed in one direction – up – so any move in the opposite direction places tremendous pressure on the instruments that support this system. Thomas Homer-Dixon (*The Upside Of Down*, Souvenir Press, 2007) writes: "The American economy, for example, must expand 3% to 5% annually just to keep unemployment from rising [the unemployment being created by increases in technological efficiency, population growth and immigration]. And to get this growth, our leaders and corporations – operating on the implicit assumption that people can be inculcated with insatiable desires and ever-rising expectations – relentlessly encourage us to be hyper-consumers."

4. Ibid.

5. The definition of 'essential' varies according to whatever cultural system dominates. For humans; food, water, air, shelter and warmth are essential – that is all. In some measures of 'poverty', a deprived person is one who lacks a television and a refrigerator; clearly something has gone wrong if deprivation is defined in terms of consumer goods. The use in the text is merely relative; most 'essentials' are unnecessary outside of Industrial Civilization.

6. 'President Bush signed a $168 billion economic stimulus package on Wednesday that will extend rebates to U.S. taxpayers' . . . "We have come together on a single mission and that is to put the people's interests first," Bush said at a White House signing ceremony. He was flanked by members of Congress and his

cabinet.' (from Robert Schroeder, 'Bush signs economic stimulus package', Marketwatch, www.marketwatch.com/news/story/bush-signs-economic-stimulus-package/story.aspx?guid=%7BB4A3B2EB-60E8-4A21-8448-0FE3F0D85F1F%7D (accessed 14 May, 2008). Clearly "the people's interests" means maintaining the status quo of control and disconnection.

7. Kate Smith, 'Balance not calories making children fat', *Sunday Herald*, www.sundayherald.com/news/heraldnews/display.var.1945300.0.balance_not_calories_making_children_fat.php (accessed 14 May, 2008).

8. Examples include: 'Auto industry spent record $70.3m lobbying Congress', www.motorauthority.com/news/industry/auto-industry-spends-record-703m-lobbying-congress-in-2007/; 'Car Dealers Lobby Against 35 MPG', www.thecarconnection.com/Auto_News/Green_Car_News/Car_Dealers_Lobby_Against_35_MPG.S196.A12664.html; 'EU bows to car lobby on pollution limits', www.independent.co.uk/news/europe/eu-bows-to-car-lobby-on-pollution-limits-435331.html; 'Germany torn on EU climate plan as car lobby bites', http://uk.reuters.com/article/environmentNews/idUKL2368721920080423 (all accessed 15 May, 2008).

9. 'Why Bikes Are a Sustainable Wonder', Sightline Institute, www.sightline.org/research/sust_toolkit/solutions/bicycle/ (accessed 16 May, 2008).

10. The figure is derived as follows: In Europe, the average automobile emits about 170 grams of CO_2 for every kilometre. In the USA and Canada this is considerably higher, but let's take the European average as a starting point. If I were to travel from A to B by car then my vehicle would emit approximately 3.4kg of carbon dioxide. If I travelled at an average of 100kph (about 60mph), then the journey would take 12 minutes, during which time I would not exert myself, and thus personally emit only 8 grams of CO_2. The total for the journey would thus be 3.4kg of carbon dioxide, give or take a few grams. If, instead, I travelled by bicycle, then I would have to exert myself. There is no way I could cycle at 100kph, but can easily reach 20kph, making my journey last 1 hour. When I cycle I breathe at between 20 and 30 breaths per minute, so let's assume 30bpm, with no increase in oxygen intake per breath. Over that hour of cycling, a person would therefore emit only 100 grams of carbon dioxide, or just 3.4% of the carbon emitted by the combined vehicle and human.

11. Daniele Fanelli, 'Meat is murder on the planet', *New Scientist*, 2007, http://environment.newscientist.com/article/mg19526134.500 (accessed 16 May, 2008).

12. Dominic Kennedy, 'Walking to the shops damages planet more than going by car', *The Times*, www.timesonline.co.uk/tol/news/uk/science/article2195538.ece (accessed 16 May, 2008).

13. Attributed to Jim McGurn, probably in *Cycling Monthly* (now defunct), 1994.

14. For a detailed, but probably unintentional, analysis of the hopelessness of sufficiently lowering greenhouse gas emissions within Industrial Civilization, read George Monbiot, *Heat*, Penguin, 2006. Monbiot's analysis is based on a 60% global reduction in greenhouse gases by 2030; which is insufficient, based on Jim Hansen's recent work – and which Monbiot himself has recently admitted is too little. Even a 60% cut is monumentally difficult within the constraints set by Industrial Civilization.

15. 'Book Burning', United States Holocaust Memorial Museum, www.ushmm.org/wlc/article.php?lang=en&ModuleId=10005852 (accessed 20 May, 2008).

16. For example: 'China seizes books from Japan school because of Taiwan map', *Japan Today*, 28 June 2005, www.ipcs.org/Jun_05_japan.pdf; Ali Asghar Ramezanpoor, 'The Scope and Structure of Censorship in Iran', Gozaar, www.gozaar.org/template1.php?id=1017&language=english.

17. 'Every Child Matters: Change For Children', HM Government, 2004, www.everychildmatters.gov.uk/_files/F9E3F941DC8D4580539EE4C743E9371D.pdf (accessed 20 May, 2008). The 'Every Child Matters' scheme was implemented as a response to the terrible abuse suffered by young Victoria Climbie at the hands of her 'carers'; the UK Government took the opportunity to sandwich the Citizenship elements within the otherwise well-thought-out recommendations on ensuring child protection standards are raised. Of course, in a culture where caring is valued more than money, such schemes would be absolutely unnecessary.

18. Ibid.

19. Jan Lundberg, 'Unlucky to have a job', Culture Change, www.culturechange.org/cms/index.php?option=com_content&task=view&id=115&Itemid=1 (accessed 20 May, 2008).

20. Joseph Tainter, *The Collapse of Complex Societies*, Cambridge University Press, 1988.

21. United Nations Population Division statistics, http://esa.un.org/unup/index.asp (accessed 20 May, 2008).

22. For example: Tim Colebatch, 'Europe paying for ageing population', The Age, www.theage.com.au/articles/2004/04/09/1081326922168.html; 'France Moves to Encourage Large Families', Deutsche Welle, www.dw-world.de/dw/article/0,2144,1720921,00.html; C. J. Chivers, 'Putin Urges Plan to Reverse Slide in the Birth Rate', New York Times, www.nytimes.com/2006/05/11/world/europe/11russia.html (all accessed 21 May, 2008). It is interesting to observe that many politicians stress the threat to pensions and the care of those in old age, when they are clearly worried about the threat to the national economy; they are merely appealing to the public's soft spot. Interestingly President Putin (NYT article) suggests a threat to the Russian State; something that is still key in the hearts of voters.

23. Callum M. Roberst et al., 'Roadmap to Recovery: A global network of marine reserves', Greenpeace International, 2006, www.greenpeace.org/international/press/reports/roadmap-to-recovery (accessed 22 May, 2008). The reason that the section on implementation is so brief in this extensive report is that there really is no way of implementing such a grand scheme in the current regime of uncontrolled marine take – civilization would never allow it.

24. The World Commission on Protected Areas (part of the IUCN) say, of West Africa: 'Protected areas cover more than 8.6% of the land area of Africa but, in many cases, they are threatened by civil unrest, weak institutions, poorly trained staff and limited budgets.' (http://cms.iucn.org/about/union/commissions/wcpa/wcpa_work/wcpa_regions/wcpa_wcafrica/index.cfm. The Wilderness Society USA state: "For over a century, the National Wildlife Refuge System has protected America's unique wildlife and irreplaceable habitats. But several years of stagnant or declining budgets have exacerbated the more than $2.5 billion operations and maintenance backlog, and have forced a dramatic 20% reduction in staff nationwide." ('America's Treasures Wildlife Refuges on the Brink', www.wilderness.org/Library/Documents/upload/RefugeCuts-ThreatsToWildlife.pdf). Greenpeace Brazil state: "Although the organization recognizes the recent efforts of the federal government in braking the destruction of forests, as Operation Arc de Fogo and the embargo of illegally deforested areas, the report released in March shows that the government fully complied with only 30% of the activities provided for in its Plan to combat deforestation." ('Desmatamento na Amazônia cai 80% em março em relação a fevereiro', www.greenpeace.org/brasil/amazonia/noticias/desmatamento-na-amaz-nia-cai-8). (All accessed 21 May, 2008).

25. Steve Connor, 'Researchers "seed" ocean with iron to soak up CO_2', The Independent, www.independent.co.uk/environment/climate-change/researchers-seed-ocean-with-iron-to-soak-up-co2-447211.html (accessed 22 May, 2008).

26. James Lovelock and Chris Rapley, 'Ocean pipes could help the Earth to cure itself', Nature (443), 2007.

27. I don't see a problem with the tools of civilization being used to help bring down civilization, at least in a way that the problem is not exacerbated: the Internet, for instance, has become essential to reach the huge numbers of people subjected to the Tools of Disconnection. This is one example of a necessary ethical sacrifice; something that will be encountered in the section on Undermining.

28. Richard Lovett, 'Burying biomass to fight climate change', New Scientist (2654), 2008.

29. Dmitry Orlov, 'Civilization sabotages itself', Culture Change, www.culturechange.org/cms/index.php?option=com_content&task=view&id=111&Itemid=42 (accessed 27 May, 2008).

30. Bruce Schneier, Secrets & Lies: Digital Security in a Networked World, Wiley, 2004.

31. This includes all of the metaphorical and physical machinery of civilization, not just the mechanical cogs and wheels.

32. Derrick Jensen, Endgame Volume II: Resistance, Seven Stories Press, 2006.

33. David W. Orr, 'The Greening of Education', Schumacher Lecture, Bristol, 1994, www.eco-action.org/dt/orr.html (accessed 30 May, 2008).

34. For the full analytical text, see Everett M. Rogers, Diffusion of Innovations: Fifth Edition, Free Press, 2003.

35. Gregg Orr, book review of Diffusion of Innovations by Everett Rogers, www.stanford.edu/class/symbsys205/Diffusion%20of%20Innovations.htm (accessed 31 May, 2008).

36. Carol J. Adams, *Living Among Meat Eaters: The Vegetarian's Survival Handbook*, Continuum International, 2003.

37. Malcolm Gladwell, *The Tipping Point*, Abacus, 2002.

38. It seems that educators, despite being restrained by a system that suppresses change, are some of the most radical people in society. This extends to librarians, booksellers and many people working in the social services.

39. Ibid.

40. Gil Kaufman, 'What's The Point Of Live Earth? Facing Criticism, Al Gore Says Concerts Are Just The Beginning', www.mtv.com/news/articles/1564062/20070705/id_0.jhtml (accessed 3 June, 2008).

41. There is a wonderful parody of this 'do something, do anything' attitude in a music video starring Russell Brand. It's in the movie Forgetting Sarah Marshall (2008) and at the time of writing could be seen at www.heatworld.com/Article/4994/Russell+Brand/See+Russell+Brand%e2%80%99s+amazing+music+video (accessed 3 June, 2008).

42. The campaign was launched in 2002, and is still at the forefront of HSBC's efforts to increase its global reach; such is its success. See www.hsbc.com/1/2/newsroom/news/news-archive-2002/new-campaign-for-the-worlds-local-bank (accessed 3 June, 2008).

43. Richard Dawkins, *The Selfish Gene*, OUP, 1976.

44. Richard Dawkins, *The God Delusion*, Bantam Press, 2006.

45. Take a look at the 'successes' pages of any number of environmental organizations' websites or magazines and you will see vast numbers of achievements being trumpeted when, in fact, almost nothing tangible is achieved or the organization in question played little or no part in the 'success'. Particularly eye-watering examples include: www.climateark.org/kudos/, www.earthactionnetwork.org/success.php and any number of 'press releases' pages of larger groups.

Chapter 16

1. My good friend is Joyce Emery, also known as Green Granny. You can read more of her wise words at www.greengranny.org.

2. Richard Heinberg, 'The Primitivist Critique of Civilization', paper presented at the 24th annual meeting of the International Society for the Comparative Study of Civilizations at Wright State University, Ohio, 1995, www.primitivism.com/primitivist-critique.htm (accessed 9 June, 2008).

3. Metaphor shamelessly taken from Lemony Snicket, *The Wide Window*, Egmont Books, 2003. Children's literature is awash with allegory and metaphor – my favourite allegory for our controlled, disconnected state is in *Harry Potter and the Order Of The Phoenix* (J. K. Rowling, Bloomsbury, 2003): read and enjoy!

4. Dmitry Orlov, 'Closing the "Collapse Gap": the USSR was better prepared for collapse than the US', *Energy Bulletin*, 2006, www.energybulletin.net/23259.html (accessed 9 June, 2008).

5. Brent Ladd, 'Realities of Going Primitive', *Wilderness Way* (2), www.wwmag.net/realities.htm (accessed 9 June, 2008).

6. Ran Prieur, 'How to Survive the Crash and Save the Earth', 2004, http://ranprieur.com/essays/saveearth.html (accessed 9 June, 2008). I would recommend Ran Prieur's essay above all others as an accompaniment to this chapter – it is a mine of useful information in a small space.

7. Between 1940 and 2000, the average household size in the USA dropped from 3.68 to 2.59 (www.census.gov/statab/hist/HS-12.pdf – accessed 10 June, 2008) even as population growth remained steady – in fact the population grew at its fastest rate ever in 1990-2000, during which time the household size continued to shrink. In Scotland it is projected that the average household size will fall to below 2 persons by 2024 (www.scotland.gov.uk/News/Releases/2006/05/30091955 – accessed 10 June, 2008).

8. The circumstances determine the speed of the barn-raising in Amish communities, but as many as 300-400 men could be directly involved in the building effort following a 'tragedy' (when a barn is destroyed by fire). Information from Randy Leffingwell, *The American Barn*, MBI Publishing Company, 2003.

9. Tribalism is the long-term view of community: a community can exist for a short period of time; a tribe cannot because a tribe has existed long enough to develop its own identity. Specifically, when I talk about Communities, I am talking about groups of interdependent people; when I talk about Tribes I am talking about groups of interdependent people who are no longer dependent upon other communities (although

interaction is not ruled out) due to their highly-developed ability to operate as a self-sufficient group. Religious or mystical ideas are not mandatory in tribal living, despite what some purists may think; but sustainability is mandatory, otherwise the tribe will cease to function.

10. The Transition Town idea provides a useful starting point on the journey towards the independent tribal community: the clue (intentional or not) is in the name. Information can be found at www.transitiontowns.org/ (accessed 1 July, 2008). Beware, though, as some so-called Transition Towns are nothing of the sort, having embraced many of the facets of Industrial Civilization that need to be removed. As I said, this is just a starting point.

11. One notable reference for the shorter-term skills is Ran Prieur, 'How to Survive the Crash and Save the Earth', http://ranprieur.com/essays/saveearth.html (accessed 11 June, 2008).

12. Survivalist authors and many others promoting major societal change on environmental grounds tend to demote the importance of people skills, preferring to concentrate on practical efforts, perhaps hoping that the community – whatever it looks like – will turn out fine. It will not turn out fine if you are not prepared to work at relationships and the way communities operate – that is what civilization has assumed; that it will take care of everything and abuse individuals' reliance on the imposed social structures. Seeds for Change (see www.seedsforchange.org.uk/) are a group that provide training and advice in a number of key areas related to co-operative living.

13. Permaculture is about more than just food production, but is centred on producing the basic energy units required to sustain a community of people. Permaculture principles should be applied wherever possible: advice is available from the Permaculture Institute (www.permaculture.org), Permaculture Activist (www.permacultureactivist.net/) and any book by Bill Mollison, particularly *Permaculture: A Practical Guide for a Sustainable Future*, Island Press, 1990.

14. World Health Organization Statistical Information System (WHOSIS), www.who.int/whosis/en/index.html (accessed 11 June, 2008).

15. Approximately 10 million vertebrates are used for medical experimentation each year in the EU, Japan and the USA combined according to the Nuffield Council on Bioethics, 'The ethics of research involving animals', 2005, www.nuffieldbioethics.org/fileLibrary/pdf/RIA_Report_FINAL-opt.pdf (accessed 11 June, 2008).

16. According to Survival International, "Following first contact, it is common for more than 50% of a tribe to die." www.survival-international.org/tribes/isolatedperu (accessed 11 June, 2008).

17. Bubonic plague would also not have occurred on anything like the scale it did, over three centuries, had it not been for trading ships and the exploitation of foreign resources. See Chapters One and Two for lots of other examples.

Index

Page numbers in *italic* refer to Figures.